D1072048

The World's Classics

CCLXI

A RUSSIAN SCHOOLBOY

A
RUSSIAN SCHOOLBOY

BY

SERGE AKSAKOFF

TRANSLATED FROM THE RUSSIAN

BY

J. D. DUFF

HUMPHREY MILFORD
OXFORD UNIVERSITY PRESS
London   Edinburgh   Glasgow   Copenhagen
New York Toronto Melbourne Cape Town
Bombay Calcutta Madras Shanghai

SERGHEI AKSAKOFF

Born, Ufa . . . . . 20 September 1791
Died, Moscow . . . . 30 April 1859

'*A Russian Schoolboy*' was first published in Russia in
1856; in '*The World's Classics*' it was first published in
1924.

PRINTED IN ENGLAND
AT THE OXFORD UNIVERSITY PRESS
BY FREDERICK HALL

INTRODUCTION

THESE recollections of school and college were published by Aksákoff in 1856, when he was in his sixty-fifth year. He called them merely *Recollections* : he did not then know that he would record other and still earlier memories in the book called *Years of Childhood*.

A Russian Schoolboy, the title chosen for this translation, is not a misnomer : when Aksákoff left Kazán in the spring of 1807, he was still a boy of fifteen, though his school had been promoted by imperial decree to the dignity of a university. As a student he wore a sword with his uniform, but little change took place in his occupations. His university studies are remarkable : he learnt no Greek, no Latin, no Mathematics, and very little Science—hardly anything but Russian and French ; and even to these he seems to have given less time than to acting plays in the winter and collecting butterflies in spring and summer ; fishing and shooting were reserved for the vacation. If our universities adopted such a pleasant curriculum, would they produce writers like Aksákoff ?

This is the third and last volume of these Memoirs, the right order being : (1) *A Russian*

Gentleman ; (2) *Years of Childhood* ; (3) *A Russian Schoolboy*. But the first and third of these were published together by Aksákoff in 1856, and the second followed in 1858 ; he died on April 30, 1859.

He himself did not use in this work the pseudonyms which he kept up throughout the other two. Hence in this part of the translation Aksákoff and Aksákovo appear, not Bagróff and Bagróvo ; but, to save confusion to the reader, three names—those of Alexyéi Stepánitch, Sófya Nikoláyevna, and Praskóvya Ivánovna—are here retained, though they are all pseudonyms and were temporarily discarded by their author.

The Appendix, as it describes an episode of college life, forms a natural part of this volume. It was the last thing that Aksákoff wrote, and was not printed till six months after his death. He had suffered much from disease, but his artistic faculty was not dimmed nor his temper embittered : he never wrote anything more vivid, more characteristic, more charming.

This translation was made from the Moscow edition of 1900; I know of no previous translation of the original into any language. It appeared first in 1917, and I have taken advantage of this reprint to correct some mistakes.

I have now done what I meant to do, by translating the whole of these Memoirs into English.

I can myself read with pleasure all that Aksákoff wrote—except his verse translation of Laharpe's French translation of the *Philoctetes* of Sophocles; but it will not hurt his reputation, if he is known to English readers by his best work only. What they can scarcely realize is the inimitable purity and simplicity, the *lactea ubertas*, of his Russian style.

Aksákoff is his own best critic: he wrote to a friend on April 10, 1856—

'The success of my life has surprised me. You know that my vanity was never excessive, and it remains what it was, in spite of all the praise, sometimes extravagant to folly, which has reached me in print or in letters or by word of mouth . . . To the end of a long life I have preserved warmth and liveliness of imagination; and that is why talents that are not extraordinary have produced an extraordinary effect.'

This may be over-modest, but it is not far from the truth.

J. D. DUFF.

February 7, 1924.

CONTENTS

A RUSSIAN SCHOOLBOY

CHAPTER I

MY FIRST TERM AT SCHOOL

In the middle of winter in the year 1799, when I was eight years old, we travelled to Kazan, the chief town of the Government. The frost was intense; and it was a long time before we could find out the lodgings we had taken beforehand. They consisted of two rooms in a small house belonging to a Mme Aristoff, the wife of an officer; the house stood in Georgia Street, a good part of the town. We arrived towards evening, travelling in a common sledge of matting drawn by three of our own horses harnessed abreast; our cook and a maid had reached Kazan before us. Our last stage was a long one, and we drove about the town for some hours in quest of our lodgings, with long halts caused by the stupidity of our country servants—and I remember that I was chilled to the bone, that our lodgings were cold, and that tea failed to warm me; when I went to bed, I was shaking like a man in a fever. I remember also that my mother who loved me passionately was shivering too, not with cold but with fear that her darling child, her little Seryózha,[1] had caught a chill. She pressed me close to her heart, and laid over our coverlet a satin cloak lined with fox-fur that had been part of her dowry. At last I got warm and went to sleep; and next morning

[1] A pet-name for Serghéi.

I woke up quite well, to the inexpressible joy of my
anxious mother. My sister and brother, both
younger than I, had been left behind with our
father's aunt, at her house of Choorassovo in the
Government of Simbirsk. It was expected that
we should inherit her property ; but for the
present she would not give a penny to my father,
so that he and his family were pretty often in
difficulties ; she was unwilling even to lend him
a single rouble.[1] I do not know the circumstances
which induced my parents, straitened as they were
for money, to travel to Kazan ; but I do know
that it was not done on my account, though my
whole future was affected by this expedition.

When I awoke next morning, I was much impressed by the movement of people in the street ;
it was the first time I had seen anything of the
kind, and the impression was so strong that
I could not tear myself away from the window.
Our maid, Parásha, who had come with us, could
not satisfy me by her replies to my questions, for
she knew as little as I did ; so I managed to get
hold of a maid belonging to the house and went on
for some hours teasing her with questions, some
of which she was puzzled to answer. My father
and mother had gone off to the Cathedral to pray
there, and to some other places on business of
their own ; but they refused to take me, fearing
for me the intense cold of that Epiphany season.
They dined at home, but drove out again in the
evening. Tired out by new sensations, I fell asleep
earlier than usual, while chattering myself and
hearing Parásha chatter. But I had hardly got
to sleep when the same Parásha roused me with

[1] A rouble was worth two shillings.

a kind and careful hand; and I was told that a sledge had been sent for me, and I must get up at once and go to a party where I should find my parents. I was dressed in my best clothes, washed, and brushed; then I was wrapped up and placed in the sledge, still in Parásha's company. I was naturally shy; I had been caught up out of the sound sleep of childhood and was frightened by such an unheard-of event; so that my heart failed me and I had a presentiment of something terrible, as we drove through the deserted streets of the town. At last we reached the house. Parásha took off my wraps in the hall, and repeating in a whisper the encouragement she had given me several times on our way, led me to the drawing-room, where a footman opened the door and I walked in.

The glitter of candles and sound of loud voices alarmed me so much that I stood stock-still by the door. My father was the first to see me; he called out 'Ah, there is the recruit!'—which alarmed me still more. 'Your forehead!'—cried some one in a stentorian voice, and a very tall man rose from an arm-chair and walked towards me. I understood the meaning of this phrase,[1] and was so terrified by it that I turned instinctively to run away, till I was checked by the loud laughter of all the company. But the joke did not amuse my mother: her tender heart was troubled by the fears of her child, and she ran towards me, took me in her arms, and gave me courage by her words and caresses. I shed a few tears but soon grew calm.

[1] i.e. 'Present your forehead' to be shaved. In those days the hair on the forehead of recruits for the Army was shaved as soon as they were passed by the doctors.

And now I must explain where I had been taken to. It was the house of an old friend of the family, Maxím Knyazhévitch, who, after living for several years at Ufá as my father's colleague in the law-courts, had moved with his wife to Kazan, to perform the same duties there. In early youth he had left his native country of Serbia, and at once received a commission in the Russian Horse Guards ; later he had been sent to Ufá in a legal capacity. He might be called a typical specimen of a Southern Slav, and was remarkable for his cordial and hospitable temperament. As he was very tall and had harsh features, his exterior was at first sight rather disturbing ; but he had the kindest of hearts. His wife, Elizabeth, was the daughter of a Russian noble. Their house in Kazan was distinguished by this inscription over the entrance, ' Good people, you are welcome '— a true expression of Slav hospitality. When they lived at Ufá, we often met, and my sister and I used to play with the two elder sons, Dmitri and Alexander. The boys were in the room, though I did not recognize them at once ; but when my mother explained, and reminded me of them, I called out at once : ' Why, mamma, surely these are the boys who taught me how to crack walnuts with my head ! ' The company laughed at my exclamation, my shyness passed off, and I began in good spirits to renew acquaintance with my former playmates. They were dressed in green uniforms with scarlet collars, and I was told that they attended the grammar-school of Kazan. An hour later, they drove back to school ; it was Sunday, and the two boys had leave to spend the day with their parents till eight in the evening.

I soon grew weary; and, as I listened to the talk between my parents and our hosts, I was falling asleep, when suddenly my ear was caught by some words which filled me with horror and drove sleep far from me. 'Yes, my good friends, Alexyéi Stepánitch and Sofya Nikoláyevna,'— M. Knyazhévitch was speaking in his loud positive voice—' do take a piece of friendly advice, and send Seryózha to the grammar-school here. It is especially important, because I can see that he is his mother's darling; and she will spoil him and coddle him till she makes an old woman of him. It is time for the boy to be learning something; at Ufá the only teacher was Matvyéi Vassílitch at the National School, and he was no great hand; but now that you have gone to live in the country, you won't find any one even as good.' My father said that he agreed entirely with this opinion; but my mother turned pale at the thought of parting with her treasure, and replied, with much agitation, that I was still young and weak in health (which was true, to some extent) and so devoted to her that she could not make up her mind in a moment to such a change. As for me, I sat there more dead than alive, neither hearing nor under-standing anything further that was said. Supper was served at ten o'clock, but neither my mother nor I could swallow a morsel. At last the same sledge which had brought me carried us back to our lodgings. At bed-time, when I embraced my mother as usual and clung close to her, we both began to sob aloud. My voice was choked, and I could only say, 'Mamma, don't send me to school!' She sobbed too, and for a long time we prevented my father from sleeping. At last she decided that nothing should induce her to part from me, and towards morning we fell asleep.

We did not stay long at Kazan. I learnt afterwards that my father and the Knyazhévitches went on urging my mother to send me as a Government scholar to the school in that town. They pressed upon her that at present there was a vacancy, and there might be none later. But nothing would induce her to give way, and she said positively that she must have a year at least to gain courage, to become accustomed herself and to accustom me to the idea. All this was concealed from me, and I believed that I should never be the victim of such a terrible calamity.

We started on our long journey, taking our own horses, and travelled first to the Government of Simbirsk where we picked up my brother and sister, and then across the Volga to New Aksákovo, where my infant sister, Annushka, had been left. In those days you might travel along side-roads in the Government of Ufá for a dozen versts [1] without passing a single village ; and a winter journey of this kind seems to me now so horrible that the mere recollection of it is painful. A side-road was merely a track over the snow-drifts, formed by the passage of a few sledges ; and the least wind covered it entirely with fresh snow. On such a road the horses had to be harnessed in single file, and the traveller had to crawl on for seven hours without a break, the stages being as much as thirty-five versts or even longer; and the length of each verst was by no means a fixed distance. Hence it was necessary to start at midnight, to wake the children from their sleep, wrap

[1] A verst is three-quarters of a mile.

them up in furs, and pack them into the sledges.
The creaking of the runners on the dry snow was
a constant trial to my nerves, and I always suffered
from sickness during the first twenty-four hours.
Then the stoppages for food and sleep, in huts full
of smoke and packed with calves and lambs and
litters of pigs, the dirt, the smell—Heaven preserve
any man from even dreaming of all this! I say
nothing of the blizzards which sometimes forced
us to halt in some nameless hamlet and wait
forty-eight hours till the fierce wind fell. The
recollection is bad enough. But we did at last
reach my dear Aksákovo, and all was forgotten.

I began once more my life of blissful happiness
in my mother's company and resumed all my old
occupations. I read aloud to her my favourite
books—*Reading for Children, to benefit the Heart
and Head*, and also *Hippocrene, or the Delights of
Literature*—not, indeed, for the first time but
always with fresh satisfaction. I recited verses
from the tragedies of Sumarókoff, in which I had
a special preference for messengers' parts, and put
on a broad belt for the purpose, with a window-
prop stuck in it to represent a sword. I played
with my sister whom I had loved dearly from
infancy, and my little brother, lying about with
them on the floor, which for warmth was covered
with a double thickness of snow-white Kalmuck
mats. I began again teaching my sister to read;
but at first she made slow progress and would not
try, and I had naturally little notion how to set
about my task, though I was tremendously in
earnest over it. I well remember that I found it
quite impossible to explain to my six-year-old

pupil how to spell whole words.[1] I gave it up in despair, sat down on a stool in the corner, and began to cry; and when my mother asked what I was crying about, I answered, 'Sister does not understand anything.' As before, I took my cat to bed with me; she was so attached to me that she followed me everywhere like a dog; and I snared small birds or trapped them and kept them in a small room which was practically converted into a spacious coop. I admired my pigeons with double tufts and feathered legs, which had been kept warm in my absence under the stoves in the houses of the outdoor servants. I watched the huntsmen catching magpies and pigeons or feeding the hawks in their winter quarters. The day was not long enough for the enjoyment of all these delights!

So winter passed by, and spring began with its green leaves and blossoms, revealing a multitude of new and poignant pleasures—the clear waters of the river, the mill and mill-dam, the Jackdaw Wood, and the island, surrounded on all sides by the old and new channels of the Boogoorooslan, and planted with shady limes and birches. To the island I ran several times a day, hardly knowing myself why I went; and there I stood motionless, as if under a spell, while my heart beat hard and my breath came unevenly. But what attracted me most of all was fishing, and I gave my whole soul to this sport, under the eye of my attendant, Yephrem Yevséitch. Fish swarmed in the clear and deep waters of the Boogoorooslan, which flowed right under the windows of the room built on to the old house by my grandfather in his life-time, in order that his daughter-in-law might have

---

[1] Russians spell by syllables, not by single letters.

a place to herself to live in. Close under the window there grew a spreading birch, leaning over the water, and one thick crooked bough formed with the trunk a kind of arm-chair in which I loved to sit with my sister. But the river in the course of time bared the roots of the tree, so that it grew old prematurely and fell on its side ; yet it is still living and puts forth leaves. A young tree was planted beside it by a later owner.

Ah, where is it now, that magic world, the fairy-tale of human life, which so many grown-up people treat roughly and rudely, shattering its enchantment by ridicule or premature enlightenment ? The happiness of childhood is the Golden Age, and the recollection of it has power to move the old man's heart with pleasure and with pain. Happy the man who once possessed it and is able to recall the memory of it in later years ! With many that time passes by unnoticed or unenjoyed ; and all that remains in the ripeness of age is the recollection of the coldness or even cruelty of men.

I spent that whole summer in the intoxication of a child's happiness, and suspected nothing ; but when autumn came and I began to sit more in the house, to look more at my mother and listen to her more, I soon noticed a change of some kind in her. Her beautiful eyes were directed at me sometimes with a peculiar expression of secret sorrow ; I even noticed tears, though they were carefully concealed from me ; and then, in grief and excitement, with all the caresses of passionate love, I besieged her with questions. At first she assured me that it was nothing and of no importance ; but soon, in the course of our conversations, I began to hear her lamenting that I had no proper

teacher, and saying that teaching was indispensable
for a boy. She would rather die, she said, than
see her children grow up in ignorance ; a man
must serve the state, and was not fit to do so
without education. My heart sank when I understood the drift of these words and realized that
the dreaded calamity had not passed away but
had come close, and that the school at Kazan was
inevitable. My mother confirmed my surmise :
she said that her mind was made up, and I knew
that she did not readily change her resolves. For
some days I could only weep, not listening to what
she said, and pretending not to understand it.
At last her tears and entreaties, her sensible
arguments accompanied by the tenderest caresses,
and her eager desire to see me grow up an educated
man—all these became intelligible to me, young
as I was, and I submitted with an aching heart to
the destiny that awaited me. But all my country
amusements suddenly lost their charm : I felt
drawn to none of them ; everything seemed to
me strange and repulsive, and only my love for my
mother increased so much as actually to frighten
her.

And now my preparation for the school course
began. I could read excellently for my age, but
my writing was childish. In arithmetic, my father
had tried earlier to impart to me the first four rules,
which were all he knew himself ; but I was so dull
and idle a pupil that he dropped it. Now there
was a complete change : in two months I mastered
these four rules, and, though I have forgotten
all the rest of my mathematics, I remember the
four rules still. The rest of the time until our
departure for Kazan was spent in revising old

lessons with my father. In the writing of copies also I became very proficient. All this I did under my mother's eye and wholly and solely for her sake. She had said, that she would burn with shame if I did not pass with credit the entrance-examination which had to be taken in these subjects, and that she was sure I would distinguish myself; and I needed no other inducement. I would not go one step from her side. When she tried to send me out to play or look at my pigeons and hawks, I refused to go anywhere and always gave the same answer, 'I don't want to, mamma.' In order to accustom me to the thought of our parting, she spoke constantly to me of the school and of education; she said that she was quite determined to send me to Moscow later, and place me at a boarding-school connected with the University, the school to which she had sent her brothers straight from Ufá, when she was herself a girl only seventeen years old. My intelligence was beyond my age; for I had read many books to myself, and still more aloud to my mother, some of them too advanced for my years. To this I must add, that my mother was my constant companion; and it is well known how the companionship of grown-up people develops the minds of children. Hence it came about, that she was able to speak to me of the advantages the educated have over the ignorant, and that I was able to understand her. She was remarkably intelligent and had unusual powers of expression; she could speak what was in her mind with a passion which it was hard to resist, and her influence over me was absolute and supreme. At last she inspired me with such courage, such zeal to carry out her darling wish as

soon as possible and justify her hopes, that I even
looked forward with impatience to our journey to
Kazan.   My mother seemed courageous and
cheerful ; but how much the effort cost her ! She
grew thinner and paler daily ; she never shed
tears, but she shut herself up in her own room
more than usual and prayed.   This was the real
proof of her love for her child, the real triumph of
that infinitely disinterested and self-sacrificing
passion ! As a child, I had been long ill, and there
was a time when for whole years she never left
my bedside ; when she slept, no one knew, and
no hand but hers was suffered to touch me.   And
again, at a later time, when she heard that I had
broken down at school and was lying sick in
hospital, she crossed the river Kama at the time
of the spring thaw, when all traffic over it had
ceased and the discoloured and swollen ice might
be expected to break up at any moment.   But all
this falls short of her determination to send her
child to school ; the school was under Government
and 400 versts away, and the child, whom she
literally idolized, was only eight and not strong
and had been tenderly reared ; yet she did it,
because there was no other means of procuring
education for him.

Winter came round once more, and in December
we started for Kazan.   In order that the return
home might be less sad for my mother, my father
insisted on taking my elder sister with us ; my
brother and younger sister were left at home with
our aunt Tatyana.   At Kazan we had the same
lodgings as the year before, in the house of Mme
Aristoff.   Before leaving, my parents had been in
correspondence with M. Knyazhévitch and had

ascertained that there was a vacancy in the school for a Government scholar, and they had got ready all the papers required for my election. So, after a fortnight, when he had made acquaintance through M. Knyazhévitch with all the officials concerned, my father, after fervent prayer to God, sent in his petition to M. Peken, the Rector of the school.

The governing-body of the school appointed the head master, M. Kamásheff, to examine me in my proficiency, and a Dr. Benis to conduct a medical examination. Kamásheff was then on leave, and his duties were discharged in part by Vassili Upadishevsky, master of one of the dormitories; while the inspection of studies, of which Kamásheff had charge, was carried on by Lyoff Levitsky, the senior teacher of Russian Literature. Both these men proved kind and friendly, and Upadishevsky soon became a real guardian-angel to myself and my mother : I do not know what would have become of us, but for this kind old friend. When my father went to the Rector's house to give in his petition, he took me with him, and the Rector proved very friendly. Next, as Levitsky was unwell and could not attend the meeting of the governors, I was taken to his lodgings by my father. He too was very amiable and cheerful; he had a high colour and, in spite of his youth, a considerable development behind his waistcoat. He charmed both of us by his reception. He began by kissing and embracing me. Then he set me something to read—prose by Karamzín and verse by Dmitrieff—and was delighted to find that I read with intelligence and feeling. Next he made me write ; and again my performance delighted him. In the four rules of arithmetic also I distinguished myself; but Levitsky, in the true spirit of a teacher of literature, expressed straight off his contempt for mathematics.

When the examination was over, he praised me without stint, and expressed surprise that a boy of my age, living in the country, could be so well prepared. ' Now who, pray, taught him to write ? ' he asked my father with a good-humoured laugh : ' your own handwriting is hardly a model.' My father, charmed and moved almost to tears by hearing his son praised, replied in the fullness of his heart, that I owed it all to my own hard work, under the supervision of my mother, from whom I was almost inseparable ; and that he himself had taught me nothing but arithmetic. He added that we had only lately moved to the country, that my mother was a great lover of books and poetry, and had spent all her youth in a provincial capital, where her father held an important position. ' Ah,' exclaimed Levitsky, ' now I understand the stamp of refinement, even of elegance, which marks your charming boy ; it is the fruit of a woman's work of education, the result of a cultivated mother's labours.' We left the house enchanted with him.

Dr. Benis, who owned a fine house in Ladsky Street, received us very politely and made no difficulty about giving me a certificate of health and bodily vigour. On returning home, I noticed that my mother had been weeping, though her eyes had this peculiarity that tears did not cloud their brightness and left no trace behind them. My father eagerly reported all that had happened to us. My mother looked at me with an expression which I shall never forget, even if I have still a hundred

years to live. She took me in her arms and said,
'You are my happiness, you are my pride!'
What more could I ask? In my own way, I was
proud and happy too, and took courage.

My mother called on the wife of Dr. Benis and
made the acquaintance of the doctor himself. It
was hard to deny sympathy to my mother's youth
and beauty, her intelligence and her tears: they
both quite fell in love with her, and the doctor
promised her, that in any illness, however trifling,
I should enjoy all the resources of the medical art
—a dangerous promise, according to my present
ideas, when I dread an excess of medical attention;
but it served then to comfort my poor mother to
some extent.

Vassili Upadishevsky was a widower, and two
of his own sons were Government scholars. My
father made his acquaintance and invited him to
visit us at our lodgings. My mother received him
so kindly that he took a great fancy to her and
was able to appreciate her maternal devotion.
At their very first interview he promised her
two things: to transfer me within a week to his
own dormitory—to have done this at once for a
new boy would have been thought a clear case
of favouritism; and to look after me more closely
than after his own 'pair of scamps', by whom
he meant his sons. Both promises were scrupulously fulfilled. I seem to see him now, with his
kind courteous face, and his right arm slung in
a broad black ribbon; the hand had been blown
off by the bursting of a cannon, and he wore
a black glove stuffed with cotton-wool attached
to the arm. He could write, however, very well
and distinctly with his left hand.

At last all the formalities were complete, and the governors decided to admit me to the school as a Government scholar. I was measured for my uniform, and the uniform was made. The strain which my mother and I were feeling did not grow less. We drove to the Cathedral and offered prayers to the three wonder-working saints of Kazan, Gury,[1] Varsonofy, and Herman; and I was taken straight from the Cathedral to the school, and given over by my parents into the personal charge of Upadishevsky. My attendant, Yephrem Yevséitch, came with me, taking service in the school as a dormitory man. The parting was, as may be supposed, accompanied by tears and blessings and good advice; but nothing remarkable took place. I was taken to the school at ten in the morning, when second lesson had just begun and all the boys were in the class-rooms upstairs.[2] The bedrooms downstairs were empty, and my mother was able to examine them and to see the very bed in which I was to sleep; she seemed satisfied with all the arrangements. As soon as my parents had gone, Upadishevsky took my hand and led me to the writing-class, where he introduced me to the teacher as a very well-disposed boy and begged him to pay special attention to me. I was put down with other new boys at a separate desk, and we were made to

[1] i.e. George.
[2] In winter, first lesson began at 8 and second lesson at 10; work ended at noon and dinner came half an hour later. In summer, work began at 7 and ended at 11, and dinner was at noon exactly. At all seasons, afternoon school began at 2 and ended at 6; supper was at 8, and we went to bed at 9. We rose at 5 in the summer and 6 in winter. (*Author's Note.*)

S + his mother.

copy pot-hooks and hangers. I was quite dumb-founded, and felt as if it was all a dream ; but I had no sensation of fear or grief. After dinner, of which I remember nothing, I was made to put on a uniform jacket, with a cloth stock round my neck, and my hair was cut close. Then we were placed on parade in a line two deep—the boy next me was Vladímir Graff—and we were taught at once how to march. I went mechanically through it all, as if I had nothing to do with it personally. When lessons were over, Upadishevsky met me at the door and said, ' Your mother is waiting for you '. Then he took me to the reception-room where both my parents were standing.

When my father saw me, he laughed and said, ' Well, one would hardly know Seryózha again ! '—but my mother, who had failed to recognize me at the first moment, threw up her hands, cried out, and fell fainting to the floor. I cried out wildly and fell at her feet. Upadishevsky, who had been looking through the chink of the door, was alarmed and hurried to our aid. My mother's swoon, which lasted about half an hour, terrified my father and had such an effect upon poor Upadishevsky that he summoned from the hospital Ritter, the doctor's assistant, who gave some medicine to my mother and made me swallow something too. When my mother came to herself, she was very weak ; and the kind-hearted Upadishevsky volunteered to give me leave to go home for the night. ' M. Kamásheff ', said he, ' may be angry with me, when he comes back and hears of it ; and he would never have given leave himself. But never mind—I will take all the responsibility ; only please bring

him back to-morrow at seven, just before breakfast.' We could not find words to thank him for
such kindness ; and off we went to our lodgings.
At home my mother, on reflection, plucked up
courage herself and breathed courage into me. She
forced herself to look calmly at my close-cropped
head, where her hand sought in vain the soft fair
curls, and at the stock, which had already begun
to rub the tender skin of my neck, unused even to
a silk handkerchief. For everything she found
a good reason which we had to submit to. Our
mutual firmness and determination took hold of
us with fresh power. I was at the school next day
before seven o'clock. My mother paid me two
visits every day—before dinner at midday, and
again at six ; the morning visit lasted only half
an hour, but I could stay with her in the evening
for an hour and a half. While we were together,
she seemed peaceful and even happy ; but I
guessed from my father's sad face that matters
were very different in my absence.

Within a few days, my father became convinced
that things could not go on as they were, and that
these constant meetings and partings were only
a source of useless suffering ; he took counsel with
M. Knyazhévitch, and the two decided to take my
mother back to the country without delay. It was
easy to decide, but hard to carry out the decision,
and this my father knew very well ; but, much to
his satisfaction and contrary to his expectation,
my mother soon yielded to the entreaties and
arguments addressed to her. Dr. Benis took an
interest in the matter, and his words were undoubtedly of great weight. He assured her that
these constant interviews were a trial to my nerves

and dangerous to my health, and that, unless she went away, it would take me a long time to get accustomed to my new life, and perhaps I never should settle down at all. Even the soft-hearted Upadishevsky urged the same course : when he declared that I could not work properly in such a condition of affairs, and that my teachers would form a bad opinion of me, then my mother consented to go away on the very next day. But there is one thing that still puzzles me—how she could make up her mind to play a trick on me. Before dinner she told me that she would leave the next day or the day after, and that we should meet twice more ; she said too that she was spending that evening with the Knyazhévitches, and would not visit me. To depart secretly and without saying good-bye—that was an unlucky idea, urged by Benis and Upadishevsky. Of course, they wished to spare us both, and me especially, the pain of a final parting ; but their calculation was not verified. Even now I am convinced that this well-meant deception had many sad results.

It was the first time that my mother had omitted her evening visit, and though she had forewarned me, yet my heart ached with grief and a presentiment of some unknown calamity. I slept badly that night. Early next morning, when I began to dress, Yevséitch handed me a note ; it was my mother's farewell to me. She wrote that, if I loved her and desired her life and happiness, I must not grieve but work hard at my lessons : she had left the town at eight on the previous evening. I remember that moment clearly, but I cannot describe it : a feeling of pain pierced my heart and compressed it, and stopped my breathing ; and this was immediately followed by severe palpitation. I sat down on the bed half-dressed and looked round the room, dazed and despairing. Upadishevsky, who had moved me into his dormitory two days before, knew of my mother's departure and consequently understood the cause of my condition. Ordering that no one should touch me, he took all the other boys upstairs at once, handed them over to one of the masters, and hurried back to me. He found me sitting on my bed in the same position, and Yevséitch in tears standing beside me. To all that he could say I turned a deaf ear : I could not form a single thought, and my eyes, as I was told afterwards, stared wildly. I was taken to the hospital ; there too I sat down mechanically on a bed, and stared in silence as before. Within an hour Dr. Benis came ; he examined me, shook his head, and said something in French ; I heard later from others that the words were ' pauvre enfant '. I was given some repulsive medicine to swallow, undressed, and put to bed, where I was rubbed with flannel ; and soon a violent fit of shivering restored me to consciousness. I called out loudly, ' Mother has gone away ! ' and the streams of pent-up tears gushed from my eyes. This evidently relieved the doctor : he sat down beside me and began to speak of my mother's departure and of its necessity for the sake of her health, of the danger of a final interview, and of the way in which a sensible boy should behave in such a case, if he loved his mother and wished to set her mind at rest. His words were a real inspiration from above ; for the doctor, though a very worthy man,

was not exactly remarkable for gentleness of
disposition. Though my tears flowed still faster,
yet I felt better. The doctor left, and I sobbed on
for two hours till I cried myself to sleep ; and
kindly sleep did something to restore my strength.
Upadishevsky came to see me several times and
brought a book for me to read, *The Child's Instructor*, which I had never seen ; he knew my
passion for reading, but I was in no mood for it
then. I asked leave to write, and wrote to my
father and mother all that day and all the evening,
crying most of the time. Yevséitch never left me.
Next morning the doctor found me in better health,
and discharged me from the hospital, thinking the
society of invalids and the inactivity bad for me ;
but he directed that I should not be worked hard.

Upadishevsky himself took me back into school,
where I found a writing-class going on ; and this
was followed by a divinity lesson with the priest.
For two hours I listened, while the other boys
repeated their lessons on the Catechism and Bible
history, and the priest set a fresh lesson and
explained some difficulty at great length ; but
I could not understand his explanations either on
this occasion or on any other while I remained at
the school. I had not learnt the lesson for that day,
and the priest had been informed of my illness ;
a strict and severe man, he did not go beyond
a reprimand, but told me to have my lesson
prepared next time. After dinner, in order that
I might not remain idle and a prey to sad thoughts,
Upadishevsky handed me over to one of the older
boys who drew well, Ilya Zhevanoff, that he might
amuse me in that way ; as a child I had had a great
fancy for drawing. I myself heard the kind old

man say to Zhevanoff : ' Please do me a great
kindness which I shall never forget, and amuse
this poor home-sick boy by drawing with him ' ;
and Zhevanoff consented. But neither then nor
later did my drawing come to anything : the
copying of circles, eyebrows, noses, eyes, and lips,
had set me against drawing for good and all.

At the end of afternoon school, Upadishevsky,
still my good genius, made me repeat my lessons
beside him ; and when he saw that I did not
understand what I was saying, he began to talk
to me of my life at home and of my parents, and
even allowed me to cry a little. I do not know
how life would have gone on with me ; but at this
point there came a complete and sudden change.
The next day but one, during dinner, Yevséitch
handed me a note from my mother, which said
that, after travelling ninety versts from Kazan, she
had come back to have at least a momentary
glimpse of me ; to leave without a proper parting
had proved too much for her. I cannot explain
to myself why I did not at the first moment feel
the immense happiness which I surely ought to
have felt. I suppose I was afraid to believe it and
took it for a dream. There was a note also for
Upadishevsky : my mother asked him to give me
leave from six till nine in the evening ; or, if that
was impossible, she would come herself ; she
added that she would only spend one night in
Kazan. He told me to write to my mother, that
she was not to be anxious and not to come herself ;
he would send me with Yevséitch, perhaps before
six, as the teacher of the last lesson was not well
and would probably not turn up ; and I might stay
with her till seven next morning. As I wrote all

this, I felt sure that I was in a dream. Yevséitch hastened off with my letter, and returned in an hour and a half with an answer of such joy and gratitude to Upadishevsky that the old man's eyes grew wet as he read it. Yevséitch told us that his mistress had returned alone; she had turned back at a village ninety versts away along the post-road; his master had remained there with the young lady, who was not well; and my mother had travelled with post-horses in a light courier's sledge, accompanied by one maid and one man. I began to realize the situation and to believe in my good fortune, and was soon so completely convinced of it that the last hour of suspense was a terrible trial. The teacher sent notice that he would not come; and at five minutes past four I got into a hired sledge, attended by Yevséitch and crazy with happiness beyond description.

My mother was staying with some friends whose name I forget; but it was certainly not at an inn. When I ran into the room, I saw her, looking pale and thin, wrapped up in a warm cloak, and sitting beside a newly lighted stove, as the room was very cold. The first moment of our meeting it is impossible for me to describe; but never in after life did I experience a thrill of happiness to compare with that. For some minutes we were silent and only wept for joy. But this did not last long: the thought of coming separation soon drove all other thoughts and feelings from me, and made my heart ache. With bitter tears I told my mother all that had happened to me since her sudden departure. I was frightened by the effect of my story. How my poor mother blamed herself, and repented of her promise to deceive me and go away without saying good-bye ! Then she told me about herself. She had fainted on getting into the sledge, and had no recollection of leaving Kazan. As she got farther away, her suffering increased every hour, and soon the idea of returning took hold of her ; but my father's arguments and her own good sense restrained her for some time from the course on which her heart was set. At last she was unable any longer to withstand her feelings, and she returned alone ; my sister, unwell already and unfit for travel, needed rest, and was to wait with my father till my mother rejoined them. That whole evening, with most of the night, was spent by us in talking and in weeping ; but, as there are limits to all things, we came to an end of our tears and went to sleep. I remember how I started in my sleep several times and began sobbing, till my mother took me in her arms and laid my head on her breast, and I fell asleep again. We were wakened at six o'clock. We were calmer and braver by that time. My mother promised that, as soon as the roads were open in summer,[1] she would come to Kazan and stay till the examina-tions were over ; and after the speech-day, which was always near the beginning of July, she would take me home for the holidays which would last till the middle of August. A feeling of comfort filled my heart ; and we said good-bye calmly enough. At seven my mother got into the sledge she had come in, and Yevséitch and I into another, and we all started together. She drove to the right, towards the town-gate, and I to the left, towards the school ; we soon turned off the

[1] The spring thaw makes travelling impossible for a time.

main street, and her sledge vanished from my sight.

My heart ached, and a load of pain lay on my breast; but my head was perfectly clear, and I fully understood all that was going on around me and all that lay ahead of me in the future. The great white building of the school, with its bright green roof and cupola, stood on a hill, and the sudden appearance of it surprised me as much as if I had never seen it before. It seemed to me like a terrible enchanted castle such as I had read of, or a prison where I was to be shut up as a convict. The great door between columns at the top of a high flight of steps, which, when it was opened by the old pensioner, I felt had swallowed me up—the two broad high staircases, lit from the cupola and leading from the hall to the first and second floors—the shouting and confused noise of many voices that came from all the class-rooms to meet me, the teachers being still absent—all this I saw and heard and understood for the first time. I had already spent more than a week in the school, but had never realized it; now for the first time I felt myself to be a Government scholar in a Government school.

The whole day each thing that happened was new and surprising, and oh! how repulsive it all seemed to me! We rose at the sound of a bell, long before daylight, when there was an intolerable smell in the rooms from the guttering or extinguished night-lights and tallow candles; the cold in the dormitories [1] made rising even more

---

[1] The temperature of the dormitories was kept at 53°, as is still the custom in all Government schools. In my

unpleasant for a poor child who could barely keep
warm under his frieze coverlet ; we washed all
together at copper basins which were always the
scene of quarrels and fights ; we marched two
and two to prayers, to breakfast, to lessons, to
dinner, and to everything ; our breakfast consisted of a roll and a glass of milk and water in
equal proportions, with a glass of *sbiten* [1] instead
of milk and water on fast-days ; we had three
courses at dinner and two at supper, but they
were not better meals than breakfast. How was
all this likely to strike a boy whom his mother
had petted and made much of and brought up as
luxuriously as if we had been very rich ? But
more terrible to me than anything else were my
companions. The oldest boys and those in the
middle of the school took no notice of me ; but
those of my own age or even younger, who were at
the bottom of the school, were for the most part
intolerably rude and rough ; and, though there
were exceptions, I had so little in common even
with them, and we differed so much in ideas and
interests and habits, that I could not make friends
with them ; and I remained solitary in the midst
of numbers. They were all healthy and contented
and unbearably cheerful, and not a single one of
them was in the least degree depressed or thoughtful or likely to sympathize with my constant
sadness. If there had been, I would have rushed
boldly into his arms and shared my secret with
him. ' How strange it is ! ' I said to myself ;
' these boys cannot have father or mother, brothers

opinion, this is positively harmful to children ; it ought
not to be lower than 58°. (*Author's Note.*)
  [1] A drink made of honey and hot water.

or sisters, nor house and garden in the country,'
and I was inclined to pity them. But I soon
found out that almost all of them had parents
and families, and some had even homes in the
country with gardens; but one thing they had
not—that feeling of intense attachment to home
and family that filled my own heart. As a matter
of course, I at once became an object of ridicule
to my companions : I was a nincompoop, a cry-
baby, and a milksop who was always ' blubbing
for his mammy'. Upadishevsky never ceased to
watch over me night and day, but neither his
authority nor his moral influence could shield me
from this form of persecution. He told me himself
never to complain of the boys' mockery, as he
knew very well how ' sneaks ' are hated in schools,
and that this label is attached to any persecuted
boy who ventures to complain to the authorities.
He put my bed between the beds of two much
older boys ; their names were Kondiryoff and
Moréyeff ; both were well-behaved boys and also
hard workers. He handed me over to their
protection, and, thanks to them, no young scamp
ventured to approach my bed. I should mention
that in those days our accommodation was so
limited, that the Government scholars and
pensioners [1] spent in their dormitories all the time
that they were not in school.

After definitely parting from my mother, I began
at once to work hard at my lessons. Through
Upadishevsky I asked my teachers to set me twice
or thrice as much as the usual tasks, in order to
catch up the older boys and get promotion from

[1] i. e. Boys who paid for their education and maintenance.

the newcomers' bench. My memory and power of understanding were already strongly developed, and within a month I had not only distanced my contemporaries but was placed on the top bench in all subjects, side by side with the best scholars. This circumstance made me even more unpopular both with those whom I had passed and those who were still my rivals.

Just at this time the head master, Nikolai Kamásheff, returned to his duties. He was considered a very able man. I do not know if he deserved this reputation; but he certainly was a cold hard man, who always spoke low and with a smile, but always acted with inflexible determination. All without exception feared him much more than they did the Rector. He loved power, knew how to acquire it, and was exacting to pedantry in his use of it. Upadishevsky had foreseen that he would get into trouble; and, in fact, Kamásheff at once discovered all the departures from school rules which had been sanctioned by his representative for my mother and me—interviews with parents at times not recognized by the rules, unlawful leave home, and (worst of all) leave for the night. My benefactor got such a reprimand that the old gentleman walked about for a long time looking very serious. Kamásheff had said to him with his quiet smile; 'If anything of the kind ever occurs in future, I shall request you, my dear Sir, to retire from your service in this school.' When I heard of this, I shed bitter tears and conceived an invincible aversion and horror for the very name of the head master. And I had some reason; for he took a dislike to me without cause and became my

persecutor, and his oppression cost my poor
mother many tears in the sequel.

Three days after his return, Kamásheff summoned me out of the ranks to the centre of the
hall and delivered for my benefit a rather long
address : a spoilt boy, he said, was a regular
nuisance ; and it was mean to take advantage of
undue indulgence shown by authorities, and wrong
to be ungrateful to the Government which gener-
ously took upon itself the considerable expense
of my education. Though mild and quiet by
disposition, I was naturally sensitive and excitable.
I stood there, with my eyes on the floor, while
a feeling hitherto unknown swelled within my
breast, a feeling of anger at undeserved insult.
' Why do you not look at me ? '—Kamásheff
called out ; ' it is a bad sign, when a boy hides his
eyes and dares not, or will not, look his master in
the face.' Then he raised his voice and said in
a severe tone, ' Look at me ! ' I raised my eyes ;
and I suppose they expressed pretty clearly the
feeling of insulted pride which filled my young
breast ; for he turned away and said, as he went
out, to Upadishevsky, ' That boy is by no means
as mild and good-tempered as you make out.'
I heard afterwards that he wished to remove me
from the dormitory I was in, and demanded
reports from all my teachers and masters ; but
when he found in all of them ' Conduct and diligence exemplary, proficiency remarkable,' he left
me where I was. During the whole of my first
term, he constantly examined my books and
note-books in form and made the teachers question
me in his presence ; sometimes he found fault
with me for trifles or told the masters that they

must make me play with the other boys, adding,
' I don't like your silent solitary boys.' I understand now that such a criticism is justified in some
cases, but it was quite unsuitable to mine and
only increased my natural irritation. Upadishevsky really loved me and watched over me with
a mother's care ; every day he inspected my
clothes and bedding, and saw that my hands were
clean and my books in good order. He often
impressed upon me that I must look the head
master straight in the face and bear his remarks
and reprimands in silence ; and I carried out these
instructions exactly, because I loved Upadishevsky.

But this did not conciliate Kamásheff. By the
school rules, none of the boys might have private
property or money of their own ; if they had
money, it was kept by the dormitory master and
might not be spent without the head master's
consent. To buy food or sweets was strictly
forbidden ; of course, there were breaches of this
rule, but they were carefully concealed. There
was also a rule that boys' letters to their parents
and relations should pass through the hands of
the masters ; each boy was obliged to give up his
letter, before it was sealed and sent to the post,
to the dormitory master, who had a right to read
it, if he felt any distrust of the writer. Though
this rule was in practice disregarded, Kamásheff
instructed Upadishevsky to show him my letters.
The kind old man had always added a postscript
to my letters home, without reading them ; but
now he was obliged to harden his heart and act
as censor of what I wrote. My first letter which
he read placed him in a very difficult position :

I described the grief I suffered daily, I complained of my companions and even of my teachers, and I expressed a burning desire to see my mother, and to leave the hateful school as soon as possible and spend the summer in the country ; and that was all. There was nothing wrong in it ; but the reader felt sure that every word would be criminal in the eyes of the head master : he would find there discontent, criticism of authority, calumny against the school, and ingratitude to Government. What was to be done ? Upadishevsky was unwilling at once to reveal to me the actual state of affairs, for that would be much the same as conspiring with a boy against his superior. He felt also that I would not understand him, and would be unable to write a letter of the kind that Kamásheff would approve ; but to deprive my mother of my frank and full letters which were her only consolation, was impossible to his kind heart. For a whole night and day he puzzled over the difficulty without finding a solution—he told me this himself afterwards ; and at last he made up his mind to tell me the whole truth and at the same time to play a trick upon his senior and superior. Accordingly, he dictated to me another letter in a purely formal style, and showed this to Kamásheff, who naturally could find nothing in it to blame me for. Both letters were sent together to the post. After this I wrote two letters every time, one for show and the other private, and I went on with this, even after my tyrant had ceased to read my correspondence. Upadishevsky himself wrote at once to my mother, to explain the reason of this contrivance. Yevséitch took the letters to the post in person. I could not then

appreciate the full extent of my benefactor's
self-sacrifice, but my mother could, and she wrote
to Upadishevsky and expressed the most ardent
gratitude that a mother's heart could feel. I need
hardly say, that, though she did not know all the
details of it, she was much agitated by Kamásheff's
persecution of her son.

Things continued to go on as before ; but a
change took place in me which ought to have
seemed strange and unnatural to those around me.
For though in the course of six weeks I ought to
have become accustomed to the new life, I became
thoughtful and sad ; and then sadness led on to
fits of misery and finally to illness. The change
was probably due to two causes. When I had
caught up my class-mates in all our lessons, I was
given ordinary tasks which were so short that
I often learnt them before we were let out of
school, and consequently had nothing to do in
our free time ; and my active mind, deprived of
proper nourishment, turned exclusively in one
direction. I was constantly turning over and
considering my present situation, constantly
picturing all that was going on at home, dwelling
on my mother's longing for me, and recalling the
old days of bliss spent in the country. In my
heart I hated the school and was convinced in my
own mind that the process of education was
entirely useless and only served to turn innocent
children into objectionable boys. The second and
perhaps the main cause of the change was the
unfair persecution of Kamásheff. Each time he
appeared in the place, he gave a shock to my
nerves ; and he paid two visits every day at
unfixed times : there was no hour, either by day

or night, at which he might not make a perfectly sudden and unexpected appearance in the school. I am able now to do justice to his ceaseless activity, though it was too strict and mechanical ; but then he seemed to me a mere tyrant, an ogre, an evil spirit, who appeared to spring out of the earth even in places that were safe from the eye of the other masters. His terrible image haunted my young brain, and the oppression of his presence was always with me. In the meantime, my secret letters to my mother became much shorter than before, and I wrote them with ever-increasing anxiety and caution. For I now understood the constraint which Upadishevsky was putting upon his honest and open nature, and the risk he ran. A third reason for the change in me was produced by the course of time. By the end of March and beginning of April the sun became very hot, the snow melted, and streams of water flowed through the streets ; there was a breath of spring in the air, and this was a trial to the nerves of a child who had a passionate if still unconscious love of nature. It is a known fact that the sun's rays in spring have a disturbing effect on the constitution ; and I distinctly remember that I was much more depressed on sunny days than when the weather was dull.

Be that as it may, I became ' absorbed ' : I mean that I ceased to listen to the talk of others ; I learned my lessons and repeated them without interest ; I heard the criticism or approval of my teachers ; and all the time, while I was looking them straight in the face, I was fancying myself at dear Aksákovo, sheltered by my mother's love in my peaceful home. This always passed for

C

mere inattention. To give greater reality to my dreams, which grew move vivid every day, I used to shut my eyes, and was often jogged by my neighbours who thought I was sleeping. One day, during a lesson in Russian Grammar, a malicious boy named Rooshka called out, 'Aksákoff is asleep!' The teacher asked other boys whether this was true, and nearly punished me by making me kneel down, when they said that it was. I did not shut my eyes in school after that; but when I had said my lesson, I often made use of a familiar pretext to leave the room; and then I could sometimes stand in peace for a quarter of an hour in some passage-corner, and close my eyes, and dream. When afternoon school was over, the boys romped for half an hour in the reception-hall, while I kept out of it, if I was allowed; and then we had all to sit down, each at the little table by his bed, and learn the lessons for next day. I too sat down and placed a book before me; and, amid the murmur of boys' voices conning over their lessons, my thoughts always travelled to the same spot, the Paradise of my country home on the bank of the Boogoorooslan.

Soon, however, this violent strain upon the imagination reached a pitch which proved injurious to my health. I began to suffer from hysterical fits, accompanied by such violent weeping and sobbing that I lost consciousness for some minutes; and I was told later that at such times the muscles of my face were convulsed. I was able at first to conceal my condition to some extent from observation. I did this unconsciously; perhaps a secret feeling told me that I should be prevented from giving myself up to those dreams which were my only comfort. The trouble generally came upon me in the evening; I felt it coming, and used to run down the back stairs to an inner yard, where all the boys might go in case of necessity; or sometimes I hid behind a pillar, sometimes in the corner formed by the high staircase where it rose from the centre of the building; sometimes I ran upstairs and sat in a corner of the landing on the first floor, which was dimly lighted from below by a hanging lamp. The cold air probably helped to shorten the attack, and I could go back to my place in my usual condition. But once I took refuge in an open class-room which was being cleaned out, and hid, though I cannot remember doing this, under one of the desks. I fancy that this fit lasted unusually long, and perhaps this was due to the close atmosphere of the room where it came on. A porter noticed me and tried to turn me out; but when I did not answer him, he told a tutor, who recognized me and informed Upadishevsky. The old man ran upstairs in great alarm; but it happened that I recovered at that very moment and went quietly back with him to the dormitory.

Before this incident Upadishevsky had felt fairly easy about me: I had been nearly two months in the school and was showing diligence in my studies; and, though he noticed that I was often either inattentive or absorbed in some way, he attached no special importance to this. Now he questioned me minutely; and I told him fully and frankly all I knew of my own condition; but there was much I could not understand, and much I could not remember. Throughout the night, he and Yevséitch watched over me; and I slept quite peacefully till morning. I ought to say that throughout the first period of my illness I always slept well at night ; I mention this because in the later stages sleeplessness was one of the chief symptoms. Early next morning, Dr. Benis came as usual to the hospital, where I had been taken by Upadishevsky ; he questioned me and examined me attentively, and found me rather thin and pale and my pulse irregular. Yet he prescribed no medicine and let me go back into school ; I was not to work too hard—he did not believe me when I said my lessons were too easy—and he gave directions that I was to be watched and not allowed to go anywhere alone. He added that he wished to see me every morning at the time of his visit to the hospital. Upadishevsky took all necessary measures : he visited me constantly himself, and put me in charge of two boys who were to keep an eye on me whenever we were out of school ; and Yevséitch was told to go with me, every time I went out to the back-yard. A report spread throughout the school, that I was catching the ' black sickness,' [1] and I was frightened, though I did not understand the meaning of the words. It seemed to me very unpleasant that outsiders should keep constant watch over my every movement ; and I felt listless and sad all that evening. The pleasure of my day-dreams was now familiar, and the thought that I was being watched by several pairs of eyes prevented me from enjoying this pleasure and burying the bitter reality out of sight ; but, for all that, the evening passed off successfully—I had no violent distress or hysterical attack. Upadishevsky and Yevséitch were delighted ; the doctor also was much pleased when

[1] i. e. Epilepsy.

I visited him next day in the hospital and he was told that I had spent the whole day and night in peace. Though he found my pulse as irregular as before, he gave me no medicine and let me go, declaring that things would come right and that Nature would overcome unaided whatever was amiss.

But next day it turned out that the evil was not cured but only changed : at nine in the morning, during a lesson in arithmetic, I felt a sudden severe oppression on the chest, and a few minutes later burst out sobbing, and then fell senseless on the floor. There was a great stir, and Upadishevsky was sent for ; by good fortune, he was in the house,[1] and he had me carried to the dormitory, where I came to myself in a quarter of an hour, and even went back into school. But in the evening there was a second fit which lasted much longer. My kind benefactor and my devoted attendant were excessively alarmed. This time the doctor gave me some drops, which I was to take whenever I felt the oppression coming on ; on fast-days I was to have ordinary food from the hospital and a roll instead of brown bread ; but on no account was he willing that I should stay in the hospital. The drops did me good at first, and I had no fainting-fit for three days, though I was depressed and cried at times ; but then, whether it was that my system became accustomed to the medicine or that the illness was gaining strength—the fits grew more frequent and more violent.

[1] Of the four ushers, two were always on duty and on the spot ; but the other two might absent themselves during schooltime ; at dinner and supper all four were present. (*Author's Note.*)

No period of my childhood do I remember with more perfect distinctness than my first term at school. I could describe accurately and with every detail—though I certainly have no intention of doing so—the whole course of my strange malady. Like everyone else, I believed at the time that no cause could be assigned for the coming-on of these fits ; but now I am convinced of the contrary : they were always produced by some sudden recollection of that past life, which presented itself to me in a moment, with all the liveliness and clearness of dreams at night. Sometimes I reached these manifestations consciously and gradually, by plunging into the inexhaustible treasury of recollection, but at other times they visited me without any wish or thought of mine. When I was thinking of something quite different, even when I was entirely taken up by my lessons, suddenly the sound of someone's voice, probably like some voice I had heard before, or a patch of sunlight on wall or window, such as had once before thrown light in just the same way upon objects dear and familiar, or a fly buzzing and beating against the panes, as I had often watched them do when I was a child—such sights and sounds, instantly and for one instant, though no consciousness could detect the process, recalled the forgotten past and gave a shock to my over-strung nerves. In some cases, however, the explanation was clear at once. Thus I was saying a lesson one day, when suddenly a pigeon perched on the window-sill and began to turn round and coo ; at once I thought of my pet pigeons at home, and the oppression on my chest came on immediately and was followed by a fit. Another time

I went for a drink of water or *kvass* [1] to the room used for that purpose; and there I suddenly caught sight of a plain deal table which I had probably seen many times before without noticing it. But now it had been newly planed and looked notably clean and white; and instantly there flashed before me another wooden table which looked like that and was always perfectly white and smooth. It had belonged to my grandmother and afterwards stood in my aunt's room; and on it were kept various trifles, precious in a child's eyes—packets of melon-seeds with which my aunt used to make wonderful little baskets and trays; little bags of carob-beans and pebbles out of crayfish; and, above all, a large needle-book, which held not only needles but also fishing-hooks which my grandmother dealt out to me from time to time. In former days I used to gaze at all these treasures with intense interest and breathless excitement. As soon as the likeness between the tables struck me, the past flashed into life and brightness before me; and the familiar sensations of uneasiness were soon followed by a severe attack. The result was the same, when I happened to see a sleeping cat curled up in the sun, and was reminded of my own pet cat at home. These instances are, I think, sufficient to justify the hypothesis of similar causes in the other cases of the kind.

My condition went from bad to worse. The fits became more frequent and lasted longer; I lost appetite and became paler and thinner daily, and I lost also my eagerness for study; I owed my remaining strength to sleep alone. As the watchful

[1] A drink of malt and rye.

eye of Upadishevsky had noticed that early rising was bad for me, one day he tried the experiment of not waking me till eight; and all that day I felt much better. Yevséitch waited on me with the tenderness of a father. Kamásheff tried another method: he lectured me severely more than once, and even threatened to punish me, if I did not behave as a well-conducted boy ought to do. My illness, he said, was only the fancifulness of a spoilt child, and a bad example to the rest. At last, he gave a positive order that I should be moved to the hospital; I wished this myself, and so did every one else; and Dr. Benis, who alone took the opposite view, was now obliged to give way, and I was removed to the sick-room.

When my mother was leaving Kazan for the second time, she made Yevséitch swear before a sacred picture that he would let her know if I fell ill. For a long time he had been burning to fulfil his promise, and spoke of it to Upadishevsky, but the master always kept him back. Now, however, he decided to act without consulting any one, and got one of the servants, who had acquired the art, to write a letter, in which, with no precautions and without due regard to the facts, he reported that his young master was suffering from epilepsy and had been removed to the hospital.

It is easy to imagine how this letter dropped like a thunderbolt upon my parents. The post was slow, and the letter reached them at the time of the spring thaw, when the roads are in a state quite inconceivable by people who live near Moscow. At every step the traveller came on places where the road was washed away, and every hollow was filled by melting snow-drifts; for a carriage to pass was almost impossible. But nothing could keep my mother back : she started the same day for Kazan, attended by her devoted Parásha and Parásha's young husband, Theodor. She drove day and night in a rough peasant's sledge drawn by one horse without shoes ; [1] they had three sledges, each holding one passenger, while a fourth was given up to the baggage ; they had only such horses as the peasants could supply. This was the only way in which it was just possible to push on step by step ; and even so, they had to take advantage of the morning frosts, which fortunately went on that year till the middle of April. Ten days of this travelling brought my mother to the large village of Murzicha on the bank of the Kama ; the main road used by the post went this way, and it was more possible to travel along it, as it was hardened by traffic. But, on the other hand, it was necessary to cross the Kama, in order to reach the village of Shoorant which is situated, I think, about eighty versts from Kazan. The river had not melted yet, but the ice was blue and swollen ; the post had been carried across it the day before by runners on foot ; but rain had fallen in the night, and the villagers all refused to convey my mother and her companions across to the other side. She was forced to spend the night in the village. Dreading every moment of delay, she walked herself from house to house, imploring kind people to help her, explaining her grief, and offering all she possessed to recompense them. And she did find kind and brave hearts, who understood a mother's sorrow ; they promised

[1] At this season, when the snow is deep on these side-roads, horses travel better unshod. (*Author's Note.*)

that, if the rain stopped in the night and there was the least trace of frost in the morning, they would land her in safety on the farther bank, and would accept whatever she pleased to give them for their trouble.

The whole of that night my mother spent upon her knees before the sacred picture which hung in a corner of the hut where she lodged. Her fervent prayer was heard : a wind rose and dispersed the clouds, and by morning frost had dried the road and covered the pools with a thin coating of ice. At daybreak six stout fellows presented themselves, all fishermen by calling, born on the banks of the river and accustomed to deal with it in all its aspects ; each was armed with a pole and carried a light burden bound on his back. Before starting, they crossed themselves, turning towards the Cross on the church. They gave Theodor a pole and also a creel which he was to drag by a rope ; the creel was a large basket with a projecting peak, and they took this in case the lady should be too weary to walk. Then they took by the hand the two women, who had put on men's long boots, and started, after sending ahead the most active of their mates to feel the way before them. The track over the ice was slanting, so that it was necessary to cover nearly three versts. To cross a great river on foot at that season is so dangerous, that only an adept can perform the feat, using all his courage and presence of mind. Theodor and Parásha simply howled, and said good-bye to this world and all their nearest and dearest ; and in some places force had to be used to compel them to go on ; but my mother's courage and even cheerfulness increased with every step. Her guides kept wagging their heads in astonished admiration, when they looked at her. They had to go round gaps in the ice, and to cross crevasses on the poles laid side by side. My mother for long refused to make use of the creel; but when they were approaching the opposite side, and the track led over shallows close to the bank, and all danger was past, then she felt her strength leave her. Pillows and a fur-lined coverlet were at once placed upon the creel; and my mother lay down upon it and nearly fainted on the spot; and in this condition the fishermen dragged her as far as the post-house of Shooran. She gave her guides a hundred roubles, just half the money she had upon her; but the honest fishermen would not take it, and asked five roubles apiece. They listened with wonder to the thanks and blessings which my mother showered down upon them, and they said at parting, ' God bring you safe to the end of your journey!' Then they started at once on their homeward way; and there was need for haste; for the ice broke up the next day. All these details I heard later from Parásha. My mother travelled from Shooran to Kazan in forty-eight hours; she stopped at the first inn she came to, and she was in the school-building an hour later.

And now I go back to myself. I was very comfortably installed in the hospital, in a small room by myself; it was intended for severe cases, but there happened to be none at the time. Yevséitch was transferred to the hospital to work there, and slept in my room. Andréi Ritter— a surgeon or assistant-surgeon, I am not sure which—had a room near me. He was a handsome lively fellow, tall and ruddy. He was at home only in the mornings until Dr. Benis came, and then went off immediately to visit his patients—for he actually had some practice among the merchant class ; he was very dissipated and often returned home late at night and far from sober. I wonder that the head master tolerated him ; he paid more attention, however, to the sound than to the sick, and Upadishevsky had greater influence in the hospital. I have entirely forgotten the name and surname of the good-natured old man who was then in charge of the place, though I have a clear recollection of his kindness to me. Upadishevsky took care that time should not hang heavy on my hands, and at once provided me with books—*The Child's Instructor* in several volumes, *The Discovery of America*, and *The Conquest of Mexico*. How delighted I was with quiet and peace and books to read ! A dressing-gown instead of uniform, perfect freedom in the disposal of my time, no bell to listen for, and books to read—all this did me more good than any medicine or nourishing diet. Columbus and Pizarro aroused all my interest, and the hapless Montezuma all my sympathy. In a few days I had finished *The Discovery of America* and *The Conquest of Mexico*, and then set to work on *The Child's Instructor*.

While I was reading this I came across something that puzzled me very much ; indeed, I was much older before I found a complete solution of the difficulty. In one of the volumes I found a fairy tale called *Beauty and the Beast*. The first lines seemed to me familiar, and, the further I read, the more familiar it became, till at last I felt certain that this was the story which I knew by the title of *The Scarlet Flower* [1] and had heard a score of times from our housekeeper Pelagéya.

This Pelagéya was a remarkable woman in her way. While very young, she had run away with her father from her owners, the Alakayeffs, to Astrakhan, where she lived more than twenty years. Her father soon died; she married, and lost her husband, and then went out to service in merchants' families. Growing tired of this, she somehow learnt that she had become the property of a different owner—my grandfather, in fact—a strict master but just and kind-hearted; and, a year before his death, the truant turned up at Aksákovo. My grandfather respected her for coming back without compulsion, and received her kindly; and soon, as she was a notable woman and could turn her hand to anything, he took a great fancy to her and made her his housekeeper, a kind of post which she had held before at Astrakhan. Apart from her skill in household management, Pelagéya brought with her a remarkable gift for telling fairy-tales, of which she knew an immense number. It is obvious that the natives of the East have imparted to the Russians at Astrakhan a strong taste for hearing and telling these stories. In the comprehensive repertory of Pelagéya, there were not only Russian stories but a number of Eastern tales, including some from *The Arabian Nights*. My grandfather was delighted to possess such a treasure; and as he was beginning to fail in health and slept badly, Pelagéya, who could boast of another valuable quality, the power of staying awake all night,

[1] This story is given in full in an Appendix to Aksákoff's *Years of Childhood*.

did much to ease the old man in his suffering.
From her I too heard no end of fairy-tales in the
long winter evenings. The image of Pelagéya,
with her fresh healthy face and stout figure, and
with the spindle and distaff in her hands, is
ineffaceably engraved upon my memory ; and if
I were an artist, I could paint her to the life this
very minute. The story of *Beauty and the Beast* or
The Scarlet Flower was to surprise me once again :
some years later I went to the theatre at Kazan to
see an opera called *Zemira and Azor,* and found
it was *The Scarlet Flower* over again, both in the
general story and in the details.

Meantime, in spite of interesting books and
delightful confabulations with Yevséitch about life
at home with its fishing and hawks and pigeons ;
in spite of removal from school with its tiresome
noise and troublesome companions ; in spite of
the quantity of pills and powders and mixtures
I swallowed down—my illness, which seemed at
first to be yielding to treatment and rest, did not
grow less, and the fits recurred several times
a day ; but for some reason, they did not frighten
me, and when I compared it with the past,
I was quite content with my condition.
The hospital was on the second story, with
windows looking on the court. The school-
building, now the University, stood on a hill and
commanded a fine view : all the lower half of the
city with its suburbs, and the great lake of Kaban,
whose waters mingle in spring with the overflow
of the Volga—this was the picturesque panorama
that spread out before my eyes. I remember
clearly how the darkness settled down upon it, and
how the morning dawn and the sunrise used little

by little to light it up. In general, my stay in the hospital has left on my mind a lasting recollection of peace and consolation, though none of my schoolfellows ever visited me. The Knyazhévitch boys came only once ; I was not very intimate with them then, because we did not meet much : they were half-way up the school and lived in the ' French dormitory,' where Meissner was tutor. Besides, I was so much taken up with myself, or rather with my past life, that I never showed or felt the least attachment for them. But we became close friends in my second term at school, and, still more, in our college days.

I wrote home by every post, and always said that I was quite well. But a Monday came without bringing me a letter from my mother. I felt anxious and sad, and when there was no letter on the following Monday, I was miserable. Yevséitch tried to reassure me : he said that owing to the season and state of the roads it was impossible to send a carriage from Aksákovo to Boogoorooslan—our country-town, twenty-five versts distant from our house. But I would not listen to him : I knew perfectly that in all weathers they sent once a week to the post without fail. I don't know what I should have done if my letter had failed me a third time. But in the middle of the week—the exact date was the 18th of April, in the morning—my kind Yevséitch began in a roundabout way to this effect, that the absence of letters might be accounted for by a visit from my mother herself, and that perhaps she had actually arrived. After this preparation, he announced with a beaming face, that Sofya Nikoláyevna was now in the school, and that, though she might not visit me in the absence of the doctor, the doctor was coming at once. Though I had been prepared for this news, I fainted away. When I recovered, my first words were, ' Where is mamma ? ' But Dr. Benis was standing by me, and scolding Yevséitch. He was not in the least to blame : however cautiously I had been told of my mother's arrival, I could not have received such joyful and unexpected tidings without strong emotion, and any emotion would have brought on a seizure. The doctor was quite convinced that permission must be given for the mother to see her son, especially when the son knew of her arrival ; but he did not venture to give it without being authorised by the head master or Rector ; and he had sent notes to them both. The Rector's permission came first, and my mother was actually in my room, when an order came from Kamásheff, to await his arrival.

For want of words, I shall not attempt to describe what I felt when my mother came into the room. She was so thin that I might not have known her ; but her joy at finding her child not only alive but much better than she expected—what did not her anxious heart forebode ?—shone so radiantly in her eyes, which were always bright, that an onlooker might have supposed her both well and cheerful. All my surroundings were forgotten ; I clasped her in my arms and for some time would not let her go. A few minutes later Kamásheff appeared. With cold politeness he told my mother that the regular rules of the school had been broken on her account : that relations or parents were not permitted to enter the inner rooms of the establishment but only the reception-room specially provided for the purpose ; and that admission to the hospital was absolutely forbidden, and especially undesirable in the case of a lady so young and so attractive.

The blood rushed to my mother's face; she was naturally impulsive, and she now told Kamásheff more home-truths than were necessary. Among other things she said: 'Your school must be the only school in the world that has such a barbarous rule! A mother's presence is desirable in any place where her son is lying ill! I am here by permission of the Rector, your immediate superior, Mr. Head master, and all you have to do is to obey!' She had plunged her knife into the tender spot. Kamásheff turned pale. He then said: 'The Rector has given leave for once only, and his order has been obeyed; it will probably not be repeated, and I beg that you will now go away.' But he did not know my mother; nor did he understand the feelings common to all mothers' hearts. She told him that she would not leave that room till the Rector, either in person or by letter, ordered her to go; until that happened nothing short of actual violence should part her from her son. And this was said with such vehemence and in such a tone, that it was quite certain she would carry it out to the letter. She took a chair, pushed it up to my bed, and sat down on it, with her back turned to Kamásheff. What he would have done I do not know, had not Dr. Benis and Upadishevsky induced him to go to another room, where, as I heard later from Upadishevsky, the doctor spoke firmly to him.

'If,' said he, 'you venture on any violent measures, I will not be responsible for the consequences; it may even kill the boy, and I am anxious about

the mother too.' Upadishevsky also implored him
to be merciful to a poor woman, who was in such
despair that she did not know what she was
saying, and still more to have pity on a poor sick
boy; and he promised that he would persuade
my mother to go away before long. Kamásheff
gave way very reluctantly, and went off with the
doctor to report the whole affair to the Rector.
Upadishevsky went back to my mother and tried
to quiet her by saying that she might stay with
me two hours. She did stay till dark, till nearly
six in the evening. The scene with Kamásheff
frightened me at first, and I was beginning to feel
the familiar pressure on the chest; but when he
left the room, the fit was stopped by my mother's
presence, her conversation and caresses, and my
own happiness. At parting, my mother said
positively that she would remove me from the
school altogether and take me back home; and
I believed her implicitly. I was accustomed to
think that she could do whatever she liked, and
a bright future began to shine before me in all the
rainbow colours of the happy past.

On leaving the school, my mother went straight
to Dr. Benis's house. He was not at home; and
she threw herself, literally threw herself, at the
feet of his wife and implored her with tears to
help in rescuing her son from the school. Mme
Benis understood a mother's feeling and was
keenly interested: she said that her husband
would do what he could, and she would vouch for
his assistance. The doctor soon came in, and
both ladies, each in her own way, pressed him
hard. But he needed no convincing: he said
that he quite agreed and had hinted at this course

to the Rector; but, unfortunately, the head
master was there too, and his strong opposition
to the plan had apparently prevailed with the
Rector, a weak but not ill-natured man; nevertheless, success was not beyond hope. Next, my
mother described all the unfairness and petty
tyranny which I had suffered from the head
master. As Benis himself disliked the man for
his usurpation of power that did not belong to
him, he served to increase rather than allay
my mother's exasperation, till she positively
hated Kamásheff as the cruellest of enemies to
herself and her son. The doctor and his wife
treated her with the kindness of friends or relations: they made her lie down on a sofa and take
some food, twenty-four hours having passed since
she had tasted even tea; they gave her some
medicine, and, above all, they assured her that
my illness was purely nervous, and that I should
soon get perfectly well in my country home. It
was decided to wage open war against the head
master. It was next settled that my mother
should call on the Rector early next morning,
before he received Kamásheff's report; she was to
ask permission to visit me twice a day in hospital,
and then to ask him to promise, that, if the doctor
thought it necessary, I should have leave to go
home and stay there, with my parents to look
after me, till I had quite recovered. Benis only
asked of her not to complain of Kamásheff, not
to abuse him, and not to allude to his personal
dislike and persecution of me. My mother called
down Heaven's blessing on the doctor and his wife,
and expressed all the gratitude that a mother's
heart can feel; and then she went back to her

lodgings to rest. Rest was a positive necessity for her : a day filled with such painful anxiety, after travelling twelve days under such conditions with little sleep or food, would have been enough to prostrate even a strong man ; and she was a woman, and not in robust health.

But God reveals His power and might in the feeble ; and, after some hours of sleep, she awoke full of courage and determination. At nine in the morning she was already seated in the Rector's drawing-room. He came at once, and his manner clearly showed that he was prejudiced against her. But his mood soon changed, when the sincerity of grief and the eloquence of tears found the way to his heart. Without raising much difficulty, he gave her leave to visit her son in hospital twice a day and stay there till eight in the evening ; but her request that I might leave the school met with more opposition. Tears and entreaties would perhaps have won a second victory ; but suddenly the head master came in, and the scene changed. The Rector now raised his voice and said that it was an unheard-of proceeding to let Government scholars go home, either on the ground of ill-health, or because they suffered from home-sickness. In the former case, it would be an admission that there was insufficient medical attendance and care for the boys when ill ; and in the latter, it would be simply absurd : what boy, especially a spoilt boy accustomed to seek only his own amusement, would *not* feel home-sick when sent to school ? Kamásheff at once chimed in and supported the Rector : he said a great deal, and there was much good sense in what he said, and as much ill-nature. He referred to the harm

done by women as educators and by mothers who spoilt their children; he spoke of dangerous examples of disrespect, insubordination, presumption, and ingratitude. Finally he said, that when the Government spent money on the salaries of the staff and the maintenance of the scholars, it did not intend that the boys should leave the school before passing through the whole curriculum and making themselves competent to serve the State in the teaching profession. He added that the authorities of the school must attach special importance to a boy whose excellent ability and conduct made it likely that he would turn out in future a successful teacher. This Jesuitical duplicity was too much for my mother: forgetting Benis's warning, she burst out with great warmth and little prudence:

'It surprises me that M. Kamásheff should praise my son, because he has never ceased, since the poor boy entered the school, to vex and torment him for trifles, to rebuke him when he did not deserve it, and to make fun of him. He has applied to him many insulting nicknames, such as 'cry-baby' and 'mammy's darling,' which of course have been taken up by all the boys; and this unjust persecution on the part of the head master is the only reason why ordinary home-sickness has developed into a dangerous illness. I recognize the head master as my personal enemy. He usurps power that does not belong to him: he tried to turn me out of the hospital, although I had the Rector's permission. He is a partial judge, and has no right to decide this question!'

The Rector was a good deal disconcerted; but

Kamásheff retorted angrily, that she herself and her unreasonable impetuosity were entirely to blame. 'In my absence,' he said, 'she took advantage of the weakness of my substitute, and constantly took her son home or visited him here. Then she broke off her journey and came back to Kazan, and after two months has come back again. In this way she never gives the boy time to get accustomed to his new position. She herself, and not the severity of his masters, is the cause of his illness; and her present visit will do a great deal of harm; for her son, who was recovering, had a serious relapse early this morning.' At these words, my mother cried out and fainted away. The good-natured Rector was horribly frightened and perplexed. The swoon lasted long: it was nearly an hour before she became conscious; and her first words were, 'Let me go to my son!' The Rector, very sorry for her and frightened about her, was glad that at least she was not dead— he much feared that she was, as he used to tell afterwards—and he gave a positive order to Kamásheff that she was to be admitted at all times to the hospital; and there she accordingly went at once.

The doctor met her there and did his best to calm her fears. He gave her a solemn assurance that my new symptom, fever, was of no importance, being due merely to nervous excitement; it might even have a good influence on my regular attacks. In fact, the first fever-fit was very mild, and though the second was more severe and was followed by others during the next fortnight, yet the hysterical seizures never returned. Nearly the whole of every day my mother spent with me.

The Rector visited the hospital several times, and each time that he found her there, showed much kindness to both of us : he could not look without pity at my thin pale face ; and the expressive features of my mother, which clearly revealed her thoughts and feelings, also awakened his sympathy. But when Kamásheff tried to enter my room next day, she locked the door and would not let him in ; and afterwards she asked the Rector to prevent the head master from visiting me in her presence. ' I cannot control myself,' she said, ' at the sight of that man, and I am afraid of frightening the patient by an attack such as I had in your house.' The Rector, who had a lively recollection of that event, expressed his willingness ; and Kamásheff, much insulted, ceased coming to see me at all.

Meanwhile the plan of removing me from the school, which had gained strength from the doctor's consent and then been postponed by my fresh illness, was proceeding in due form. My mother wished to begin by discussing the plan with her friends, and went to see M. Knyazhévitch. That kind-hearted but rather gruff and positive Serbian disapproved of her purpose. ' No, no ! my dear lady,' he said ; ' I cannot advise you to take your son and wrap him up in cotton wool, to coddle him and feed him on sugar and carry him off to the country, that he may run about there with the village boys and grow up ignorant and good-for-nothing. You will make nothing of him that way. I tell you frankly that, if I were in your husband's place, I should not allow you to do it.' My mother was displeased ; she said that she did not intend her son to grow up a dunce

and a country bumpkin, but she did certainly wish to save his life and restore him to health. She had no further interviews with M. Knyaz-hévitch. Next she turned to a distant relation of my father's who lived at Kazan : his name was Mikhéyeff, and he was a lawyer. Though he also disapproved of her plan and declined to take any active steps in support of it, he was willing to do one thing she asked—to write a petition for my release, to be submitted to the Governors. In the petition, my mother asked that her son might be restored to her for a time, with a view to the recovery of his health ; and she pledged herself to place me again in the school as a Government scholar, as soon as I was well. This petition was accompanied by a report from Dr. Benis, in which he said that, in his opinion, it was absolutely necessary to send young Aksákoff home to his parents ; the country was specially indicated, because my illness was of a kind which nothing but country air and home life could overcome ; treatment in the hospital would be quite useless ; my attacks threatened to develop into epilepsy, and epilepsy might end in apoplexy or injury to the brain. How far all this was true, I cannot tell ; but the doctor was not content to stop there. He asserted that I had some swelling of the knees and a tendency to crookedness in the bones of the leg ; and these symptoms called for exercise in the open air and a prolonged course of some syrup—I don't remember its name—which he offered to supply out of the stock of medicines provided by Government for the school. I believe that all this last part of the report was fictitious : I really had very thick knees ; but many children

have, and it passes off without treatment. Nevertheless, these trifling external symptoms were treated with great respect in the later stages of this affair.

The business began at a meeting of the Governors. The Rector was in the chair, and the others present were Kamásheff and the three senior teachers. Kamásheff, who generally settled everything, asserted his influence, and the three teachers sided with him. The Rector could not make up his mind. The majority were for instructing Benis to invite to a consultation the senior medical officer in the town, and then to continue his treatment of me; but Benis explained beforehand that he would not carry out such an instruction, and would report to the Governors in favour of letting me go at once; for, as soon as the fever had passed off, symptoms had appeared, portending a renewal of the previous attacks. This, indeed, was perfectly true. My poor mother, seeing that things were not going well, became quite desperate. Finally Benis advised my mother to put this request before the Rector—that he should order me to be examined in his presence by the school doctor and other doctors from outside, and that he should be guided by their opinion; and she drove off at once to the Rector's house. Wishing to protect himself from tears and petitions, of which he was heartily weary, the Rector sent a message that he could not possibly receive her that day, and hoped she would come back another time. But this rebuff was not the first, and my mother was prepared: she had brought with her a letter, in which she said: ' This is my last visit. If you refuse to see me, I will not leave your

drawing-room till I am turned out. But I do not believe you will behave so harshly to an unhappy mother.' The Rector could not help himself: he emerged into the drawing-room, and again he was not proof against the expression of genuine grief and even despair. He pledged his word to carry out all my mother's wishes, and he kept his word. The very next day the Governors of the school passed a motion in perfect agreement with Benis's suggestion and my mother's request. But the Rector himself was the only person who was aware of this: everyone else thought that Benis would resent an examination by outside doctors, and they were convinced that these doctors would disagree with Benis.

Two of the leading physicians in the town were called in. Benis, confident that they would concur in his opinion, waited calmly for the issue of events, and his confidence did something to calm my mother, who tried in her turn to soothe me. She repeated to me in minute detail all she had done and all she had said, and tried to convince me that, in spite of obstacles, she had not given up hope of success. I could share this hope only at times and not for long: deliverance from my stone prison, as I called the school, and restoration to my home in the country, seemed to me bliss beyond attainment and beyond possibility. The choice of doctors involved much correspondence with the authorities; and the Rector, urged by Kamásheff, ordered that I should be discharged from hospital, the fever having entirely left me. Benis was forced to give his consent. So I went back to Upadishevsky's dormitory, where I found my bed empty. After a considerable spell of

freedom in the peace and quiet of the sick-room,
I disliked more than ever the regular rules and
constant noise of school life ; and also the move
struck me as a bad sign, unfavourable to my
hopes of release. I saw my mother daily, but
only in the general reception-room and not for
long. All this brought depression back upon me,
and my attacks began again as violent as before,
as if there had been no cessation of them. But
this painful situation did not last long, thank
God !

Just a week after my return, when supper was
over and the boys came down to the dormitories
and began to undress, Yevséitch pushed into my
hand a note from my mother and said, ' Don't let
any one see you reading this ! ' My mother told
me not to get up next morning ; I was to tell
Upadishevsky that my legs, and especially my
knees, were aching, and to ask sick-leave to the
hospital. I was told to burn the note, and I did
so at once. I was very much surprised by these
instructions ; for I was quite unaccustomed to
tell lies, and my mother never passed over untruths
without punishment. Though I had a dim suspicion
in the back of my head, that this lie would help
to set me free from school, yet I lay awake a long
time ; I was made unhappy by the thought, that
to-morrow I must tell an untruth, and that
Upadishevsky and the doctor would at once see
through it and detect me. But, when Yevséitch
woke me next morning, I told him that my legs
were aching and that I wished to return to hospital.
A suppressed smile curled the lips of my good
Yevséitch, as he went off to inform Upadishevsky.
To my surprise Upadishevsky took it very coolly.

'Very well,' he said, 'let him stay in bed. I shall just take the boys upstairs and then come back for him and take him off to hospital.' But the boys would not leave me in peace; and a number of them, pulling off the coverlet which I had purposely drawn over my head, asked me why I did not get up. Blushing and confused, I was forced to repeat my lie several times. They laughed and said, 'You're shamming, you're too lazy to work, you like hospital better.' Then the crowd of noisy boys fell in and marched upstairs in order. Upadishevsky soon came back, and without asking any questions about my ailment, took me to the hospital and handed me over to the charge of Ritter, the assistant-surgeon, and the superintendent. My old room was assigned to me, and at nine o'clock Benis came. On beginning his examination, he put this leading question: 'I suppose you feel pain in the legs? I quite expected it.' Then he made the superintendent and the assistant-surgeon look at my knees, and added, 'See how swollen they are in one week, and the inflammation is worse.' There was not the least change in the state of my knees, and I felt no inflammation; but I noticed with surprise, that there seemed to be a general conspiracy to keep up the pretence. I was even more surprised when my mother arrived soon after Benis, and discussed quite calmly with him and the others my new and fictitious symptoms. When we were alone, I looked at her with wonder and asked what it all meant. She took me in her arms and said: 'My dear, we cannot help it: it is the only way; it is what Benis told us to do. You will soon be examined by the other doctors, and you must tell them that

you have pains in your legs. Dr. Benis is positive
that this will secure your discharge.' A ray of
hope flashed before my mind, though I saw no
special reason to rely upon it. Two days later,
my mother told me at night that the examination
would take place to-morrow ; she repeated all that
I was to say about my afflicted legs, and urged me
to answer boldly and without hesitation.

At eleven next day a whole party entered my
room—the Rector, the head master, Benis, and
two strange doctors, the three teachers who were
members of the governing body, and Upadishevsky. They filled my room, which was not large ;
chairs were placed for them all, and they all sat
solemnly down beside my bed. I was so confused
that I began at once to feel faint, but I soon
recovered without any medicine, and listened while
Benis told his colleagues the history of my illness,
sometimes speaking in Latin but chiefly in Russian.
He referred again and again to Upadishevsky ;
and the others cross-examined the dormitory-
master on the spot. Yevséitch also was summoned,
and several questions were put to him about my
state of health before I entered the school. I too
had to answer a great many inquiries ; the doctors
came up to my bed again and again, sounded my
chest and stomach, felt my pulse, and looked at
my tongue. When my knees and leg-bones came
under consideration, all three of them came round
me, and all three suddenly began to prod me in
the part supposed to be affected ; and they talked
very earnestly and got very excited. I remember
that they often repeated the terms, ' serum,'
' lymph,' ' scorbutic habit.' The examination
lasted for an hour at least, and I was quite worn

out by it; but it ended at last, and I fell asleep as soon as they had all gone.

When I woke, my mother was sitting by me, and my dinner was standing cold on the table. My mother was hopeful, but knew nothing yet for certain. She went off immediately to call on Benis, and when she returned in two hours her face was radiant with happiness. The doctors had gone straight from my room to a meeting of the Governors, where they all signed a certificate, to this effect: ' In complete agreement with the opinion of Dr. Benis, we consider it absolutely necessary that the Government scholar, Aksákoff, should be sent home to the country, to be cared for by his parents. A syrup has already been prescribed for the patient; but we think it as well to add certain other medicines, to be followed by a course of cold baths to recuperate the strength.' The Rector gave his consent in plain terms, and the three teachers followed his example; only Kamásheff would not budge, and refused to sign the minutes; [1] but that did no harm.

And so the desired event, which for so long had seemed a mere castle in the air, really came to pass. My mother was radiant with bliss; she laughed and cried and embraced everybody, especially Upadishevsky and Yevséitch, and she thanked God. I was so happy at times I could not believe in my happiness: I thought it all a beautiful dream and feared to wake up; I clasped my mother close and asked if it was really true. She sat with me longer than usual that evening, till Upadishevsky came in more than once, to ask

[1] Copies of all the papers were long preserved in our house. (*Author's Note.*)

her to go. Kamásheff behaved like himself to the last : he proposed to the Governors to require my mother, in view of the five months I had spent at the school, to refund the whole cost of my maintenance and education. But the Rector did not agree : he said that I was not being expelled but only sent home for convalescence. Three days after the consultation the Governors summoned my mother to appear before them, and made her sign a promise to send me back when I was well ; then they gave her leave to take me. She came straight from the meeting to visit the hospital for the last time ; Yevséitch had dressed me in my own clothes, returning my uniform and books and all other Government property. We said good-bye to Upadishevsky and to the hospital superintendent with tears of ardent gratitude. Then my mother took my hand, and she and Yevséitch brought me out upon the steps.

I gave a cry of joyful surprise. The carriage from home was standing in front of the steps, drawn by four of our own horses bred at Aksákovo ; I knew the coachman on the box, and I knew the postillion still better, for he used always to supply me with worms for bait. Theodor and Yevséitch placed me at my mother's side in the old carriage, and we drove off to our lodgings. In spite of the joy which filled or, I might say, intoxicated my heart, I cried so when taking leave of Upadishevsky, that I went on crying even in the carriage. And surely this good man's unselfish kindness to us who had been mere strangers, and his tender sympathy which did not shrink from self-sacrifice, deserved the truest gratitude ; and it should be added, that his many years of service at the school

could not fail to accustom him to cases of the kind, and there are few hearts that are not hardened by custom. At our lodgings Parásha was awaiting me with tears of joy; and the lady of the house, our old acquaintance Mme Aristoff, showed in the same way the interest she took in our situation.

That same evening my mother and I called on Dr. Benis, to thank him and say good-bye. I must do full justice to him too: for some reason he passed in the town for a cold selfish man, but his conduct to us was obliging and disinterested. He would not take one penny from us, and even refused the present which my mother offered him as a souvenir of our obligations; of course she repaid the 25 roubles which he had paid as consultation-fee to each of the doctors who had examined me. All she could do was to thank Benis by words and tears and prayers for his welfare; and she did this with such warmth and sincerity that he and his wife were deeply touched. So far as I was concerned, I was somehow not touched; and though I knew very well that I owed my deliverance from school to Benis alone, I shed no tears, and my expression of thanks was so languid and trivial that my mother scolded me afterwards. Early next day we went to the Cathedral and then to the church of Our Lady of Kazan, and offered thankful prayers. We called on the Rector; but he was either away from home or unwilling to receive us. On returning home, we found Upadishevsky, who had come for one more parting interview. He also refused to accept any souvenir. His answer to my mother was short and clear: 'Please don't insult me, Sofya Nikoláyevna.' I did not part with him as I had parted with the

doctor : I cried so terribly that for a long time I could not be stopped ; and one of the old attacks seemed to be coming on, when my excitement was soothed by some new drops. I ought to say of this medicine, that three times during these days it was successful in arresting a fainting-fit. When Upadishevsky left, we had a hasty dinner and then set to work at once on our packing. We were afraid to stay in Kazan, and each hour before our departure seemed like a long day. By evening all was ready. The evening set in warm, a real summer evening, and my mother and I went to bed in the carriage. At dawn the horses were put in very quietly ; and I was still asleep, when we drove slowly out of Kazan.

When I awoke, bright sunlight was pouring into the carriage. Parásha was asleep ; my mother was sitting beside me, weeping tears of joy and gratitude to God ; and her eyes showed her feeling so clearly that any spectator of her tears would have rejoiced and not grieved. She embraced her darling child, and a torrent of tender words and caresses showed what she was feeling. It was the 19th of May, my sister's birthday. It was a real May day ; the spring morning was warm, even hot, and flooded all the landscape with burning light. The green fields of young corn, the meadows and woods, peeped in at the carriage windows ; I felt such a desire to survey the whole wide prospect, that I asked to have the carriage stopped. Then I sprang out, and began to run and jump like a playful child of five, while my mother watched me with delight from the carriage. For the first time, I felt that I was really free. I embraced Yevséitch and Theodor ; I exchanged

D

greetings with the coachman and postillion, and the latter found time to tell me that when he left Aksákovo the fish were beginning ' to bite fine '. Next I greeted all the horses : Yevséitch held me up in his arms while I patted each of them. There were six of them, a splendid team of bays and dark-browns, of a breed which has long been quite extinct ; but, twenty years ago, it was still remembered and often spoken of in the Government of Orenburg. They were big horses, standing over sixteen hands high, and strong beyond belief. They generally trotted but could gallop without distress, and they never tired ; they used often to draw a heavy carriage eighty or ninety versts in a day.

Ah, how delighted I was ! When I was obliged to get back into the carriage, I stuck my head out of the window and kept it there till we reached our halting-place, greeting everything we passed with cries of joy. At last a streak of water sparkled before us : this was the Myosha, not a very large river, but deep and abounding with fish. A rather crazy raft worked by a rope crossed it ; and we took a long time to get over. Only one pair of horses could cross at a time, and the carriage could hardly be managed at all : even when all the heavy trunks were taken off it, it made the raft sink low in the water. My mother and I crossed first. The far side was covered with trees and bushes, whose fragrant blossom drove me nearly mad with delight. Our postillion was very fond of fishing, and had brought with him from home a rod and line ready for all emergencies. This was quickly unfastened from its place under the carriage ; and while the horses were crossing,

I was fishing with bread for bait and pulling out roach. Except the Dyoma, I never saw a river better stocked than the Myosha : the fish swarmed in it and took as fast as you could bait your line and throw it back. Is it wonderful that to me, delivered from the prison of school, this halt seemed like heaven ?

On the river-bank behind us there was a gentleman's estate, where we got hay and oats, a chicken and eggs, and all other necessary provisions. Yevséitch was a bit of a cook, and he cooked us a splendid dinner on a gridiron. The fish, fried in a pan, tasted excellent. We had driven thirty *versts* from Kazan, and we stopped four hours before starting again. Clouds came up, thunder began to roll, the ground was sprinkled with rain, the heat and dust disappeared. We started at a slow pace, but afterwards trotted so fast that we covered ten versts in an hour. The sky soon cleared, and a splendid sun dried up the traces of rain. We drove on forty versts farther and camped out for the night, having procured all we needed at our last stoppage. A fresh supply of pleasures and enjoyments for me ! The horses were taken out and hobbled, and allowed to crop the juicy young grass ; a bright fire was lit, and the travelling *samovár*—really a large teapot [1] with a funnel —was placed on it ; a leather rug was spread out beside the carriage, the canteen was brought out, and tea served ; how good it was in the fresh evening air ! In two hours the horses had cooled down and were watered ; their nose-bags were

---

[1] The *samovár* is an urn with a central receptacle for charcoal : here the receptacle is inserted where the lid of the teapot should be.

opened and fastened either to the carriage-pole or to posts driven into the ground ; and then the horses were let loose upon the oats. My mother and I and Parásha lay down in the carriage ; and as I sank into a delicious sleep, I listened to the horses munching their oats and snorting when the dusty particles got into their nostrils.

Early next day we crossed the Kama, which was still in flood, a little above Shooran. I was afraid, as I am still, to cross a great river ; and a tolerable breeze was blowing that day. There was a large new ferry-boat, on which room was found for all our horses and the carriage. Parásha and I were shut up inside the carriage, with the blinds down, to prevent my seeing the rushing water ; and I tied a handkerchief round my head as well ; yet even then I shook with fear till we had got across. But there were no unpleasant consequences. We landed at Murzicha ; and my mother hunted up the fishermen who had guided her over the ice ; she had brought handsome presents for them all, and the presents were received with no surprise but with pleasure and gratitude. Fifteen versts brought us to our next halt. And so our journey went on, till on the fifth day we arrived at Baitoogan, a village on the river Sok and not more than twenty versts from Aksákovo, where we spent a night. Though this is a good river for fishing, my mother feared the evening damp and would not allow me to go ; but our postillion took a run to the riverside, and came back with some perch and roach. By rising at dawn as usual, we avoided stopping at Nyeklyoodovo where relations of my grandmother lived ; they were asleep when we passed, and so were we. Four versts from Aksákovo, just where our estate begins, I woke up suddenly, as if I had been roused on purpose; we drove on between the two woods and came out on the slope of the hill; from there we were bound soon to see Aksákovo—the large pond and the mill, the long line of peasants' huts, our house and the birch woods beside it. I kept asking the coachman whether he could see it, and at last he bent down to the front window, and said, 'There is our Aksákovo, as clear as if it lay in the palm of one's hand!' Then I begged so eagerly to sit on the box beside the coachman, that my mother could not refuse me. I shall not try to describe what I felt when I saw my dear Aksákovo. Human language has no words adequate to express such feelings!

I continued throughout my life to feel, when approaching Aksákovo, the same emotion as I did then. But some years ago I was getting near the place after an absence of twelve years. Again it was early morning; my heart beat fast with expectation, and I hoped to feel the happy excitement of former days. I called up the dear old times, and a swarm of memories came round me. Alas! they brought no happiness to my heart but only pain and suffering, and I felt heavy and sad beyond expression. Like the magician, who sought in vain to hide from the spirits he had called up but could not control, so I did not know how to banish my recollections and lay the storm of my troubled heart. Old bottles will not hold new wine, and old hearts are unfit to bear the feelings of youth. But *then*—ah, what were my feelings *then*!

Several times I felt the oppression on my chest

and was pretty near falling; but I said nothing and held tight to the rail of the box and pressed against the coachman; and the trouble passed off naturally. The carriage rolled quickly down the hill and crossed the rickety bridge over the river. We nearly stuck in a swampy place, but our strong horses pulled the carriage through it, and we passed the reed-beds, the pond, and the village. And there was our house at last, and standing on the steps were my father and my dear little sister. When we drove up, she clapped her little hands and screamed out, ' Brother Seryózha is on the box ! ' My aunt hurried out, bringing my brother ; and my baby sister was carried out by her foster-mother. How many embraces and kisses ! how many questions and answers ! how much happiness ! All the outdoor servants collected, and even the labourers who happened to be at home, and a crowd of boys and girls from the village. My father was delighted. He was doubtful whether it would be possible to get me away from school ; and we were too busy during our last week in Kazan to let him know what was happening.

CHAPTER II

A YEAR IN THE COUNTRY

THE first days were days of unthinking and unresting activity. My earliest visit was paid to my pigeons and the two hawks which had lived through the winter. Then I ran round to every dear and familiar spot, and there were plenty of them. Round the house, in the garden and kitchen-garden, and in the wood with the jackdaws' nests near the house, my sister kept constantly at my side and held my hand; sometimes she even pointed out to me, as if I were a stranger, some alteration which I had missed by my absence—for instance, a steaming hot-bed, very large and high, planted with melons and gourds. We went together to the store-room, where some pretty boxes were kept; they were made of copper or iron and adorned with carved ivory, and contained a number of specimens and fossils presented to my mother long ago by some friend who held an important position in the mines. We paid a visit also to the cellar, where Pelagéya, the housekeeper, feasted us on cool thick cream and brown bread.

To the river and across the river my sister might not go with me; and Yevséitch took her place for the time. He and I went over the gangway to the first island, where our summer-kitchen was, and a wide bark floor where the wheat was dried after it was washed clean. This little island was surrounded on two sides by the old channel of the river, which was now overgrown with osiers and beginning to dry up. We crossed this channel on planks and came at once to the other island. It was larger, and the old channel which surrounded it on one side was still deep and clear. This was a favourite spot with my aunt Tatyána ; it was divided in the middle by a lime avenue, and birches grew all along the river bank. My grandfather must have had a fancy for the place in old days ; for he planted the trees there long before the birth of his youngest daughter, Tányusha [1] as he used to call her ; the trees were now fifty years old, and she was thirty-five. Like all her sisters, my aunt had received no education, but she loved nature and kept in her heart a kind of leaning towards culture. She possessed a few stray books, chiefly old novels, probably procured for her by her brother, and some plays. Of course, I read them all through, with permission or without permission ; I remember in particular a kind of vaudeville, called *A Trifle for the Stage*. My aunt was fond of sitting on the island, where she read a book and fished in the deep water of the old channel. On many of the birch-trees she had carved her own name and various dates, and even verses from her song-book. How I loved this island ! How pleasant it was in summer heats to sit there in the cool shade with the water all round ! On one side the new cutting from the mill-dam joined the stream that raced from under the mill-wheel ; and on the other side the old channel of the Boogoorooslan, then deep and clear, made a bend round the island. To this day my heart is strongly stirred when I recall summer afternoons which I spent there. Now, all is changed. The

[1] A pet-name for Tatyána.

old channel is almost dry ; a fresh cutting carries away the water from the pond in another direction ; the osiers and alders have spread everywhere ; and the island, though it keeps the name, no longer deserves it. In a loose sense, indeed, the name may be applied to the whole plot of land extending to the mill-dam.

When I had admired the island sufficiently, had examined each tree and read all my aunt's inscriptions, and had looked long enough at the chub and carp darting below me or hanging motionless in the water—then I started off with Yevséitch for the mill ; but first I paid hasty visits to two other spots, ' Antony's gangway ' where I used to catch gudgeon, and the forge where I liked to watch the red-hot iron and the sparks leaping from under the hammer. When at last the expanse of the pond opened out before me with its green reeds and burdock-leaves, and the long mill-dam over-grown with young alder and teeming with a bird and fish population of its own, I was mute with wonder and delight and stood there some minutes, as if rooted to the ground. I was a favourite with the miller, who was nicknamed Boltunyónok ; [1] and he had prepared a surprise for me. Knowing that I was sure to come, he had set some wire lines among the weed for pike and left them unvisited till I came. Now he made Yevséitch and me get into a boat and rowed us to the place ; the water was very shallow, and I was not frightened this time. I drew up each line myself, and on one of them was a large pike which I pulled out with Yevséitch to help me, and carried in triumph all the way home in my own hands.

[1] i.e. ' Little chatterbox ' ; *boltún* = chatterbox.

Two days later my father took me further afield to fish; he also drove with me to ' Antony's dyke ', where an active spring spouted from the top of a hill, making a foaming waterfall; to Koloda, where the water ran from a spring into wooden troughs ready to receive it; to the Mordoff dyke, where a spring burst out of a rocky fissure at the foot of the hill; to the lime-tree wood, and the ' Sacred Wood ',[1] and the place between them where the bee-hives were kept. The old bee-man, another great friend of mine, lived there summer and winter in a low turf hut; and he had a tom-cat called Alka and a tabby called Sonya, which he had named, as a compliment, after my father and mother.

Such were the pleasant occupations that took up my time during the first fortnight after our arrival at Aksákovo. I need not say how happy my mother was, when she saw me cheerful and enterprising and, to all appearance, well. Before leaving Kazan, in order to prevent my life in the country being spent in complete idleness, she had procured copies of the text-books used in the school. She never forgot, that, if by God's mercy I recovered my health, I must be sent back to school at the end of a year; and she set apart two or three hours a day, in which I was to revise what I had learnt, and practise writing, and read aloud to her various books suitable to my age. I carried out this plan very willingly, and my outdoor amusements pleased me all the better after my tasks. I also began again to teach my dear little sister and pupil to read;

[1] i. e. A wood preserved from the ravages of thieves by a religious service celebrated by the priest on the spot.

and this time my efforts were crowned with complete success.

I said above that I was apparently quite well ; but it did not in fact turn out quite so. It is true that I had not a single seizure after leaving school ; and the feeling of oppression and palpitation passed away on our journey, and there was no return of these symptoms at home. But I now became excessively restless and began to talk in my sleep every night. At first my mother attached no importance at all to this, attributing it to over-exercise and the liveliness of a child's impressions ; this was all the more natural, because I had often talked in my sleep before I went to school, and many children are apt to do so. But now the thing began by degrees to assume a different character.

In the first place, I began to talk every night, and several times on some nights, and to talk very excitedly. In the second place, I began also to cry and sob in my sleep, to jump out of bed and try to walk out of the room. I slept with my parents in their bedroom, and my bed was close to theirs. The door was now locked on the inside, and Pelagéya the housekeeper slept in the passage outside the door, to make it impossible for me to leave the room. My nocturnal distress grew worse every day, or rather every night, till at last it bore an evident resemblance to the fits from which I used to suffer, during the day only, at school : once again I cried and sobbed till I became unconscious, and this was followed by ordinary sound sleep. But these fresh attacks by night were much more violent and alarming than what I had experienced before ; and there was more variety in the

symptoms. Sometimes I cried quietly and moaned,
with hands always clenched against my chest and
inarticulate muttering; this went on for whole
hours, and passed into spasmodic and furious
movements in case an attempt was made to wake
me. As time went on, these attempts were given
up. When I was tired out by tears and sobbing,
I went quietly to sleep. But it was very difficult,
especially at first, for the bystanders to look on
at such suffering without trying to wake me and
afford me some relief. I was told afterwards, that
not only my mother, who suffered terribly at the
sight, but my father and my aunt and all my
attendants, broke down themselves and could not
witness my distressing symptoms without tears.
At other times I sprang to my feet with a piercing
cry and stared wildly round, repeating again and
again disjointed and meaningless phrases, such as,
' Let me go! '—' Go away! '—' I can't! '—' Where
is he? '—' Where shall I go? ' Then I dashed to
the door or window or corners of the room,
trying to get past, and battering the wall with
hands and feet. At such times I was so strong
that two or three people could not hold me, and
I dragged them about the room, with the sweat
pouring from me. This kind of attack always
ended with a severe fainting-fit, in the course of
which it was hard to determine whether I was still
breathing; the swoon by degrees passed off into
sleep, rather disturbed at first, but then sound
and quiet, and sometimes lasting till nine in the
morning. After such a night I woke up as fresh
and lively as if I had been peacefully asleep all
the time; and though the furious excitement and
exertion left me rather weak and pale, these

symptoms soon passed off, and I was quite cheerful all day, learning my lessons, running about, and giving myself up to my amusements. On waking, I had no clear recollection that anything had happened; sometimes I fancied vaguely that I had dreamt of something falling upon me and smothering me, or of monsters pursuing me; sometimes, when the people holding me could not help coaxing me with kind words to lie down and be quiet, their efforts roused me for an instant to a sense of reality; and then, when I was wide awake next morning, I remembered waking for some reason in the night, to find my parents and others standing by my bed, while the nightingales sang in the bushes under the windows and the corncrakes cried across the river.

My mother was at her wits' end; she was specially alarmed by the way in which my face was convulsed and I foamed at the mouth, while unconscious. These were ominous signs; and the idea, that my trouble might really be that epilepsy which Yevséitch had foretold in his letter long before, filled her with horror. She ceased to give me the drops prescribed by Dr. Benis; the medicine for purifying the blood, which had been supplied from the Government stock of drugs, she never used at all, though Benis advised that it should be tried; he suspected scrofula, which I never had. She allowed me to bathe in the river, thinking that bathing might make me stronger; but, though I enjoyed it exceedingly, it did me no good. Next my mother had recourse to Benis: she sent him a description of the course of my illness, a description so admirable that the doctor was charmed by it; he thanked her for it and sent me some pills and a kind of tea, and prescribed a diet. All his directions were precisely carried out, but the illness was not relieved : on the contrary, the attacks became more obstinate, and I grew weaker. The medicines were now given up, and the 'wise women' and 'wise men' of the countryside were tried. They all agreed that I was bewitched and had been 'overlooked' by some one ; they tried baths and ointments and fumigations, but all to no purpose.

I am not in the least opposed to popular medicine. I believe in it, especially in connexion with mesmerism ; and I have long ago renounced the contemptuous view which many take of it, from their superior position of enlightenment and science. I have seen so many remarkable and convincing cases, that I cannot question the efficacy of many of the remedies used by the people. But they did me no good then, perhaps because they did not suit my ailment, or perhaps because my mother would not allow any but external applications to be tried. I remember, however, that on the advice of a lady who lived near us I took powdered fern for a long time ; only the youngest sprouts were used, those which look like a comb and spring immediately from the root, between the large indented leaves of the plant. But the fern also did no good. In the end, the commonest of all medicines was tried ; it had been constantly used in our house in my grandparents' time, and my aunt had often suggested it ; but my mother had a prejudice against it, and for long would not hear of its being tried. It was called 'fit-drops' or 'storax-drops',[1]

---

[1] These are apparently what Aksákoff elsewhere calls 'Haarlem Drops': as 'Dutch Drops', they are to this day regarded as a panacea by sailors.

because the resin of storax was the chief ingredient; ten drops were poured into half a glass of water, and the water turned as white as milk. The number of drops was increased by two each day, till twenty-five were taken at one dose; it was always given at night. After twenty-five drops had been reached, the dose was lessened by two drops each day till it finally came down to ten. The very first dose did me good; and in a month the illness had completely disappeared and never returned. I went on bathing all the time, and ate just what I pleased. What a noise it would have made, if some famous doctor had cured me with such marvellous success! What a relief it was to my poor mother and father and all the household, especially to Pelagéya the housekeeper, who was constantly occupied with me during the attacks, beginning to tell me fairy-stories as soon as I went to bed, and going on with them even after I fell asleep. My mother was as happy as if she had rescued me from school a second time. My case shows how often we go far afield in search of healing, when it is close beside us all the time. I shall now go back a little in the course of my narrative.

In spite of the alarming nature of my illness, I went on all the time with my lessons and outdoor amusements also; only, when the attacks became more severe, I was more moderate in the amount of exercise I took, and my mother kept a careful eye on me, and would not let me go far away or for long. Every morning before the great heat came on, I went out with Yevséitch to fish. Our very best fishing was in the garden, and almost under our windows, because there was a mill and

a very large pond below Aksákovo in the village
of Kivatsky, and the overflow caused by the dam
extended nearly as far up as our garden. Every
sportsman knows how good the fishing is, under
such conditions. Now for the first time I became
acquainted with the fisherman's chief delight—
the catching of large fish. Up till then I had caught
only roach, perch, and gudgeons ; it is true that
the two former fish often attain considerable size,
but, for some reason, I never happened to hook
a very large one ; and if I had, I could not have
landed it, as I used thin lines and small hooks.
But now Yevséitch plaited two lines for me, each
of twenty horse-hairs, attached stout hooks to
them, and tied the lines to strong rods ; then he
took his own line as well, and guided me through
the garden to a pool which he kept a secret from
others, and which he called ' The Golden Pool '.
He baited my hook with a piece of brown bread-
crumb about the size of a large hazel-nut, and cast
my line right under a bush in the deep water, while
he dropped his own by the bank near the weed and
rushes. I sat quietly, never daring to take my
eyes off my float, as it swayed gently up and down
in the eddy that formed under the bank. Before
long, Yevséitch suddenly sprang up and cried out,
' I've got him, *bátyushka* ' ; [1] then he began to
struggle with a big fish, holding the rod in both
hands. Yevséitch had no idea of scientific fishing :
he merely pulled with all his might, trying to jerk
the fish out over his shoulder. But the fish had
probably got fixed behind some weed or rushes ;
the rod was no more than a stick, and the line

---

[1] The word means ' father ', but is used as a general
title of respect or affection.

broke, so that we did not even see what sort of a fish it was. Yevséitch was much excited; and I too, as I watched him, was almost shaking. He vowed that it was the largest fish he had ever hooked in his life; but it was probably a carp or chub of ordinary size, which seemed so heavy to him because it had got entangled in the weed. Then he shook free my other line and cast it as quick as he could into the same spot: ' I believe I was a little too hasty,' he said: ' next time I won't pull so hard; ' and down he sat on the grass, to wait for a second bite; but none came.

My chance came next, and fortune resolved to do me a good turn. My float began gradually to rise on end and fall again; then it remained on end and finally disappeared under water. I struck, and a very large fish began to move heavily, as if reluctantly, through the water. When Yevséitch ran to my aid and caught hold of my rod, I remembered what he had just said, and told him again and again not to pull so hard. At last, as the rod, which I never let go, was not very supple,[1] and the line was new and strong, we landed somehow by our united efforts a very large carp. Yevséitch fell on it at full length, crying out, ' Now we've got him, my little falcon; he won't escape now.! ' In my joy I shook like a man in a fever—indeed this often happened afterwards when I caught a large fish; for long I could not calm down, but kept constantly running to look

---

[1] In order to land big fish, a supple rod is generally much better than a stiff one. But in this case, contrary to all the rules of art, the fish was jerked out over the shoulder; and therefore the stiff rod did good service, as the line was tough enough to support the fish. (*Author's Note.*)

at my prize, as it lay on the grassy bank at a safe distance from the water. We threw in the line again; but the fish had ceased to take, and half an hour later we went home, as I had only leave to be out a short time. This early success confirmed once for all my passion for fishing. We tied the carp to a branch, and I carried it home to show my father, who liked to fish at times himself. In those days it was not our custom at Aksákovo to weigh big fish; but I believe that I never afterwards caught so large a carp, and that it weighed at least seven pounds.

My father sometimes took me with him when he went out shooting, but he went very seldom. I took a strong interest in the proceedings, and these expeditions were red-letter days for me, although my share was confined to performing the duties of a retriever: I mean that I ran to pick up the dead birds and handed them to my father. I might not even hold the gun. But in the summer holidays three years later—I shall describe this period when I come to it—I fired a gun for the first time, and my fate was fixed; all other sports, even fishing, lost their charm in my eyes, and I became and remained throughout life a passionate lover of the gun.

August was ending before I was quite well again, and the large fish had long ceased to take; but I managed to pull out some of considerable size, and, as a matter of course, lost twice as many; the perch-fishing, on the other hand, was still at its best. Besides, I was much interested at that time in hawking. As early as July, the old hawks were taken out in pursuit of quails, and the young birds taken from the nest had long been in training. The sport was carried on with great success. The old hawks were managed by Mazan and Tanaichónok, the young ones by Theodor and Yevséitch. I had a little hawk of my own, very well trained, with which I caught sparrows and other small birds. I sometimes drove to the fields on a long car with one of the falconers, most often with Yevséitch, and I liked to watch the pursuit of the fat autumn quails and landrails. And so I passed the summer and beginning of autumn, constantly engaged in country occupations and amusements, among which I may reckon expeditions to pick berries and, later in the year, mushrooms.[1]

My mother had no taste for such expeditions, and could seldom be persuaded to drive with my father and me to field or forest. I remember, however, that she was sometimes tempted out to the fallow lands near the house by the wild strawberries which grew there in wonderful profusion in those days; she was very fond of them and thought them good for her health. Occasionally we drove in a family party to the picturesque springs in the hills and drank tea in the shade of the birches; but my mother was bored beyond endurance by picking mushrooms, though my father and aunt were very fond of it, and I shared their taste. But the worst thing of all was, that my mother did not love our dear

[1] I did not then foresee that picking mushrooms would provide one of the standing amusements of my old age. In gratitude for this, I long ago took a fancy—and I do not yet give it up—of writing a little book about mushrooms and the pleasure of picking them. (*Author's Note.*)

He did write an article on the subject, which is included in his works.

Aksákovo. In her view, its position was low and damp—she was right there to some extent; the smell from the pond and mill-dam was repulsive; and the water of the springs was chalky and hard. She considered all the conditions positively dangerous to her health; and though there was much truth in her views, there was also much prejudice and exaggeration. It must be remembered that she was born and grew up in a town and would have found the country anywhere lacking in interest. My father and I listened with mortification to the eloquent invectives which she often aimed at Aksákovo, and though we did not venture to defend it, our hearts were not convinced. Though my mother lived in the country, she did not adopt country ways: she occupied herself with her children, or read, or carried on an active correspondence with former acquaintances, most of them notable people, who, after visiting Ufá or living there for a short time, had kept a lasting feeling of friendship and respect for my mother. She liked also to read medical books, Buchan's *Domestic Medicine* being her chief stand-by; while nursing her sick father for several years, she had become used to read books of this kind. She kept a medicine-chest in the house and treated sick people herself, and not only those on our own estate, so that not a few patients used to be brought from the surrounding villages; in this good work my father gave her his active assistance. To the management of the household she gave hardly any attention.

Autumn now came on, and my outdoor amusements, one after another, ceased to be possible. The days grew short and dark; rain and cold soon drove everyone indoors, and I began to spend more time with my mother and to do more lessons in the shape of reading aloud, and writing. In the long evenings, my father used to read to us, and occasionally my mother, who was a remarkably good reader. Though my father had not acquired the habit of reading in his early life at home—my grandparents had no books except almanacs and some pamphlets recommending 'Haarlem Drops' and 'The Elixir of Life'—yet he had a natural taste for literature, as is proved by a very large collection of songs and other verses of that day, copied out by him with his own hand, which is still in my possession. My mother was able to develop this natural taste; and so the readings went on every evening and interested us all. It gives me keen pleasure to recall these evenings, at which my aunt Tatyána was always present. The enjoyment of reading was enhanced by roasted chestnuts, of which my mother was very fond, though they were very bad for her. A copper box [1] containing the chestnuts made its appearance each evening; and nut-crackers and bits of stick were brought in to crack the chestnuts and open them with. But as soon as my interest was excited by the reading, I resented the extra entertainment, because it distracted attention and made it difficult to listen. When my mother was in a happy frame of mind and felt better than usual, her gaiety

[1] The history of this box is worth recording. When my mother was married in 1788, it held her ribbons and laces : in the nineties and as late as 1801, it was our receptacle for roasted chestnuts ; in 1807 it contained more than 100,000 roubles in notes and bills, and diamonds and pearls worth a great sum ; and now it lies under my son's writing-table, crammed with old papers. (*Author's Note.*)

was infectious : she laughed a great deal and made
us laugh too. There were two stories in particular,
Francicico Petroccio and *The Adventures of Ilya
Bendel*,[1] so silly in themselves and so absurdly
translated into bad Russian, that they excited our
hearty laughter ; and then my mother's lively
and pointed comments worked us up to such
a state that we all literally rocked in a paroxysm
of merriment which stopped the reading for some
time. But there were also books which excited
keen interest and sympathy, and even brought
tears to the eyes of the listeners.

The approach of winter with its first snow-
showers and slight frosts made it possible for me
to go back for a time to my outdoor amusements.
We walked up hares, the large grey kind and
the white, over the snow. My father took me with
him, and we were accompanied by a miscellaneous
crowd of beaters. The method was to place nets
almost all round a hare lying in her form ; then the
beaters with loud shouts moved forward along the
open space, till the frightened hare sprang up and
got entangled in the netting. I ran too, and, as
may be guessed, made more noise and got more
excited than any one. I was very fond of this
amusement and liked to talk about it with my
father. When my mother was busy over something and found my constant questions troublesome, or when she was not feeling well, she often
sent me off to my father with the words, ' Go and
talk to him about your dear hares ! '—and then we
two had endless conversations on the subject.

---

[1] Apparently novels of the 18th century, the first
Italian, the second German. I have not been able to
trace them.

Another great occupation of mine was to lay traps for small animals—martens, ermines, and stoats. The soft pretty skins of my victims were hung up as trophies by my bed.

But soon heavy snowstorms began, the ground was covered with deep drifts, and all my outdoor pursuits came to an end for good. A winter snowstorm is a sad and even alarming sight, not only to the wanderer on the steppe, but also to those who sit warm indoors. The snow covers the windows, blows in through the doors, and obliterates all the paths from the house to the servants' cottages, so that they have to be dug out; at forty paces off a man is invisible. At last the snowdrifts become so huge that one cannot believe they will ever disappear, and a feeling of depression is inevitable. Dwellers in the capitals can have no conception of this, but country people will understand and share my feeling. I was confined to the house for good and all: nothing would induce my mother to let me go out with my father on his expeditions to the river. He sometimes went in a sledge to places by a ford, where a barrier or close hedge of stakes, with wicker traps in the middle, had been stuck in where the stream ran deep. Between Christmas and Epiphany, or even earlier, the fish called *nalim* [1] began to get caught in these traps, and some of them were very large. They were brought to the house stiff with the hard frost, and thrown into a large trough full of water; then the fat, mottled, dark-green fish began to thaw by degrees, to splash, and to move their tails covered over with soft down. I stood long beside the trough, admiring their movements,

[1] The English name seems to be ' burbot '.

and starting back each time that the drops of water flew from their fins or tails. My father kept a number of these captives in large tanks, and soup made out of them or, still better, pies made out of their livers, appeared nearly every day at our table, till we all got heartily tired of them. When they ceased to be popular, they became an occasional dish, and the whole stock was exhausted before the end of Lent.

As I have said already, my mother had formerly lived in a town; she had also suffered much oppression and sadness in her childhood and early youth; and then she had gained what may be called some external contact with culture by the reading of books and by acquaintance with people of intelligence and education, according to the standards of those days—a contact which often arouses a kind of pride and contempt for the simple life of the poor. From all these causes combined, she did not understand and did not like the dances of the people, or their songs at weddings and festivals, or their Christmas revels; she did not even know much about them. She was therefore very unwilling to give her consent, when my aunt begged that I might have leave to watch the servants acting. My aunt herself, who had grown up in the country, had a strong taste for everything of the kind: she sometimes got up singing and acting in her own room, and the sweet enchanting sounds of the songs native to the people, as they floated to my ear from two rooms off, filled me with excitement and gave me thoughts which I could not fully understand. I was very much vexed that I was not allowed even to be present at the acting, far less to take part in it; and, as

a consequence of this strict prohibition, I was
tempted at last to deceive my wise mother whom
I loved so well. I began, of course, by begging
to go, and besieged my mother with questions,
asking why she objected to my looking on. She
answered positively and sternly : ' A great deal
that goes on there is silly and repulsive and
undesirable, and you have no business to hear or
see such things, because you are still a child,
unable to distinguish good from evil.' But, as
I saw nothing bad or did not understand it if I saw
it, I obeyed her reluctantly, without inward
conviction and even with a feeling of injury. My
aunt, on the other hand, and her own maids, gave
quite a different account : they said that my
mother was naturally inclined to be discontented
with everything ; that she disliked everything
about country life, and that her bad health was due
to this cause ; that, because she was not cheerful
herself, she wished no one else to be cheerful either.
These words made a secret impression on my
young mind ; and the consequence was, that my
aunt induced me to go for once without leave and
look on at the acting. This was the way in which
it was arranged. From Christmas till Twelfth
Night, my mother was either not very well or not
in good spirits ; instead of reading to us all, my
father read to her, merely to send her to sleep,
some book she did not care for or knew already ;
and after tea, which was always served at six
o'clock in the evening, she slept for two hours or
more ; and during this time I used to go to my
aunt's room. It was on one of these convenient
occasions that she persuaded me to come and see
the mummers. She wrapped me up, head and all,

in a fur coat, put me in the strong arms of her maid, Matrona, and went off with me to the carpenter's cottage, where all the maids and girls of the village were waiting for us, dressed up as bears or turkeys or cranes, old men or old women. In spite of the evil smell of tallow candle-ends, the dim light which a smoky pine torch threw round the large room, and the stifling atmosphere, how much real merriment there was in these simple revels! Those Christmas songs, surviving from remote antiquity and telling of a vanished world, still preserved their living power to charm and captivate the hearts of the people through countless generations. All present were filled with a kind of intoxication of merriment. Both songs and speeches were constantly drowned by bursts of ringing hearty laughter. Those were not actors and actresses representing a part for the amusement of others—the dancers and singers expressed their own feelings, and danced and sang to please themselves out of the abundance of their hearts, and each excited spectator was an actor too. The singing and dancing, talking and laughing, were universal; but just when the fun was most fast and furious, the same strong pair of arms wrapped me up in the fur coat and carried me quickly away from that magical fabulous world. On those nights I lay long awake, and strange forms long danced and sang round my bed and kept company with me even in my dreams.

On the first occasion, I was drawn into this act of deception suddenly and almost forcibly; and after I went back to the house, it was long before I could look my mother in the face; but the fascination of the sight had taken such hold of me that I readily agreed to go a second time, and afterwards took the first step myself, begging my aunt that I might go and see the mummers.

At last the severity of the winter came to an end, and the frost became less intense. As we had no thermometers in those days, I cannot say how many degrees of cold we reckoned; but I remember that birds were frozen, and some bodies of sparrows and jackdaws were brought to me, which had fallen dead in flight and turned stiff in a moment; in some cases they were revived by warmth. In general, I ought to remark that the winters of my childhood and early youth were much more severe than they are now; and this is not merely an old man's prejudice, for during my residence at Kazan before the beginning of the year 1807, mercury was twice frozen, so that we could hammer it like hot iron. But this has become a mere legend of the past now at Kazan.

The sun began to give some warmth, and the roads to glitter in his rays. Shrove-tide came and brought tobogganing with it. To my regret, my mother would not let me toboggan with the village children. As I coasted down with my sister and sometimes with my little brother, I cast envious glances, as we ran past, at the crowd of village boys and girls, all ruddy with the air and exercise, who sped boldly down all the way from the stack-yard at the top of the hill on their small sleds or toboggans or skates. For toboggans, they were content with old sieves or round wicker baskets, shod with ice. The merry active children, often dressed up in strange costumes, talked and laughed their loudest, especially when a skater flew head over heels, or a toboggan span quickly round and upset, and the girl-passenger began to shriek long before the shipwreck of her vehicle. How I longed to join in their merry noise and laughter, and, after seeing them, how tiresome it seemed to me to toboggan in solitude on the little ice-run which had been made in the garden, in front of the drawing-room windows ! But I had one consolation, that my sister used to go there with me.

When Lent began, our winter sports, of which we had not many, all came to an end. It cannot be said that Lent in our house was spent in prayer and fasting. My mother did not observe fasts, on the ground of health ; I certainly did no fasting ; and as to my father, though he ate no meat during Lent and the Fast of the Assumption (August 1 to 15), yet his dinner was much more dainty then than at other times,[1] owing to the abundant supply of frozen sterlets and sturgeon from the Ural district, fresh caviare, and *nalim* from the tanks. In those days the nearest church was nine versts away, in the village of Mordovsky Boogoorooslan. For some reason the priest was not well-disposed to us, and we went there only for the great festivals. In general, it must be said, our family were not indifferent to religious ordinances, but the distance of the church had the usual effect, and we were not accustomed to attend divine service. Thus I spent the season of Lent in working as usual, or rather harder than usual, at my books. My own pupil was no longer

---

[1] ' Even their fast days—they ca' it fasting when they hae the best o' sea-fish frae Hartlepool and Sunderland by land carriage, forbye trouts, grilses, salmon and a' the lave o't, and so they make their very fasting a kind of luxury and abomination ' : *Rob Roy*, chap. vi.

a cause of vexation but gave me pleasure by her progress. With her I made buildings out of bricks or played with dolls, and sometimes I read fables for children and explained them to her.

During all this time, my mother had something on her mind and was at times obviously unhappy; and she was less with me, so that I had more time for quiet reflection. School life had given a shock to the sweet security of childhood, and my return home had not obliterated the new impressions. I found that I had lost the old freedom from care and the old passion for outdoor amusements; I began to pay more attention to what went on around me, and to understand some things which I had never before noticed. The radiance of some objects began to fade for me, and a peculiar feeling of sadness, such as I had never experienced before, began to cast a shadow over all the amusements and occupations I had loved so well. This is a sad subject, and I do not intend to dwell upon it; but some allusion to it is necessary, in order to explain why life at Aksákovo ceased after some months to be to me the bright paradise it had been once, and why I no longer dreaded returning to school; besides, I was not to go there as a Government scholar.

Winter was long and obstinate, and spring slow in asserting her rights. April was ending, before a warm air, together with wind and rain, attacked the terrible snow-drifts in earnest, and routed them in the course of a single week. At Easter the roads were utterly impassable: and we could not even attend the morning service on the great festival. Easter Week brought little happiness to me; for my mother was unwell and depressed, and my father, unusually silent, was constantly poring over documents in connexion with a lawsuit against the Bogdánoffs about some land ; in the end, he won his case. He went every day to the mill, to observe the rise of the water.

One day he came home unexpectedly soon and said to me : ' We intend to let the water out of the pond at once, Seryózha ; ask your mother if you may come.' Off I ran to ask leave, and I was more fortunate than usual ; for my mother let me go, when she had taken some precautions against wet feet and chills. We drove to the mill on a long country car, and found the labourers waiting for us on the mill-dam, armed with implements of different kinds. All Russians love to watch moving water, and the population of Aksákovo had collected in a body to watch the process of empty-ing the pond. A mill-race with a sliding gate to exclude the water was unknown in our country in those days, and the opening made in the dam to let out the flood water was filled up again and rammed tight every year. The ice on the pond was swollen and dark and uneven ; it had cracked and broken away from the sides ; and hardly any water found its way to the machinery. Axes, crowbars, and iron shovels set to work to hack away the frozen dam along the edges of the hole made the year before ; and the men had hardly cleared away the surface to a depth of two feet, when the water began to flow and went to work so effectively, with no further help from man, that in half an hour it had cleared a path for itself. The muddy waves rushed forward impetuously, and turned instantly into a powerful river which refused to confine itself to the new channel and inundated the surrounding land. The people saluted with shouts of joy the element they loved, as it tore its way to freedom from its winter prison; the shrill voices of the women rose above the rest; and their cries, the splashing of the water as it fell from a height, and the cracking of the ice as it settled down and broke—all this presented a picture full of life; and had not a message come from the house that it was long past dinner-time, my father and I would probably have stayed till the evening to watch it.

Next morning we went back to the dam and found a different scene there, though the noise and merriment were as great as before. The violence of the water's first onset had calmed down a good deal; the level of the pond had fallen noticeably; small blocks of ice had broken against the posts and been swept along, while large blocks had settled at the bottom of the pond where it was shallow. The ground outside the hole in the dam had formerly been almost dry, though a great volume of water was running there now; and short stout stakes had been driven in here before the flood came down. Now the men were wading waist-deep into the water, to tie or hang upon the stakes traps of different kinds; and the fish driven downstream by the pressure of the water, and, still more, the fish that made their way upstream as far as the opening in the dam till they were beaten back by the might of the falling waves, got caught in the traps set for them. The men were dripping wet and shivering with cold; yet they bandied jests and loud cries with one another, as they kept drawing out their spoil upon the bank; and the women and old people and children carried it home, using baskets and sieves for the purpose, or sometimes merely their petticoats. We picked out some large fish and started homewards. My mother was vexed with us for staying so long, and it was some time before I got leave to visit the mill again.

Before long all traces of winter had disappeared; the bushes and trees were clothed with green, the young grass grew up, and spring appeared in all its beauty. As before, our garden was soon populous with songbirds of all kinds which had a special fancy for the old gooseberry-bushes and barberries; again the nightingales began to sing, and the mocking-bird to imitate their song. The previous spring I had spent in close confinement, in a narrow room in hospital; and it would have been natural for me to feel a special pleasure in the contrast; but I had a constant heartache, and, though I did not clearly understand the cause of it, yet all my occupations, to which I seemed to devote myself as usual, were poisoned by a feeling of sorrow.

While it was yet winter, my father determined to make a new outlet for the mill-dam, provided with a sluice, and to build a better mill. For this purpose he employed a miller called Krasnoff, a great talker, who turned out eventually to be a great impostor. During the whole of Lent, our labourers were preparing timber of all kinds— large and small beams, joists, planks, and posts; it seemed that all these were required in large numbers. As soon as the flood-water had run down, they began to pierce the dam and build a new channel for the water in a different place. At the same time, hired labourers began to drive in piles and then to build a large mill, also in a new position, which was intended to hold six pairs of grinding-stones; there was also to be a crushing-machine in a building of its own. The work went on nearly all summer. My father had a blind belief in Krasnoff, but the old miller Boltunyónok, and some of our peasants, who knew something about the building of mills, grinned and shook their heads, when they were by themselves. When my father said : 'What do you think of Krasnoff? How well he understands his job! He has made a plan of it all on paper ; he trusts to his eye in making the piles, and they all fit perfectly!'—our men always answered with the innocent cunning of the Russian peasant : ' Oh, he's all alive, *bátyushka*, and a capital hand at his job. He works it all out in his head ; and everything fits into its place just as it ought to fit. Only one can't tell how the mill is going to work ; the water may run slow along that channel, slower than it did when it came straight from the current. We only hope it won't freeze in winter.' Krasnoff smiled at these criticisms and refuted them with such perfect assurance that it never entered my father's head for a moment to doubt of success. I too listened with reverence and awe to the eloquence of Krasnoff.

Meanwhile the building operations made it necessary to let the water out of the pond ; and such fishing followed as was never known either before or since. All the fish in the pond made for the river which fed it, and the fish were as thick as they are in a tureen of good fish-soup. The number caught was fabulous. I and my attendant Yevséitch never left the place, and never cast

E

a line anywhere else. My father also, who very seldom had time for it, could fish now from morning till night, because he had to spend most of the day by the mill, watching the building operations; so it was quite easy for him, while fishing, to keep an eye on all the works and examine them from time to time. Chub, carp, perch, pike, and large roach (three or four pounds weight) took constantly and at all hours. The size of the fish depended on the size of the bait: a large bait always secured a large fish. My father liked especially to catch perch and pike, and I remember that he sometimes tied two hooks on one line and used small fish as bait; and he often had two perch on at once, and once a perch and a pike. The pike were generally caught in traps which were baited with fair-sized perch; and some of these pike weighed nearly twenty pounds. We were not scientific anglers and had no landing-nets; so, in spite of thick lines and strong hooks, it is not surprising that the largest fish often broke our rods or tackle and made off. Yevséitch, whose excitement over fishing even in his old age often made me laugh, suffered more than anyone from this cause; and, thanks to him, I also often lost a large fish, because I could not pull it out without his help, and his help was in most cases a hindrance. By the middle of July the best of the sport was over, and the chub and other large fish ceased to take. But the smaller fish still gave excellent sport; and the others would probably have gone on taking, if we had known then to use whole crayfish as a bait.

Throughout this year, my mother corresponded regularly once a month with Upadishevsky. During the twelvemonth a number of changes had taken place in the grammar-school at Kazan. The Rector had retired, and his duties were now performed by the senior teacher of Russian History, Ilya Yakovnin; Kamásheff also had retired, and the new head master was Upadishevsky: Our old friend had discussed the matter with the new Rector and with the inspector, and now informed us that I might, if my parents approved, be removed from the list of Government scholars and enter as a pensioner. This would enable me to live with one of the teachers; and he told us that there were two excellent young men, Ivan Zapolsky and Grigóri Kartashevsky, both graduates of Moscow University, who rented a large house for their common use and took boarders, whom they made exceedingly comfortable at a moderate charge. This news, and especially the disappearance of Kamásheff, gave much pleasure to my parents; and though it was a serious burden on them to pay three hundred roubles a year for me and to spend two hundred more on my clothes and books and attendant, they resolved to run into debt for the sake of my education. They owed already 2,500 roubles—in those days even so small a sum was considered 'debt'; and they would not have ventured to borrow more, but for their expectations from my father's aunt, Praskóvya Ivánovna. The school term began on the fifteenth of August, but boys were entered a fortnight earlier. So it was settled that we should start for Kazan at the end of July. I accepted this decision calmly enough, because the secret burden upon my mind had become heavier and more painful. But when our preparations were completed and the day of departure fixed, I began to grieve so at leaving Aksákovo, that everything about it suddenly recovered in my eyes all, or more than all, its old preciousness and charm. Feeling that I should never see it again, I said good-bye to every building and every spot, every tree and bush, and I said good-bye with tears. I distributed all my wealth: my pigeons I gave over to our cook Stepán and his son; of my cat I made a present to Sergéyevna, the wife of our blind man of business, Pantelyéi Grigóritch, a capital hand at all business and learned in the law; my fishing-tackle and traps I divided among the village boys; while my books, dried flowers, pictures, and so on, became the property of my sister, between whom and me there had grown up during this year as close a friendship as can exist between a girl of nine and her brother of eleven. To part from her was a great grief to me, and I begged my mother to take her with us. My mother refused at first, but gave way at last to my eager wish.

I ought to mention that the new mill was set going a week before we went away. Alas! the doubts of Boltunyónok and his mates were justified: as they had prophesied, the current was weaker than before, and the six pairs of stones were too much for it; even when a single pair was used, the mill worked much worse than the old one. My father could believe no longer in Krasnoff's skill: he turned the man off, and charged the old miller to mend matters as best he could.

At last, on the 26th of July, the same roomy carriage as before, with the same coachman and postillion and drawn by the same six horses, was standing by the front steps ; and the same crowd of indoor and outdoor servants collected to see us off. My father and mother, with my sister and me and Parásha, took their places in the coach ; Yevséitch took his seat on the box and Theodor on the rumble ; and we started slowly from the house, leaving behind us on the steps my aunt Tatyána, my brother with his nurse, and my youngest sister in the arms of her foster-mother. Our road went for some distance along the pond, over which flocks of white and pied sea-gulls were already flitting. How I envied each village boy ! *He* was not obliged to go off anywhere, or to part with any person or thing ; he was staying at home, with full power to sit where he liked on the dam with his fishing-rod, and angle for perch and roach under the close shade of the alders, with never a care in his head. He was left in undisturbed and undisputed possession of the pond, which, because it had been emptied so late in spring, was free this year from the growth of weed and rushes. For want of exercise, our horses were hot and restless, but the strong and practised arms of the coachman controlled them and forced them to keep to a walk for a long time. Inside the carriage, we all seemed sad, and no one spoke. I pushed my head out of the window and watched my dear Aksákovo until it disappeared from my sight ; and silent tears flowed down my cheeks.

CHAPTER III

MY RETURN TO SCHOOL

ON our arrival at Kazan in the summer of 1801,
instead of staying as before with Mme Aristoff, we
took somewhat better lodgings. I forget the name
of the street, but I remember that we occupied the
whole of a small detached house which belonged,
I think, to a M. Chortoff. Upadishevsky came at
once to see us, and this friend and benefactor was
greeted by us all as a near kinsman. He told us
that Yakovnin was still performing the duties of
Rector, but that reports were going about the
town to the effect that M. Likhachoff, a rich
landowner of the district, would soon be appointed
to the post. This was a good opportunity, he said,
to enter me as a pensioner at the school ; for,
though Yakovnin and all the Governors had given
their consent, the future Rector might take
a different view of the matter and prove obstinate.
Upadishevsky was warm in his praise of two of
the senior teachers, Ivan Zapolsky and Grigóri
Kartashevsky ; [1] the first taught Physics and the
second Pure Mathematics, and both had come to
the school some time before from Moscow University. He spoke highly of their intelligence,
learning, and regular habits. The two were friends

[1] Kartashevsky and Aksákoff, the tutor and the pupil,
both married in 1816, within one month of each other ;
and Kartashevsky's bride was Nadyezhda Aksákoff, the
sister of whom the author speaks so often and with such
affection. Kartashevsky died in 1840 at Petersburg.

and lived together in a fine stone house, where they took seven boarders, all pensioners at the school; the board and lodging was very good, and much attention was paid to the boys' progress in their school work. It was not their intention to take more boarders, but Upadishevsky had told them about me, and had given such a glowing account of the whole family, that the young men, unable to resist his entreaties, had agreed to make an exception in my mother's favour and to include me among their pupils.

My father took me to call on the acting Rector, and got permission for me to enter as a pensioner; we next called on the two young masters and met with a friendly reception in each place. Kartashevsky explained that they divided the pupils between them, and that the three oldest boys, who were under his immediate supervision, would complete the school course within the year and go away to enter the Civil Service. As it was his intention to set up house for himself after that, and take no more pupils, he said that I ought to apply to his friend and colleague, Zapolsky. To my father it was all one, which of them took me; but he pressed both the young men to come and make the acquaintance of my mother. They came next day, and my mother, whenever she saw him, formed a very favourable impression of Kartashevsky, and much regretted that I was not to be under him. But my father and I much preferred Zapolsky: he seemed to us more cordial and friendly and sociable than his solemn colleague. All my mother's friendly expostulations—that the two friends, instead of parting, ought to live together and help one another in the performance of such sacred duties, were ineffectual: Kartashevsky replied very firmly, that he found this duty too serious and too absorbing; that to be responsible for the education of young people was a burden he could not discharge to his own satisfaction, even if the parents were satisfied; and that his study of science, in which he was still a learner, was hindered by such ties. His reply was so positive that any attempt to continue the discussion would have been useless and awkward as well. When the two young men left us, my mother expressed her disappointment with her usual vivacity. She was always too much carried away by her instinctive feelings, and now she praised to the skies the merits of Kartashevsky, while she found many defects in his colleague. The sequel proved that my mother's eager enthusiasm was not at fault. For, though Zapolsky was quite a ' good ' man, in the ordinary sense of that word, the other belonged to a select class among mankind—those who have an exceptionally high standard of duty and spend all their lives in rigid observation of that standard. But I was delighted to think that the good-natured Zapolsky was to be my tutor, and that I was to live, not with the big boys who had quarters of their own, but with my equals in age, lively and good-natured boys like myself. Thanks to the interest taken by Upadishevsky, all our business was settled without difficulties of any kind; and within a month my parents and my sister went back to Aksákovo. But during this month Kartashevsky, though he passed for a confirmed recluse, paid us many visits; he could appreciate my mother, and a lasting friendship was formed between them, a friendship founded on mutual respect and tested in the course of time by many events of importance.

This second parting from my mother did not cost me anything like the pain and misery which had accompanied our former separation. I noticed the difference in myself especially; and, young as I was, I was impressed by it and had some regretful thoughts. But before long the new life absorbed all my attention. I occupied a room with three brothers called Manasséin, and we became good friends at once; a small room near ours was occupied by a single tenant, a boy called A. He was very rich, and I think he was the only son of his mother, a widow. In spite of his wealth, which was obvious from his clothes and bedding and all his belongings, he was not at all generous. He kept a large iron-bound chest in his room and always carried the key in his pocket. This chest excited general curiosity, and my schoolfellows believed that its contents were very valuable and precious.

At last I set eyes again on the school buildings which I had once feared and hated; and I was much pleased to find that the sight did not produce in me either fear or any unpleasant feeling. I was placed in the Junior Class as before. Most of my former companions had been promoted to the Middle Form, and their places were filled by new boys, less well prepared than I had been, while those who had failed to get their remove were either idle or stupid. Hence in a very short time I was top of the form in all subjects except in the Catechism and *Outlines of Sacred History*. The priest continued to keep up a sort of ill-will against me, though I always knew my lessons for him very accurately. This fact seems worth noting: when

Upadishevsky asked him later, why Aksákoff, who worked very hard at other subjects, was not at the top with him, and added, ' I suppose he does not know his lessons '—' No ' said the priest ; ' his work is very well done, but he has no liking for the Catechism and Sacred History.'

The course of a few months dispersed the last traces of home-sickness and longing for the freedom of the country : by degrees I became accustomed to school-life, made some real friends among the boys, and became fond of the school. This change of feeling was largely due to the fact that I did not live in the school and only went there for lessons. Life in my tutor's house was not so entirely unlike my life at home as my former condition, when I was shut up permanently in a Government institution and surrounded by a number of companions of all classes.

At first A. avoided intercourse with me and the Manasséins, and indeed with all the boys ; but when he noticed how quiet and peaceable I was, he began to talk to me and invite me to his room ; he went so far as to treat me to some of the dainties from home which he generally devoured in secrecy. At last he offered to show me his chest, but it must, he said, be done in such a way that no one else should know of it. My imagination, full of fairy tales, pictured this receptacle as full of precious stones or ingots of gold and silver ; and I was delighted. It was arranged that I should come to his room when all were asleep ; and I did so that same evening. The Manasséins did not keep me long waiting, for they soon began to snore ; and I went off to A.'s room, where there was always a lamp burning at night before a large sacred picture in a rich gilt frame. When he had lit a candle and locked the door, he made me promise to tell no one of what I was about to see, and then carefully unlocked the mysterious chest. But a great surprise awaited me. It turned out that the chest was packed full of inferior pictures! There were engravings and drawings, landscapes and portraits in oil, the latter like the signs displayed over barbers' shops. Though I was a lover of pictures myself, I paid no attention to them now, because I was expecting something entirely different; and I was hoping all the time that the real treasure would be revealed at the bottom of the chest; so, when the last sheets had been taken out and the bare boards met my eyes, I could not help calling out, 'Is *that* all!' This was a terrible disappointment to A., who expected me to be surprised and delighted. Talking in a whisper, I frankly confessed the belief which we all entertained about his chest. 'You are a pack of fools,' said A. angrily, and he almost turned me out of the room; and that was the end of our boyish friendship. Some time later, I broke my promise and disclosed the contents of the chest to the Manasséin boys; and we looked several times through the chinks in the locked door and watched A., while he spread out his pictures on the bed and tables and chairs, and even on the floor. He looked at them, dusted them, and admired them, as Pushkin's *Avaricious Knight* gloated over his treasures; he gave himself up to this pleasure almost every night for whole hours. We began to make fun of him, and spread in the school the story of his passion for pictures; and soon he was pestered by mischievous boys who called upon him

to share his riches with others, and to let them see
' The Mice burying the Cat,' or ' Yeruslan defeating
a Horde of Unbelievers.' A. abused them in his
wrath, and even used his fists ; but nothing would
stop them. At last he became so weary of this,
that he wrote to his mother, and she soon took him
away from the school for good. Of course, there
may have been other reasons as well for his
removal. Not long ago I heard that A. was very
eccentric in later life also ; but that does not
prevent him from enjoying a high reputation for
the practical management of his land.

During the first few months after my entrance,
Zapolsky gave a certain amount of attention to me
and his other pupils. He asked us beforehand
about the lessons set for us to learn, and he taught
us some French and German ; and that was all.
But he gradually ceased to pay us any attention
at all, and began to absent himself, though we did
not know where he went. To tell the truth, our
studies profited by his absences, because Kartashevsky took us in hand at such times, and he taught
us, as I could see very well, much more carefully
and much better than his colleague. At last
Yevséitch told me in confidence that Zapolsky
was courting a young lady of good family and
possessed of some means ; that she herself and
her mother were favourable to his views ; but
her father was unwilling to give her hand to a
teacher, who had no money and was also the son
of a priest. This information turned out to be
quite accurate.

As was expected, M. Likhachoff was appointed
Rector ; but the boys in boarding-houses did not
even know him by sight for a long time, because

he commonly visited the school at the dinner-hour and never even looked into the class-rooms. I learnt my lessons and drove or walked to the school very cheerfully. I do not know whether my present companions were different or if the difference was in myself—anyhow, I felt nothing of the teasing and bullying which I had found so unbearable before ; I found common interests with others, and a desire sprang up within me for social intercourse with them, so that I began to look forward impatiently to school-hours. I ought to add that most of my time at the school was spent in form, where my vanity was constantly flattered by the approval of the teachers and a certain measure of respect on the part of my school-fellows ; but this last did not prevent me from joining their noisy games during all our free time and on every suitable occasion. I wrote home every week, and every week I received very affectionate letters from my mother, to which my father sometimes added a postscript. My mother assured me that she was not grieving over our separation, and that she was glad to get from Zapolsky and Upadishevsky such good accounts of my conduct and diligence. When she said that she was not grieving, I believed her. In every letter she sent her kind regards to Zapolsky and Kartashevsky, and from time to time corresponded with them herself. And so things went on for nearly a year—till June of 1802. The examinations took place in June, and they resulted in a complete triumph for my youthful vanity ! I was promoted to the Middle Form in all subjects. At our speech-day, which was at the beginning of July, I received a prize with a gilt inscription on

the boards—'For diligence and proficiency';
I also got a Certificate of Merit.

A plain-covered cart and three horses with
a coachman had been sent for me from home some
time before; and after dinner on speech-day I set
off with Yevséitch for our dear Aksákovo. We
travelled along the same road as two years before,
when my mother carried me off in triumph from
my prison, and we halted at the same places for
food and sleep. The breath of nature soon
penetrated my being, driving out of my head all
thoughts of school, of boys and masters, books
and lessons. After a period of apparent forgetful-
ness or indifference, I fell in love with the beauties
of God's world more fervently than ever and more
consciously. At home, all my family greeted me
with tender love, and my mother's happiness it is
impossible to describe. My sister had grown much
taller and much prettier in the course of the year,
and she was delighted to see her brother again.
How many questions there were to ask, how many
stories to tell! She told me for one thing that my
mother had made herself quite ill by her grief at
parting from me; and I felt a kind of pain to think
that I had suffered so little this time from the
separation.

All the days which I spent at Aksákovo during
these holidays melt in my memory into one happy
day of splendid weather; I could not, if I wished,
tell what I did—I only know that I enjoyed myself
from morning till night. In the swarm of my
pleasures, fishing, bathing, and hawking are the
most prominent. My mother made me repeat
every trifling detail of my life at school during
the year, and, as I went on, she said again and

again to my father, ' You see, Alexyéi Stepánitch, I was not mistaken about Kartashevsky. He is as far above Zapolsky as the sky above the earth; he is the man whom I should like to have for Seryózha's tutor, and I shall use every effort to bring that about.' She was confirmed in this purpose by what Yevséitch told her; and I myself understood the importance of the change and wished it to be made. My mother was attracted chiefly by the high standards and strict principles of Kartashevsky.

From my sister I hardly ever parted at this time; our friendship became even closer and more tender. But the happy days flew by on wings; and on the 10th of August, the same covered cart with the same horses and the same coachman carried me off with Yevséitch on our way to Kazan.

On my arrival I found all the boys had returned. But Zapolsky was absent, and we were told that he had gone off to be married to Nastasya Yelágin, the young lady whom he had been courting. After their honeymoon, the young pair would come to Kazan and receive us in a house of their own which they intended to take; Kartashevsky would look after us till then. I was delighted by this prospect, but the Manasséin boys were not, especially the youngest brother, Elpidifor, a fine boy but very mischievous and idle then, though the mischievous boy grew up to be an active and useful man.

I remember very well the eager anxiety to learn with which I entered the Middle Form. I knew beforehand that the lessons there were much more difficult, and that this form was considered to be the critical stage of a boy's school career. It was generally believed that a scholar who distinguished himself there was sure to earn distinction also in the Senior Class, whereas it often happened that the top boys in the Junior Class never did very much in the Middle Form.[1] This belief alarmed me ; and my fears were not dispelled during the whole of the first month. The teachers were different, and we were strangers to them. The boys who had been promoted sat all by themselves on two separate benches, and little attention was paid to them at first by the teachers. Owing to the difficulty of the work, most boys spent two years in this form ; hence the classes were so large that it was physically impossible for the teacher to give equal attention to us all. One of the subjects taught in this form was Slavonic Grammar together with Russian ; and the text-book we used was written by our teacher of the subject, Nikolai Ibrahimoff, a graduate of Moscow University. He taught Russian literature and mathematics in the same form. His surname and his appearance alike clearly betrayed his Tartar or Bashkir origin ; his head was large, his eyes small and piercing, with a very pleasant expression ; he had prominent cheek-bones and a huge mouth. This man had a great influence on my literary development, and his memory is dear to me. He first encouraged me and gave me what I may call a push in the right direction. He used to dictate from his *Slavonic Grammar*, for the benefit of those who had not heard the work explained or did not possess a copy of it. The custom was for one pupil to write on the board at his dictation, while the rest copied

---

[1] It is obvious that three forms were too few. When this was proved by experience, grammar-schools were divided into seven classes. (*Author's Note.*)

down what was dictated. Ibrahimoff's explanations were not sufficiently detailed and not quite clear; his comments, though they did well enough for those who were going through the grammar a second time, were not enough for the new boys and especially for those who like myself and many others were only twelve years old. But fortunately, owing to Zapolsky's absence, Kartashevsky was supervising my preparation at this time; and he explained to me the *Introduction to Slavonic Grammar*, which contained a view of grammar in general. Without his explanations I should have understood as little of this *Introduction* as the other boys did. I possessed already a complete manuscript copy of the *Slavonic Grammar*, and I read this through on Sundays, asking my tutor to explain points that were dark to me; and this practice proved of no small service to me afterwards.

At the end of September, six weeks after the term had begun, Ibrahimoff changed his method. The little Tartar figure, after walking once or twice along the whole row, book in hand, instead of dictating as usual, suddenly drew near to the benches where the new boys sat by themselves. My heart began to beat hard. He first put questions to all the boys who had been promoted from the lower form, taking the questions from the *Introduction* and first two chapters of the *Grammar* which we had already gone through, and examining us according to the order in which we sat. The order was as follows: first came the Government scholars, then the exhibitioners, and lastly the pensioners. Questions upon the *Grammar* were fairly well answered; but of the *Introduction* no one knew anything at all—a clear proof that they did not understand it. At last my turn came. I answered questions on the *Grammar* readily and satisfactorily, and Ibrahimoff said, ' Good ! ' after each answer. He began to get interested, and asked me twenty questions instead of the usual three or four ; and I answered them all with equal success. The big Tartar mouth stretched its widest, as Ibrahimoff smiled again and again ; and at last he said : ' Very good indeed ! Now let us see what you can make of the *Introduction*.' My answers were no less satisfactory than before. Then he tried to puzzle me but failed, because I really understood the subject and was not merely repeating words which I had learnt by rote. Ibrahimoff was surprised and delighted beyond measure. He showered compliments upon me ; then he made me stand up and collect all my class-books, and led me by the hand to the top desk. ' That is your place,' he said, and made me sit third in a class of more than forty boys. Such a triumph I had never even dreamed of, and I was perfectly happy. On returning home, I sent Yevséitch to ask Kartashevsky if I might come to his room ; and when leave was granted, I told him with great joy what had happened to me. Though he was in reality much pleased both by my success and the spirit in which I took it, yet he answered dryly enough, as his system required : ' Don't be too happy over it ; possibly Ibrahimoff was in too much of a hurry. You are bound now to work still harder and confirm his good opinion.' Such an answer might have discouraged or repelled many boys—and I decidedly disapprove of such a method myself—but I understood Kartashevsky already. Before this he had praised me highly in letters to my mother without letting me see that he was pleased with me; he even asked her not to show me his letters.

Russian Literature was another subject taught by Ibrahimoff, and my success in this was no less pronounced; he taught the syntax of the Russian language and made us write exercises, consisting partly in dictation and partly in turning passages of verse into prose. The dictation was very good for us, not only as practice in writing, but because it helped to form our taste; for Ibrahimoff used to choose the best passages from Karamzin, Dmitrieff, Lomonossoff, and Kheraskoff, which he made us read aloud, and then explained their literary merit. To paraphrase of verse he did not himself attach much value and only made us do it occasionally, merely because it was one of the prescribed subjects. He preferred to give us practice in the writing of short compositions upon subjects which he set himself. As to other subjects —in general history, Russian history, and geography, which we did with Yakovnin, I did well, but was not one of the best. In languages generally, the standard attained was not high, and this was certainly due to bad teaching. In arithmetic, I was weak even in the Junior Class; and in the Middle Form it became clear that I was quite unable to learn mathematics; and this reputation I kept at the University as well as at school. In writing, drawing, and dancing, I got on well enough. In my lessons with the priest I did well, but not very well. While in this form I ceased to use a slate, which was then, and still is to some extent, a pet aversion with me: the squeaking of a slate pencil upon a slate grates on my nerves now as it used to do then.

At last we heard that Zapolsky had brought his bride back to Kazan and was staying at his mother-in-law's house. He came next day to see his pupils and was exceedingly cordial to us. Yevséitch told me in confidence that Kartashevsky was very angry with his colleague for prolonging his absence from one month to three, and said, ' I am quite tired of bothering about these brats, but I cannot leave them as you do without supervision and attention.' Zapolsky apologized, thanked him for what he had done, and tried to embrace him ; but his friend treated him very sternly and roughly, threatening to leave the house and give up the care of the boys, unless the young pair set up an establishment of their own without delay. I should add that Kartashevsky had now ceased to have any pupils of his own. In spite of these threats, it was some time before Zapolsky took any lodgings, and Kartashevsky lived on in our house two months longer, attending steadily and scrupulously to our comfort and conduct and supervising our studies. During these five months I became much attached to him, though he never once spoke affectionately to me and never dropped the appearance of dryness and severity. I was too young to appreciate his real worth, and I could not have got to care for him, if my mother had not secretly informed me that he really loved me and praised me highly, though he concealed his feelings, fearing that his praise might be injurious to so young a boy. Kartashevsky in his long and useful career held important posts where he had to associate, not with children

only but with men advanced in years; yet he
never abandoned this mistaken principle, and the
result was unfortunate. Those whom circumstances enabled to know him intimately, kept
through life a deep respect and devotion to him;
but, on the other hand, many good people were
repelled by the well-meant dryness of his manner,
and believed him, quite unjustly, to be proud and
unfeeling.

Zapolsky did at last take suitable lodgings, and
we all went to live there. I shed tears on parting
with Kartashevsky and would have embraced
him; but he would not allow it, and, though
I found out later from a letter he wrote to my
mother that he was very near weeping himself,
he said dryly and coldly: ' What is all this about ?
what are you crying for ? I suppose you are
afraid that Zapolsky will be stricter with you.'
I admit that I was hurt by such words at such
a moment.

I forgot to say that Zapolsky brought his bride
to see us; all we noticed was that she had no
eyebrows and never stopped blushing; and she
was so simple that she was unable to say a word
of greeting to the boys. In the new house the
Manasséin boys and I occupied a wing by ourselves.
We were left entirely to our own devices, and now
I realised the wide difference between our present
tutor and his predecessor. The former we never
saw except at dinner and supper: the young
husband was completely taken up either with the
arrangements required by his change of condition,
or with the management of a small property of
sixty serfs which had come to him as his wife's
dowry; the property was twenty versts from

Kazan, and he went there for two days every week. The rest of his time was spent in teaching physics to the Senior Class, or in attending to his wife's family; three of her sisters were grown-up, and they were regular inmates of his household. Yet no one attended to the management of the house, and it was very badly done. Even our food was wretched, and thus I got involved in a scrape which I must describe.

We always had supper in the large house at a common table; and one evening there was ham for supper. I cut off a piece and was just going to put it into my mouth, when Yevséitch, who was standing at the back of my chair, nudged me from behind. I turned round and stared at him in surprise; he shook his head and winked at me, meaning that I was not to eat the ham. So I laid the piece of ham down on the plate, and noticed for the first time that the meat was bad, actually crawling; I gave up my plate as quickly as I could. I was sitting quite close to Zapolsky, and he saw all that had happened. I should add that his wife, with her mother and three sisters, was sitting at table, as well as the boys. When supper was over and we all went to Zapolsky to say good night before going to bed, he told me to stay, and took me and Yevséitch off to his study. There he rebuked me with great severity for impertinent behaviour; he said that, on purpose to disgrace him, I had directed the attention of all the party to the spoilt ham, though everyone else had eaten it out of politeness. After reading me a long lecture and proving that I had committed an unpardonable crime, he next abused my worthy Yevséitch in most insulting terms. Not under-

standing in the least how I was to blame, I began
to cry, from a sense of undeserved insult. This
softened Zapolsky's heart : he said that he forgave
me ; he even wished to embrace me, but I said
very frankly, that I was not crying because I was
sorry for what I had done, but because he had
wronged me by suspecting me unjustly of a bad
intention, and because he had abused Yevséitch.
He got very angry again : he actually said that
I was a hardened sinner and should suffer exemplary punishment the next day. Then he let me go
to bed.

But it was long before I fell asleep : the thought
that a comparative stranger intended to inflict
severe punishment on me for no fault of mine,
wounded and irritated my feelings excessively.
Never within my recollection had any one laid
a hand upon me, except my mother ; and even
that was an old story. At last I fell asleep. Next
morning we dressed and went across to the house
for our tea. Zapolsky, contrary to custom, joined
us there, and explained my crime to the Manasséin
boys and Yelágin, his brother-in-law, who had
joined the school a fortnight before. Then they
were sent off to school ; but I was sentenced to be
deprived of tea, and kept out of school. I was to
go back to our wing, undress, and go to bed ; and
there I was to stay till evening, with a slice of
bread and a glass of water for lunch and dinner.
A punishment so silly and so entirely undeserved
was bound to seem, and did seem, an unbearable
insult to a boy as sensitive and precocious as I was ;
and I did really feel hardened, as I looked with
a contemptuous smile at my tutor and then hurried
off to our wing. I undressed and went to bed,

taking a book with me for occupation. My faithful
Yevséitch, though he could not grasp the injury
to my feelings and laughed heartily at so absurd
a punishment, was distressed to think that I should
not have enough to eat; and he promised to
procure for me on the sly anything tempting that
was served in the dining-room. But I angrily
forbade him to do this, and sent him out of the
room. At first I felt only rage and irritation;
then I began to cry, and finally went to sleep.
Owing to my bad night, I slept so sound that
I never woke till my companions came back to
the wing after dining with the family, and began
to make a noise over their games. Sleep had
calmed my feelings; I refused the bread and water
and stood with indifference the jokes of the boys
at my expense; they agreed with me that I was
innocent, and laughed less at me than at the
oddity of my punishment. The second Manasséin
boy was a confirmed idler, and he even envied me,
saying that he would welcome that form of punishment every day. When the others went off to
afternoon school, I began to prepare the work set
that morning in my absence, and to go over the
work of the evening before. At seven o'clock,
when the boys had come back from school and
were having tea in the dining-room, Zapolsky sent
a message to me to dress and join them; and
I obeyed.

He greeted me by saying: ' I forgive you; but
you owe it to these ladies that the time of your
punishment is shortened '—and he pointed to his
mother-in-law, his wife, and her sisters. I expressed my thanks to them. Then he and his wife
immediately left the house for some reason, and

the boys, having finished their tea, went off to the wing, but the ladies kept me. In no time a small table was laid and food brought in; the young ladies made me sit at the table and sat round me themselves. They fed me almost out of their own hands, and even produced a pot of jam, on which I regaled with a will. These benefits were conferred with so much kindness that my heart was quite melted. It turned out that, though the young ladies had never spoken a word to me till then, they had long before taken a fancy to me for my modest behaviour; and my punishment, which they and their mother thought undeserved and inhuman, had excited their warmest sympathy! Zapolsky had been unable to resist their intercession on my behalf. I was told that Katerina had even shed tears and gone down on her knees before him—which made Katerina blush terribly. They kept me in the house all the evening, and asked me all sorts of details about myself. As may be guessed, I chattered freely: not only did I tell them about my dear Aksákovo and my first term at school, but I recited to them a great deal of poetry, having long had a passion for recitation. The young ladies were sincerely delighted; they uttered cries of pleasure and showered caresses upon me. I was delighted too by the impression I had produced, and my head was turned with youthful vanity. After supper I went back to the wing, where the other boys, who knew already from Yelágin how his sisters had fed and comforted me, asked me questions and expressed their envy of my luck. I was kept awake a long time by excitement and vague fancies beyond my comprehension.

This incident seems trifling enough, but I had a purpose in describing it so fully. It made me idle, though I had worked hard till then. Mme Yelágin as well as her daughters took a fancy to me, and often asked permission of her son-in-law to invite me to spend the evening with them, and I found a couple of hours passed in their society very agreeable. On Sundays and holidays I constantly ran across to their house, and almost ceased to visit some ladies, relations of my father's, who had often entertained me in the past. The other boys went on envying me, and Yelágin, a young scamp of fifteen whom his sisters would not invite to join us, was seriously vexed with me, and showed it by caustic allusions, of which I entirely missed the point. By degrees my attention was taken off my work altogether. After three months Zapolsky hired a teacher for us, a divinity student who had finished his course; his name was Guri Lastochkin, and he was a very modest and intelligent young man, from whom I might have gained much; but my work was very badly done until spring came and the Yelágins went off to the country. There was one exception: in Russian Literature and Slavonic Grammar, the subjects taught by Ibrahimoff, I still distinguished myself, because I had a strong liking for the subject and for the teacher. Six weeks before the examinations I began to work in real earnest. Lastochkin gave zealous assistance to my endeavours, and took a great liking to me at this time; but in spite of all, I was not promoted to the Senior Class and had to stay where I was for a year longer. Only a third of my form were promoted, and some of these owed their remove not to proficiency but to seniority, after remaining two or three years in the form. No one blamed me for this, and I professed, like all the others, that it would be good for me to stay in the form two years as most boys did ; yet my youthful vanity was hurt, and still worse, I feared that my mother would be vexed.

But my fears were groundless. When I went home to Aksákovo with Yevséitch for the summer holidays of 1803, and when my mother had read the letters from Upadishevsky, Zapolsky, and Kartashevsky, she and my father were very well pleased that I had not been promoted. But when I told her fully and frankly the way in which I had been passing my time in my tutor's house, she became very serious and looked dissatisfied. She disapproved of Zapolsky and his relations, and even of Lastochkin ; for she could not endure divinity students, and here my father, who had a contemptuous nickname for them, agreed with her entirely. This prejudice was especially unfair in the case of Lastochkin, who had many good points.

I had a strange meeting with Lastochkin a few years later. I should say that we became very intimate, in spite of the difference of our ages, at the end of that term ; and he confided all his private affairs to me, telling me for one thing that the Government was urging him to enter the sacred profession, though he felt no leaning in that direction. I do not know why, but I felt convinced that he would certainly enter the priesthood, and I told him so. He denied it with some heat ; and in order to convince me of the contrary, he took a sheet of paper one day and wrote on it : ' Sooner shall the river at Kazan flow upward than Guri

Lastochkin take priest's orders.' Then he gave me the paper to keep as a guarantee that he would retain his freedom—a clear proof of his own youth at the time. Two months passed, and we parted; and then for nearly four years I never once heard of him, and had quite forgotten his existence.

One wretched autumn morning I received a note from my aunt, my mother's half-sister, whom I loved very dearly; she was living then with the B——s, and I often saw her. 'My dear Serge,'—she wrote—'Come to our house at six this evening, wearing your uniform and sword.[1] There is a wedding in this house; and you, as the bride's page, must put on her shoes and escort her to church.' The bride had been brought up by the B——s; she was poor but young and pretty. When I got there, I was scolded for being a little late, and taken at once to the bride's room where I put on her silk stockings and shoes. She was not quite dressed, but her head was in proper bridal trim; and I remember that I was struck by her beauty. I had hardly time to exchange a few words with my aunt in her room, before the lady of the house sent for me and asked me to drive at once in her carriage to the bridegroom's lodgings. I was to tell him that the bride was dressed, and that he should go at once to the church and send a message from there that he was waiting. I went off instantly and had no time to ask the bride-groom's name. A friend was with me who knew the bridegroom and where he lived; he took me to a large Government building inhabited by a number of people, led me through several rooms, and then opened a door. 'There,' he said, 'is the

[1] Students carried swords: see p. 169.

bridegroom, dressing in front of the looking-glass.'
I saw the back of a stout man; he was wearing
knee-breeches, silk stockings, and shoes, and
a servant was hastily fitting on to him a stiff white
shirt-front. When I came close, the bridegroom
turned round—it was Lastochkin, though grown
very stout. A cry of surprise burst from both of
us. 'My dear Aksákoff,' he said, embracing me,
'how glad I am to see you! But at this moment
you must excuse me. . . .' I interrupted him by
saying that I was the bride's page, and had been
sent to hurry the bridegroom. He went on dressing
in haste, talking to me all the time. 'A great
surprise to you, I suppose,' he said. 'Yes,'
I answered. 'I did not know who the bridegroom
was; but I congratulate you on marrying a good
and pretty girl.' 'Oh, you are quite in the dark
still,' said he; then he took me aside and said in
a low voice, 'You probably remember my engage-
ment in writing not to take orders. Well, to-
morrow I shall be a priest, and next day senior
curate in the Cathedral of Peter and Paul'—and
tears came to his eyes. I do not know what
circumstances altered his convictions; but he
evidently regretted the loss of his freedom. We
never met again. In the course of fifteen years
I often heard that he was universally loved for his
qualities of heart and respected for his learning.
I think he became Rector of the seminary recently
founded at Kazan.

What chiefly troubled my mother about my
school life was the absurd punishment inflicted
on me by Zapolsky. The wish to take me away
from him and place me with his former colleague
rose again in her heart with renewed strength. It

was not difficult to take me away ; but it seemed hopeless to induce Kartashevsky to break through a rule which he had laid down once for all ; and the difficulty was increased by the fact that he was not merely a colleague of Zapolsky's, but an intimate friend. The loss of his best pupil might injure Zapolsky's reputation with other parents, and my transference to Kartashevsky might, by people who were ignorant of the circumstances, be called unhandsome. My poor mother was very sad about it, but she saw no way to mend matters. To my great astonishment, she disapproved also of the notice taken of me by the kind ladies at my boarding-house, and especially of the blandishments of one of the sisters. She decided to travel to Kazan in winter ; she wished to see my manner of life for herself, and also to urge Kartashevsky by every means in her power to fall in with her plan. She had a third motive which I discovered later : she intended that I should spend with her, and not in the bosom of my tutor's family, all my free time during the Christmas holidays.

All my summer holiday I spent in the country, and I was as happy as in the previous year. But on my return to Kazan I fell in with an adventure which made a deep impression on my mind ; indeed, the traces of it remain to this day. From it I date an increased fear, which possesses me still, of ferrying across great rivers. It happened in the following way. We came in the afternoon to the bank of the Kama, opposite the village of Shooran ; during summer the river was crossed at this point. On the bank there were three loaded carts with their drivers, waiting to cross, and about a score of peasant women with baskets full of

berries which they were carrying home to the other
side. No ferrymen were to be seen; they had
all wandered off somewhere. After some discussion the peasants and my servants determined
to take us across themselves; for one of the
peasants asserted that he had been a ferryman for
some years, and offered himself to take the steer-
ing-oar. Accordingly they picked out the best
of the ferry-boats; the three carts with the
horses, and my carriage and three horses, were all
put on board, and, of course, all the women with
their baskets came too. The man who professed
to be a ferryman took his place at the steering oar;
the other four oars were taken by two peasants,
my coachman, and my servant Ivan, whose
courage and great strength made him worth ten
ordinary men. Meanwhile a black cloud was
rising quickly in the west and gradually covered the
horizon; it was impossible to help noticing it,
but we all thought that it might pass to one side,
or that we might get over before it burst. Though
the starting-point was exactly opposite Shooran,
it was necessary to punt upstream for more than
a verst, to prevent the boat from being carried
down beyond the landing-place by the swift current
of the angry Kama. This process was very slow,
and the storm came quickly nearer and nearer.
To save time, we went only half the right distance
up the stream; then the men took to their oars
again, crossed themselves, and began to row
straight across. But, before we had reached the
middle of the river, the cloud advanced with
astonishing speed till it covered the sky from end
to end, the heavens grew black and the reflection
in the water still blacker, darkness came on, and

a frightful storm burst over us with thunder and lightning and a hurricane of wind. Our steersman dropped his oar in a panic, and confessed that he was not a ferryman at all and could not steer; an eddy whirled our boat round like a shaving and carried it down the stream; the women raised a piercing shriek, and horror fell upon us all. I was so frightened that I trembled all over and could not utter a word. The rapid current carried us down several versts, and then stranded us on a sandy shoal about a hundred yards from the far bank. Ivan sprang into the water which was waist-deep; then he waded ashore, and the water nowhere came higher than his breast. Next, he came back the same way to the boat, made the quietest of our horses jump off, and mounted me on it, bidding me hold on tight to the horse's neck and mane. Then he led the horse by the bridle, while Yevséitch walked alongside and supported me with both arms. Great waves of discoloured water surged past us and drenched even our heads. Unluckily, Ivan, who was walking in front, missed the ford he had traversed twice already, and got into deep water. All in a moment he disappeared below the surface, my horse began to swim, and Yevséitch was left behind; and the fear of immediate death which came over me then I have never forgotten. I was ready to faint and almost choked by the waves; it was fortunate for me that it grew shallower after a few yards. Ivan was a strong swimmer, and he swam on to the shallows, never letting go of the horse's bridle till he brought him safely to the bank. But Yevséitch was nearly drowned, he could not swim well and had much difficulty in getting to land. I was taken off the horse almost unconscious and wet to the skin; my fingers had stiffened as they clung to the mane. But I soon recovered, and was inexpressibly rejoiced to find myself safe.

Yevséitch stayed with me, while Ivan went back to the boat. The women, crying and shrieking but refusing to part with their baskets, were jumping into the water; the peasants were pulling off their horses and carts; and at last they hit upon a safer passage and all made their way somehow to the bank through shallow water. The boat, now lightened of most of its freight, rose off the sand and began to drift down. But at this point Ivan's great strength did us yeoman's service: he held the boat fast till my coachman had got off both carriage and horses into the water; then he let go, and off went the boat down stream. The two men, up to the waist in water, harnessed the horses and brought the carriage to land. Everything in it was soaked. Wet and cold we got in and drove fast to Shooran, where we were warmed and dried and drank plenty of hot tea; and our cold bath was followed by no bad consequences. But I had had a terrible fright; and ever since, the sight of a great river even in calm weather has made me uneasy, while a storm produces in me an involuntary horror which I cannot overcome.

On returning to school, I set to work in earnest at my lessons; and, as the Yelágins were in the country, I had no distractions. Lastochkin was pleased with my diligence and coached me zealously, so that I soon rose high in all subjects except mathematics. Of the work with Ibrahimoff I need not speak; for there I was always at the top. By this time I had become strongly attached

to the school, the masters, and the boys, in whom
I found cheerful companions. I was no longer
confused by the constant bustle and running about,
the noise of loud voices and loud laughter; I was
unconscious of it all and took my part with the
best of them, and found something attractive and
orderly in the life.

The autumn was long and wet. There was
a serious epidemic of fever in the town, and I was
one of the sufferers. Dr. Benis had left the school,
and our old friend, Andréi Ritter, attended to all
the boys, including those who like myself lived in
boarding-houses. His treatment checked the fever
pretty soon, but it returned in a few days. Large
doses of quinine and Glauber's salts, at the thought
of which my gorge rises even now, routed the fever
a second time; but it returned in a fortnight in
a severer form, and the illness dragged on for some
time. Yevséitch, seeing that the remedies were
doing little good, began to doubt the skill of the
doctor, whom he had known before as a heavy
drinker, and who was sometimes ' half-seas-over',
according to Yevséitch, when he came to see me.
So my servant ventured to report this to Zapolsky
and asked him to call in another doctor. Zapolsky
was very angry: saying that Ritter was famous all
over the town for his success with fevers, he sent
Yevséitch about his business. But Yevséitch,
who was devoted to me, remembered his promise
to his mistress, and wrote to tell her of my illness.
My mother was much distressed and alarmed. She
had not yet recovered from her confinement—our
family had just been increased by the birth of
a third brother; but she started at once and
travelled alone to Kazan, where she took lodgings

for herself and me, called in the best doctor, and nursed me herself. This journey was a fresh act of self-sacrifice on my mother's part: her health suffered seriously in consequence; but her whole life was made up of such actions. Some disagreeable explanations with Zapolsky were inevitable: he was offended by my mother's moving me to her lodgings and by her changing the doctor. But while I was recovering, which took some time owing to severe pain in my right side, Zapolsky had some difficulties with the parents of the Manasséin boys, which made him give up his boarding-house and announce that he would take no more pupils.

This was a great satisfaction to my mother: she would not have left me with Zapolsky in any case; but she would have found it much more difficult or even impossible to induce Kartashevsky to take me directly from his friend. Even as it was, she met with so many difficulties that success for long seemed doubtful. I ought to say that, during all the second period of my school-time, the friendly relations between Kartashevsky and my family showed no signs of falling off, but grew steadily closer. My mother carried on a very active correspondence with him, and he could not fail to appreciate her intelligence, her steady friendship for him, founded on respect for his high character, and her exceptional devotion to her child. More than once I was within hearing in another room, while she urged and entreated Kartashevsky with the fire of heartfelt eloquence and burning tears to take me as his pupil. At last she broke down his opposition, and he consented, though very unwillingly. He took me, not as a pupil or boarder, but as a young companion—he was then twenty-seven, and I thirteen. He refused positively to accept money for his charge, and proposed that we should share the expense of board and lodging, though, for convenience' sake, I was to have my own supply of tea; all our other expenditure each of us was to manage independently. When my mother had at last secured the fulfilment of her darling wish, she was so radiantly happy that I felt deeply how far superior a mother's love is to that of anyone else in the world. I too was very glad to come under Kartashevsky. I felt a profound respect for him, and even loved him. His rather strange and dry manner did not frighten me; for I knew that this cold exterior, due to his views on education, was part of a regular system in his dealings with boys; and I thought then that perhaps it was the right system, though I certainly do not think so now.

A house belonging to the Yelágins, a fairly good and roomy house which was standing empty and on lease at the time, was taken by us at once. My mother moved there with me and made arrangements about our future housekeeping. I was now quite well again; and when she had handed me over personally to the care of Kartashevsky, she went back to the rest of the family at Aksákovo, full of bright hopes for the future. This was in February of the year 1804.

My life with Grigóri Kartashevsky is one of the happiest memories of my early youth. It lasted two years and a half; and, although its brightness suffered some eclipse eventually, yet only the happy part of it remains lively and distinct in my grateful recollection. It was long before he consented to take me; but, once he had consented, he devoted himself to me heart and soul. My school lessons, though I continued to do well in them, were now of secondary importance, and my private instruction became the main business. I had been used to attend all the classes in school regularly, but now I seldom went to lessons in arithmetic, drawing, and writing, spending these hours at home instead, under the supervision of my wise tutor. It is an odd fact that I was positively unable to learn mathematics. At first, Kartashevsky tried hard to teach me; and I cannot say that I did not understand his uncommonly clear explanations, but I forgot instantly what I had understood, so that he did not believe I had ever understood him. Knowing that I was intimate with Alexander Knyazhévitch, the best mathematician in the school, my tutor suggested that he should try his hand with me. When Knyazhévitch taught me, I understood him much better than my tutor, and I remembered the points longer. But it was all of no avail: after a few days, not a single proposition, not a single proof, remained in my head. In respect of mathematics, my excellent memory proved no better than a clean sheet of white paper, which refused to retain a single mathematical sign! Therefore my tutor took into account my natural powers and inclinations, and drew up a course of education for me in accordance with them: it was to be general, not abstruse, and mainly literary. He wrote out a long list of books for me at once. As far as I can remember, this included Lomonossoff, Derzhávin,[1]

[1] There was then only one volume of Derzhávin in print, and also a small collection of Anacreontic poems, printed,

Dmitrieff, Kapnist, and Hemnitser. Kheraskoff
and Sumarókoff I possessed already, but my tutor
never read these with me. Then there were French
books on the list : the preachers, Massillon,
Fléchier, and Bourdaloue; *The Arabian Nights*,
Don Quixote, *The Death of Abel* and *The Idylls* of
Gessner, *The Vicar of Wakefield*, and two *Natural
Histories*, one of them with pictures, but I do not
know the authors' names. To me natural history
was the most seductive of the sciences. There were
other books as well, but I forget their names too.

But the first thing my tutor did with me was to
work at foreign languages, especially French, in
which I, like most of the boys, was very weak ; and
in three months I could read it fluently and understand any French book. Words and the grammar
and conversations I learnt in the ordinary course
at school ; but at home I learnt nothing by heart :
my tutor took a book and made me read and
translate aloud. At first I was completely
puzzled, and this method seemed to me absurd and
wearisome ; but my teacher stuck to it, and I was
soon surprised and delighted by its success.
I made a separate list of words I did not know ;
then I wrote out a literal translation of the French,
a rough copy and then a fair copy. I had the
active memory of youth, and I was always able to
repeat next morning, without having learned them,
the French original, my Russian translation, and
the separate list of words. The first piece I read
and translated was *Les Aventures d' Aristonoy*,[1]
from a French reading-book ; and next I began to

according to the titlepage, in ' Petrograd '. Apparently
Derzhávin disliked the foreign name of the modern capital
of Russia. (*Author's Note.*)   [1] By Fénelon.

read and translate *The Arabian Nights,* which was followed by *Don Quixote.* Certain passages I was forbidden to read, and I obeyed orders scrupulously. What a pleasure it was to have such delightful and attractive lesson-books! Even now, after the lapse of fifty years, I recall these readings with the liveliest satisfaction; I remember how impatiently I awaited the time fixed for them, although it was nearly always immediately after dinner!

My tutor was a serious student of his own branch of science. Making use of the labours of men who were famous then in that branch of learning, he was writing an original course of lectures on Pure Mathematics to be delivered in the school. He knew modern languages very well and could write them readily; he read much German literature and philosophy. He was also constantly engaged in perfecting his knowledge of Latin; and his command of it astonished the University of Vilna with which he was connected later. To read *The Arabian Nights* and *Don Quixote* with me was a relief from his severer studies; and he joined heartily in my laughter, like a boy of my own age, or even like a child; and at first this puzzled me exceedingly. At such times my tutor was a different man: all his dryness and strictness disappeared, and I came to love him like an elder brother, though at the same time I stood in great awe of him.

When I had got a fair mastery of French, the reading of Russian authors, especially the poets, became our main occupation. My tutor explained poetry so well, pointing out the writer's meaning and the merits of his style, that my liking for literature

soon became a passion. With no effort on my part,
I learned by heart all the best poetry of Derzhávin,
Lomonossoff, and Kapnist, selected by the critical
judgement of my teacher; and Dmitrieff's poetry,
which was then considered a model of style for
purity and correctness, I could repeat almost from
end to end. Of Russian prose we read very little,
probably because my teacher was dissatisfied with
the prose writers of the time. It is worthy of
remark, that he read no Karamzin with me except
a few letters from *The Russian Traveller*, and would
not allow me to have *My Trifles* among my books.
But I knew already all that Karamzin had written,
and used to recite enthusiastically *The Parting of
Hector and Andromache*, and *The Proof of Solo-
mon's Wisdom*. I proceeded at once to display
these acquirements to my tutor; but he only
frowned and said that the first poem gave no idea
of Homer, and the second none of Ecclesiastes;
'Karamzin is no poet; better forget these poems
altogether,' he added. I was exceedingly puzzled:
I admired both poems, and continued to recite
them when I happened to be by myself in the
garden.

He did not allow me to compose, and I could
only taste this pleasure in secret or in Ibrahimoff's
class. My room was divided by a thin partition
from the drawing-room which served my tutor as
study and bedroom; and I once overheard a conversation about myself between him and Ibrahimoff. The latter praised me highly and showed
my tutor a composition I had written in class,
in the form of a letter to a friend, on 'The Beauties
of Spring'; and he added that it might be as well
to make me do more in the way of original com-

position. My tutor always exercised a kind of ascendancy over his colleagues, and he now replied very positively : ' My dear fellow, that is all utter nonsense. The boy's essay is a mere cento of phrases picked up out of different books ; and it is impossible to judge whether he has any original gift. He has a great fancy for writing, and I am sure he will soon begin to stain paper, but I shall keep him in leading-strings as long as I can. The later he begins to write, the better for my young Telemachus.' (This was a nickname given to me by all the masters, while they called my tutor ' Mentor ' or ' Minerva.') ' A young man ought to collect good examples, and form his taste by reading authors with a correct and well-formed style. Do you suppose I let him read all Derzhávin ? Not a bit of it ! He only knows twenty poems of his, but he knows the whole of Dmitrieff. I believe you will spoil him. I daresay you constantly use in school *Poor Lisa*, and *Natalya, the Nobleman's Daughter*,[1] and *Sofya, A Dramatic Fragment*.' Ibrahimoff was offended, and replied that, for all their charm, he understood perfectly that these works were unsuitable for boys. ' Glad to hear it ! ' my tutor continued ; ' but these are the very poems which Erich has made them translate into French.' (Erich, who had a great knowledge of languages, ancient and modern, used to teach French and German to the Senior Class.) This conversation went on for some time, and my youth did not prevent me from understanding the good sense of my tutor's arguments. He would not have talked so loudly about me if he had known that I was in the house. A teacher

---

[1] Novels by Karamzin, published about 1792.

having failed to appear, I had come back early from school and passed unnoticed into my room. On this occasion I learnt the high estimate Kartashevsky had formed of my mother; but alas! about myself he did not make a single flattering remark; yet how I longed to hear something of the kind! It really seemed as if he knew that I was listening behind the door.

When I reflect now upon the past, it puzzles me exceedingly, and I cannot understand why I was so warmly attached to my tutor. I was too young to appreciate fully the deep sympathy and real affection for me that were concealed under that dry manner. Never once did he show kind feeling, or flatter my vanity by any kind of compliment, or praise my diligence; and yet I loved him more than anyone outside my family. I remember that I once heard him laughing and looked into his room: he had some mathematical treatise in his hand, and the stern martinet was laughing like a child as he watched some kittens at play; and he wore an expression so kind and even affectionate that I was jealous of those kittens. When I went into the room with my book, his face changed and assumed the old expression—cold and composed, with even a trace of surliness.

And so my life went on. At times, my tutor became more approachable, and his manner of addressing me, if not friendly, was at least playful. This happened only when we were alone, and especially during the reading of *Don Quixote*—Sancho Panza was an inexhaustible source of laughter to us both; but the appearance of any third person, even if it was only Yevséitch, at once put an end to his mirth.

Grigóri Kartashevsky was the son of a Little Russian priest, who had the rank of nobility and owned about a hundred serfs, and the great-grandson of a Turk, who left Turkey for reasons unknown to me, became a Christian, and then married and settled down in Little Russia. In youth he was neglected by his mother; and his father, who loved him with a mother's tenderness, seeing that the child was unhappy at home, took him to Moscow when he was nine years old, and placed him as a Government scholar at a school connected with the University. The son was passionately attached to his father: he suffered much when left alone at Moscow, and his joy and excitement, when his father visited him a year later, were so great that he fell ill of a fever; and the poor father, called back by his duties, had to leave his darling on a sick-bed. A year later the father died. During the eighteen years that followed his entrance at the Moscow school, the boy paid only one visit to his home in Little Russia. This was shortly before he entered the teaching profession, and the impression left upon him by his visit was painful and distressing. All these facts I learnt from his servant Yashka, who had come from Little Russia with his master. In my tutor's pronunciation, in his turn of mind, and in his appearance, there was no indication whatever of his native country, and I think it had no attraction for him: I often heard him praise the good sense of Great Russians and laugh at the indolence and stupidity of his own countrymen. This gave great offence to the other Little Russians, Zapolsky and Markevitch. The latter was the school bursar, a fat and very good-natured man, a born humorist and very amusing; he was very kind to me, and I was very fond of him.

The spring of 1804 came round, and my tutor and I fasted in Passion-week and carried out all the observances prescribed by the Church for that season. Our parish church, dedicated to St. Barbara the Martyr, was close to the outside of Kazan, and the roads were in a terrible condition, owing to the thaw; yet we went on foot to all the services, even in the early morning. Zapolsky came to our house one day, and I happened to overhear him laughing at Kartashevsky for his devoutness. His words implied that my tutor had not always been equally strict in his performance of religious duties; but he got a sharp rebuke on this occasion for ill-timed jesting. Zapolsky, who set up for a freethinker, was much offended and did not come near us for a long time. I ought to say that Kartashevsky, during his whole life, was a sincere Christian. This tiff did not prevent my tutor from going with me to Zapolsky's country house, where we spent the time together very pleasantly, in the absence of the owners. We lived in a little wing of the house, on the bank of a large pond which had just lost its winter covering of ice; we read continually and took two walks every day, defying the mud. Spring distracted my attention and reminded me too much of spring at Aksákovo; the budding sportsman could not hear with indifference the cries of the returning birds. One day my tutor was reading some serious French book with me; he was sitting by the open window, trying to explain some idea which I could not quite grasp, when suddenly the musical cry of a redshank rang out, and the bird itself, with its wings raised and its slender red legs stretched out, alighted gracefully on the bank of the pond, right opposite the window. I started, dropped the book, and rushed to the window, to the astonishment of my tutor. ' A redshank ! a redshank ! ' I repeated breathlessly ; ' he perched on the bank close by ! Look, there he is, walking about ! ' But Kartashevsky did not understand the feelings of a sportsman : he told me sharply to sit down and go on with my book. I obeyed ; but, though I could not see the bird, I could hear its note ; the blood rushed to my face, and I could not take in a word of what I was reading. My tutor was displeased : he told me to put the book down and write a fair copy of an old translation which he had already corrected ; he took a book himself. An hour later he said, ' Well, has the redshank flown out of your head by this time ? ' I said it had, and we resumed the work which had been interrupted. I should add that he was always indulgent on these occasions : whenever he saw that I was tired or inattentive, he made me do some mechanical task or sent me to walk in the garden.

Examinations began with the beginning of June. Though I did very well in all the classes which I attended, yet, as I had dropped some subjects altogether, I got no prize ; but this did not interfere with my promotion to the Senior Class. Only nine boys completed the course and left the school at this time ; the rest remained, to spend another year in the same form.

A carriage and three horses had arrived before this to fetch me. Yevséitch and I got ready for the journey, and it was settled that we should start after dinner on speech-day, which was on one of the early days of July. My tutor told me the day before that he would like to go part of the way with me, and asked whether I approved of this plan. I supposed that he would go as far as the town gate, and said that I should be very glad. Next morning Yevséitch whispered in my ear : ' He intends to go with us to Aksákovo ; but he told me not to tell you.' Though I worked willingly at school, I was not altogether pleased by this news : I was looking forward to a real orgy of fishing in the holidays, and even more to shooting ; for my father had promised a year ago to get me a gun and teach me to shoot. But I knew that my tutor would not drop his lessons with me, and would make heavy demands on my time ; and also I was vexed with him for not telling me. Yevséitch too seemed discontented. When speech-day was over, we dined rather earlier than usual and drove out of the town. I pretended to be ignorant of my tutor's plan. When we had reached the country, we got out and walked for a time. My tutor was in very good humour and even gay ; he looked with pleasure at the green fields and woods and the cloudlets in the summer sky. Suddenly he smiled and said : ' This fine weather tempts me to go with you to your halt for the night ; then I shall see you catch fish for our supper.' Keeping up the pretence of ignorance, I said : ' Very well ! then let us get in again and go faster, or we shall arrive late. But when will you turn back, and how do you mean to travel ? ' ' Oh, I shall spend the night in the carriage with you, and hire a cart to-morrow morning,' he replied, looking at me attentively.

We got into the carriage and went off at a quick trot. The beauty of the evening was enchanting. We had fishing-tackle with us, and Yevséitch and I caught a quantity of fish, which was boiled or fried for our supper ; then we lay down in the carriage to sleep.

Waking early next morning, I saw that we were moving ; the sun was already high in the sky ; my tutor was sitting in the carriage opposite to me, and I saw he was laughing. I burst out laughing myself and confessed that I had known his plan all the time. He scolded Yevséitch for indiscretion ; then, reading in my face that I was not quite pleased, he said : ' You are afraid that I shall interfere with your amusements, but you need not fear that : I shall not give you lessons except when you ask me to do so yourself. We might just as well read something now, as there is nothing else to do in the carriage '—and he pulled a book out of his pocket. I was quite comforted by his words, and would gladly have embraced him ; but I dared not even think of taking such a liberty. We did a great deal of work on that journey ; beside, I repeated over again all that I had learnt, and I talked much more, and more openly, than at Kazan ; yet, wherever it was possible to fish, fish I did to my heart's content. So we travelled on till we reached Aksákovo on the fifth day. My tutor's visit was a most pleasant surprise to my mother : she was delighted to see him.

Though we did not at all expect it, we found the house full of relations and visitors and a great bustle going on. My aunt Tatyána was going to be married, and the wedding was fixed for a few days later. Though now past forty, she was very active and well-preserved. She was tired of living in her brother's house, in complete dependence upon her sister-in-law, who in days gone by had suffered much at the hands of her husband's sisters ; and Tatyána, though she was better than the rest, was not guiltless. She wished to spend her old age at least under her own roof, and to be mistress in her own house, however small that house might be. Her future husband was Vassíli Ooglichínin, who, after a life spent in the army, had recently retired as lieutenant-colonel. He was a very simple and kindly man, of an honest and friendly nature. He was well over fifty, with nothing to live on but his pension ; he belonged to a very poor but noble family, which had migrated to the district of Ufá. He had entered the army at fourteen and done good service in his quiet way—taking part in many engagements and receiving several slight wounds. He had struggled with poverty all his life and had earned no distinctions, though his formal discharge was so long and eloquent that his breast might well have been covered with medals. His last service had been in the Caucasus ; and from there he had brought home a small sum saved out of his pay, a uniform without epaulets, a hill-pony so old that his coat had turned white, rheumatism in every joint, and cataract in his right eye. The cataract was fortunately not very noticeable ; and the old soldier took pains to hide it, fearing that the loss of an eye might make the bride draw back. My aunt had a small estate of twenty-five serfs, within seven versts of where her sister Alexandra lived, and a small house on the estate. The house, which was no more than two peasants' houses run together, stood on the bank of a stream which swarmed with trout—a great attraction in my eyes! She owned a suitable amount of excellent land with all the usual accessories—land which had been bought for her from the Bashkirs for almost nothing. To the retired soldier this modest domain seemed a haven of rest; and to an old man half a loaf was better than no bread.

There was much secret laughter at the expense of an old and one-eyed bridegroom, but my parents and my tutor took no share in it: they always treated him with respect and cordiality. Evil tongues accounted for my mother's behaviour by saying that she wished to get rid of her sister-in-law. But that was false: my mother never failed in appreciation and respect for simple and guileless people; she honestly advised my aunt to marry this worthy man, and my aunt was grateful to her for that advice till the day of her death. Karta-shevsky, who shared my mother's feeling, took special pleasure in conversing with the veteran, who was excessively silent as a rule, but readily answered his questions and told us much that was curious and entertaining. My tutor lost no time in enlisting my interest and sympathy for this character, explaining to me those merits which I was too young to notice and understand.

There was no room in the house for male visitors; and even the ladies were accommodated with difficulty, because three rooms were given up to the future bride and bridegroom. In this difficulty my mother took a step for which her husband's relations never forgave her. Her own bedroom, which no one outside the family ever dared even to enter, she gave up to my tutor and put me there with him ; of course we left it as soon as the party broke up. The marriage took place with no hitch on the appointed day. My father went with the pair to their new abode, but came back at once. At last we were left alone and had our house to ourselves.

But here I break the thread of my narrative to run on ahead a little. For the married life of my uncle and aunt rises up so vividly before me that I want to say something about it.

After her marriage, my aunt became familiar with the troubles of poverty, of which she had known nothing during her girlhood in her father's house, or under the roof of my parents ; but she was perfectly happy. She felt a tender and passionate love for her old colonel, and his love for her was no less deep and tender. Unfortunately they had no children. My aunt lived to be very old ; but a kind of maidenly modesty clung to her till the last. She was rather ceremonious in addressing her husband, and suppressed every sign of affection for him, when a third person was present, though the old soldier would sometimes give a sly hint that the lady was not always quite so prudish. Be that as it may, in company they were always distant and polite to one another, never saying ' thou ' but always ' you '. A casual observer might have taken this for coldness ; but soon one became aware of a different state of things—a solicitous attention on both sides, a constant observation, an instant sympathy in each other's every word and movement ; and it became clear to all that husband and wife drew from each other the very breath of life. If there was any difference

in their feeling, it was that the husband's love was
less easily alarmed. Their little house shone like
a new pin ; it breathed of peace and attracted the
visitor by its cosiness. It cannot be said that
they had similar tastes ; but, in their case,
differences only met to make the course of life
run more smoothly. For example, my aunt liked
cats and dogs in the house ; and it must be stated
that her pets, for some reason, were guilty of no
nuisance and never tore or spoilt anything belonging to her. My uncle did not like them at all ;
yet even 'Kalmuck', a hideous lapdog that
snuffled and lolled out its tongue at one corner
of its mouth, was pleasant and actually dear to
him, because she loved it ; and he fed and caressed
this repulsive animal with satisfaction and gratitude. Then there was a marmot which passed the
winter under the stove ; it was the source of much
amusement to my aunt and as much annoyance
to my uncle, because it carried off his slippers and
hid them so cleverly that they were often missing
for a whole day, and the poor colonel had to step
out of bed in the morning with bare feet ; yet
even the marmot enjoyed his favour. In their
little house everything was in its place, and everything seemed to be somehow better than in other
people's houses : their dogs and cats were sleeker
and cleaner, the cage-birds sang louder and more
gaily, their plants were greener. If you gave them
some half-withered stick in a flower-pot, the
plant at once revived, put forth green leaves, and
grew so splendidly that you wanted to have it
back again. In her small rooms, my aunt grew
vines from seed, palms, and other plants that need
heat. The atmosphere seemed to have something

calming and life-giving in it, something suited to beast and plant, which made up in some degree for the loss of freedom or native climate. Together they attended to the management of their small estate ; and, without any pressure on their part, all the work was done twice as quick and twice as well as it was done elsewhere. Together they walked out to pick mushrooms and berries ; together they angled for the fine trout in their little stream ; and together they rejoiced over each fish they caught. But, if one of them chanced to have a slight illness, what was the state of matters then ! At once there came to the surface that deep and tender mutual affection which might easily escape notice in the ordinary course of life.

But I shall refrain from further details which might carry me too far afield. I shall only say, that, when later in life I sometimes paid a visit to this remote corner and watched for a few hours this simple modest existence, it always made a deep impression upon me, and I wondered whether this was not the true happiness for man—a life without passions and excitements, a life undisturbed by insoluble questions and unsatisfied desires. The peace and order of their life remained long with me ; I felt a vague agitation and regret for the lack of something so near at hand and so easily procured ; but, whenever I put to myself the question, ' Would you like to be what your uncle is ? '—I was afraid to reply, and my feeling of agitation vanished instantly.

My father kept his promise to me : he had got me a light gun, very handy in the stock and prettily finished ; it was inlaid with silver, the sights were of silver, and the barrel tapered like those of the English guns then used by sportsmen. He had picked it up for fifteen roubles, but, though only of Tula [1] manufacture, it was worth two or three times as much, even at the prices of those days : it did very good work at fifty yards. With my first shot I killed a crow, and that settled my fate : I went mad over shooting. Next day I shot a duck and two snipe, and my madness was confirmed. Fishing and hawking were forgotten ; carried away by my natural excitability, I ran about with the gun all that day and dreamt of the gun all night. It was just the same on the days that followed. My tutor never saw me except for a moment, and then I was busy and in a hurry ; he looked forward to a time when I should ask him for some work to do ; but that time never came.

He then told my mother of our agreement, and she issued her orders to me : I was to ask my tutor to set me some tasks to be done under his supervision for two hours every day. Though this requirement went much against the grain, I obeyed. At first my tutor could not help laughing at my dismal face and dejected figure. I opened a French book and began to translate. But I was too distracted to attend to what I was reading : visions of ducks and snipe passed before my eyes, and their cries rang in my ears. When I began to blunder in translating, my tutor frowned, took the book from me, and walked about the room from corner to corner for a whole hour, giving me a serious lecture and urging me to conquer the dangerous habit which made me forget everything else in my passionate devotion to some amusement.

[1] Tula is, or used to be, the Birmingham of Russia.

But alas! I neither heard nor understood a single word: his eloquent phrases, just sentiments, and convincing arguments, were all wasted. Seeing that his appeal had failed, he tried another plan: he left me in perfect freedom for a whole week, to run about with my gun from morning till night, till I was tired out and fit to drop. He hoped that I should come round of myself, that bodily fatigue and an overdose of this new amusement would restore me to my senses. But he was mistaken. I ate little and slept badly; I grew as brown as a gipsy and lost flesh visibly; but I never stopped shooting.

But now my tutor, fearing for my health, took decisive steps, which my mother had suggested some time before, though she wished to leave my tutor a free hand: my gun was hung up on the wall, and I was forbidden to go out shooting. I am both amused and ashamed when I think of the way I spent the first twenty-four hours. I cried and even yelled like a child of three; I rolled on the floor and tore my hair; I very nearly tore up my books and papers; indeed nothing but my mother's grief and my father's gentle remonstrances saved me from acting like a fool and a madman. Next day I came to myself, as it were; and on the third day I was able to study and to read my favourite poets aloud with attention and enjoyment. On the fourth day I had calmed down altogether, and then the cloud lifted for the first time from the face of my tutor. Till then he had hardly spoken to me; he had only looked at me with an expression either of displeasure or of insulting pity. But now he showed sympathy for me and spoke words of indulgence

and wisdom; and this time his efforts were entirely
successful. Angry with myself and ashamed
almost to tears, I now ran from one extreme to
the other and wished to give up the gun for good.
But this did not please him either: he disapproved
of my intention, and insisted that I should go out
shooting every day from breakfast to dinner or
from dinner till evening, but that I should work
diligently three or four hours a day, especially at
history and geography, in which I was rather
weaker than my chief rivals at school. And so the
time flowed by in pleasant and regular occupation.

During this month it was possible for my parents
to enjoy frank and friendly conversation with Kartashevsky without interruptions; and this increased
their appreciation and regard for him, in whom
penetrating intellect and high qualities of character
were combined with many-sided culture and sound
learning. My mother used all her power over me
to make me understand the character of the man
whom fortune had appointed to be my instructor.
She considered this to be a special instance of
God's goodness. I understood her meaning, and
I had a strong feeling of the truth of her words.
I assured her—though unfortunately I could never
quite convince her—that I was myself warmly
attached to him; that, though my attention was
distracted at home by my favourite pursuits and
especially by the hitherto unknown delights of
shooting, at Kazan my one thought was to gain
the love and approval of my tutor, and one kind
word from him made me entirely happy.

My dear sister, who was also my bosom friend,
was growing taller and prettier at a surprising rate.
Though she could no longer share my outdoor

amusements and occupations or spend so much
of her time with me, she bore this deprivation
patiently when she saw how happy I was; but
she complained of the time I spent over lessons,
and this was probably the reason why she did not
look with favour on my teacher.[1]

We left Aksákovo on the 10th of August and
arrived at Kazan on the 15th without any mis-
adventures. It was a surprise to me when Kartashevsky that same day told me not to attend classes
in the school, and made out a programme of work
for me to do at home. But he went off himself
every morning to meetings of the Governors and
stayed there a long time; he acted as their
honorary secretary. Five days later, he told me
that many of the boys had not turned up yet, and
there was little doing in the way of teaching; then
he proposed that we should go to Zapolsky's
country-house, to enjoy an extra holiday and do
some work for a week or so. This was a still
greater surprise, but I was much pleased. In the
country we spent, not a week but more than a
fortnight; my tutor drove to Kazan several times,
starting early and returning for a late dinner.
I asked no questions about these visits. We
returned at last to Kazan, and he told me the next
day to begin my attendance at school. I went off
in good spirits, but my school-fellows met me with
glum faces and told me of an unfortunate affair
that had taken place. I shall tell it here.

I should begin by saying that Likhachoff, the
Rector of the school, was a very bad Rector and
also the possessor of a ludicrous personality which

---

[1] Yet she became his wife twelve years later: see note
to p. 102. He was her second husband.

was not calculated to inspire respect : for one
thing, his lower lip was as large and swollen as if
it had been bitten by a poisonous fly or stung by
a wasp. Neither masters nor boys had any respect
for him ; and even before I went home for the
summer holidays, he was hooted by the boys one
day when he was walking about the dining-hall
during dinner ; the cause of irritation was the
quality of the porridge, in which some boy had
found a piece of tallow candle. That same night,
inscriptions in abuse of the Rector, boldly written
with red pencil in large printed characters,
appeared on many of the inside walls, on the
outer walls, and even on the cupola of the building.
These inscriptions were so high up that the artist
must have used a ladder, and the inscription on
the cupola was recognized as a triumph of boldness
and agility. Neither then nor later were the
culprits discovered ; even now I do not know
who did the writing. And now for later events.

A few days before I returned with my tutor
from Aksákovo, and when most of the boys had
already come back, an official, known for some
reason as ' quartermaster ', who had once served in
the army and controlled all the old soldiers
employed about the school, got angry with one of
his subordinates and proceeded to thrash him
without mercy. This took place in the back-yard,
which was divided from the front-yard, where the
boys could play in their free time, by a wooden
boarding ; and as it was after dinner, the boys
were all there at the time. The sufferer's loud cries
aroused such pity in their young hearts, that
Alexander Knyazhévitch and some other boys
of the Senior Class passed through the gate into

the back-yard, in contravention of the rules, and called loudly on the quartermaster to drop his stick. But this attack on his authority made the man furious : he began to shout abuse in the foulest terms at the boys ; and Alexander Knyazhévitch, a very kind-hearted boy and therefore more excited than the rest, as he was in front, bore the brunt of all this bad language. When the noise of the contention reached their ears, all the Senior Class made an appearance in the back-yard, and others followed them. The elder Knyazhévitch, Dmitri, recognizing the voice of his brother to whom he was much attached, was the first to hurry to the scene ; naturally hot-tempered, he eagerly espoused the cause of his insulted brother, and the other boys backed him with one accord. As may be supposed, there was no lack of forcible expressions and threats ; the quartermaster soon found himself obliged to drop his disciplinary proceedings and beat a hasty retreat. This trifling incident, due to a praiseworthy feeling of pity for suffering and then to reasonable anger at grossly insolent language, led to very lamentable consequences, simply because it was misunderstood and mismanaged by the Rector.

The Senior Class began by submitting a humble petition in writing : they asked that the quartermaster should be dismissed for cruelty and insolence. The Rector refused to grant this petition : he threw all the blame on the boys and even sentenced some of them to some form of punishment. This injustice naturally produced irritation : their respectful petition had been refused, and now the boys took to persistent demands and infringements of the established rules. The Senior Class struck work and refused to attend any classes until their enemy was removed from the school ; and the other two forms soon made common cause with their seniors. As the trouble was chiefly due in its origin to the insulting language addressed to Alexander Knyaz-hévitch, it was natural that his brother, Dmitri, who took the lead in every department of school life and was very popular, should become the leader of this movement. The Rector played a cowardly part : he dared not show himself to the boys ; and when he had to attend a meeting of the governors, he came by a back entrance, passing through Yakovnin's rooms ; but he sent various envoys to remonstrate with the rebels, and all these remonstrances proved ineffectual. Upadi-shevsky was loved for his kindness and respected by the boys ; and if he had been acting as head-master at the time, the whole of this unfortunate affair would have been smothered at birth ; but he had gone away some weeks earlier owing to ill-health, and his substitute was a mere cipher.

For three days the affair dragged on in the same unsettled state. On the fourth day, the boys found out that the Rector was attending a meeting of the governors ; they first posted a guard at the back entrance and then proceeded in a body to the door of the board-room, where they loudly demanded that the quartermaster should be discharged. The Rector tried to leave the building, but was told that his line of retreat was cut off by the boys posted at the back door. This news threw him into such alarm and agitation that he gave orders on the spot to draw up a resolution for the discharge of the offending quartermaster ;

and the resolution was read out to the boys. The effect was immediate : the rebels calmed down at once, expressed their thanks to the authorities, and ceased from their mutinous behaviour. Order was restored, and the ordinary routine of school life began again. At first it was supposed that this incident would not lead to any further developments ; but this belief was quite mistaken. The Rector reported the case at once in the highest quarters, and then, acting on some advice, he entered into relations with the Governor of Kazan, and took the following measures. A few days later, during dinner-time, a party of soldiers armed with rifles and bayonets entered the hall, and were followed immediately by the Governor and the Rector. The latter then called out by name sixteen boys of the Senior Class, including of course the elder Knyazhévitch, and ordered them to be taken to the school prison under the escort of armed soldiers. All the other boys were horror-struck, and dead silence reigned in the hall. Two soldiers armed with bayonets were posted at each outer door of the school, and four at the door of the prison.

I heard the whole story a fortnight after it occurred, when I came back after the holidays, or, I should say, when I returned from Zapolsky's house, and joined the depleted ranks of the Senior Class to which I now belonged. The other boys told me the bad news at once. And now it flashed upon me why my prudent tutor had first prevented me from going into school and then carried me off with him to the country. Had I been on the spot, I should beyond all doubt have been one of the most active sharers in this unlucky affair. Six weeks later the decision of the central authority was delivered at Kazan. Again the Governor appeared in the dining-hall, accompanied by the Rector and other governors of the school; and a document was read, setting forth the guilt of the rebellious boys, and declaring that, as an example to the rest, eight of the Senior Class, who were considered the ringleaders, were expelled from the school without a certificate of character. The victims were the best students of the class; Dmitri Knyazhévitch, who was one of the eight, we considered the ornament and pride of the school. We were all deeply impressed and sorely grieved by the sentence; when it had been executed, the sentries were withdrawn, and the state of siege, which we strongly resented, came to an end.

The Rector was removed from his place soon afterwards, and was succeeded by the senior teacher, Yakovnin. Dmitri Knyazhévitch long kept up a close connexion with his school-fellows. He entered the public service at Petersburg, and wrote to his brother by every post; sometimes he addressed his communications to us all, and then his letters were solemnly read aloud in the hearing of the whole form. After a period of sadness and silence, the youthful population of the school began by degrees to recover their spirits and to forget the painful affair: the old noisy activity returned, the old laughing and singing was heard again, and life sped forward as if nothing had happened.

My work in school and at home went on quietly till midwinter under the steady supervision and direction of my tutor; but at that time my uncle Alexander, my mother's brother, paid a visit to

Kazan and took me twice to the theatre, of course with my tutor's permission. We saw an opera and a comedy—the latter was called *A Sister sold by a Brother*—and the effect of these two performances upon me was nearly as strong as the effect of my first day's shooting. I had a special passion for dramatic compositions, and had formed from what I heard some notion of their performance upon the stage. But the reality far surpassed my anticipations. The two performances I had seen filled my head day and night, and I found it utterly impossible to concentrate my attention upon my books. Of course my tutor noticed this at once, and his questions soon elicited the true reason. He frowned and showed displeasure at this new folly on my part; and once more I had to listen to a long lecture. But I felt the justice of his rebukes this time; for I understood the danger of my tendency to be carried away beyond all bounds by the things I cared for. My passion for the theatre was the natural development of a tendency which had shown itself from early years in my love of recitation and of plays, both Russian and French; but I made a great effort and succeeded in checking the rising flame. I calmed down and applied myself with more than ordinary zeal to my tasks.

My tutor was much pleased. When a week had passed, he started a conversation about the stage and the art of acting, in which he gave me some real notion of the subject and told me stories of many famous actors, both living and dead, Russians and foreigners; for instance, I heard of the Moscow actors, Shusherin and Plavilshchikoff. These conversations, so delightful to me, went on

for three days during the hours of recreation.
Then, one happy day, when I had come back from
school and was drinking my evening tea, my tutor
opened my door and said in a cheerful voice :
' You have got to drive somewhere with me at
once : be quick and get done with that milk and
water ! ' (I was very fond of milk and used to put
so much in my tea that my tutor often called it
milk and water.) I was ready in a moment, and
we got into a sledge and started. I felt sure that
we were going to call on M. Voskresensky ; his son
was at school with me, and my tutor sometimes
took me to their house. At a turning, the driver
was told to go straight down Georgia Street ;
I was surprised, for this was not the way I expected.
A few minutes later we were opposite the theatre,
and the order came, ' To the theatre entrance.'
When we got there, my tutor sprang out of the
sledge, but I was so stunned by the joyful prospect
that I sat stock-still. He could not help laughing :
' Well,' he said, ' don't you want to come ? '—and
I took a flying leap to the ground. Tickets had
been taken beforehand ; we went in and sat
together in the front row of the stalls. An opera
called *The Pork-butchers* was performed. How
intensely I enjoyed that evening ! At this moment
I can see before me Mihail Kalmikoff who played
the leading part of the old pork-butcher ; and
I can hear Pritkoff singing to the guitar, though
in fact he only opened his mouth while an actress
behind the scenes sang the music, and I remember
some of the words—

> ' O loved one in whose chains I lie,
> Hark to thy pris'ner's plaintive cry ! '

Yet more than fifty years have passed since

that evening, and during all that time I have never once heard the opera of *The Pork-butchers* mentioned!

On our way home I thanked my tutor heartily, and he pleased me by saying that this treat was a reward for my sensible behaviour, and that, if *The Pork-butchers* did not upset me, he would take me to the theatre from time to time. To tell the truth, *The Pork-butchers* did fill my thoughts and upset me to some extent; but I tried hard to hide my state of mind, and got on so well with my work, thanks to an exceptionally strong memory, that my tutor remained quite in the dark. In the course of a short time I saw a good many plays— *The Hobbledehoy, Mistakes, or Morning Thoughts are Wisest*, an opera called *Nina, or The Crazed Lover*, and *Count Valtron*, a play by Kotzebue. My love of the stage grew and strengthened every day. I learnt by heart the plays I had seen, and found time to perform all the parts with myself for audience. Of this my tutor knew nothing; for I shut myself up in my own room for the purpose, or used a part of the house which was uninhabited and unheated.

In this winter of 1804 I began an intimacy with another pensioner at the school, Alexander Panáyeff, who was like me a lover of the stage and of Russian literature. Being a worshipper of Karamzin, he wrote prose idylls, in which he tried to reproduce the smooth and florid style created by the historian. His brother Ivan was a lyric poet. Alexander Panáyeff was editor at that time of a manuscript magazine called *Shepherds of Arcadia*, of which I still preserve several numbers. All the contributors signed their writings with pastoral names—Adonis, Daphnis, Amyntas, Iris, Damon, Palaemon, and so on. As Alexander Panáyeff was a skilful penman and artist, he used to write and illustrate with his own hand each monthly number of his magazine. To tell the truth, as we were children then, so was our national literature in its childhood; but it is worth remarking that the tendency and style of this magazine were exactly the same as those which prevailed in Russia for some decades after this date.

I took no share in the editing of this magazine, because, thanks to the exertions of my tutor, I was not yet an author. But alas! the example proved very seductive, and I began to write a little in secret, though I kept it dark even from my bosom friend, Panáyeff. A year later, he and I were joint editors of another magazine which will be described hereafter. In this same winter amateur theatricals took place in the school, and a tiresome priggish play whose name I forget was performed twice, and also a little comedy by Sumarókoff, *A Dowry Gained by Deceit*. I was only a spectator; for many older boys wished to act, and also I did not venture even to hint at such a step to my tutor. But the next year, which was to bring about a development of my dramatic and literary doings at school, proved that I was mistaken about my tutor's feelings.

For nearly a year reports had been going about that a University was to be founded at Kazan. The reports turned out to be true, and in December 1804 the official announcement was received, that a charter for the University had been signed by the Emperor on the 5th of November. A Chancellor was appointed, Stepan Rumovsky, a high political official; and he came to Kazan. This event, which caused much excitement in the town, was even more interesting to the school and especially to the Senior Class. Meetings were held daily, with Rumovsky as chairman; and the other members were Professor Herman and Professor Zeppelin who had come with the Chancellor, Yakovnin the Rector of the school, and all the senior teachers. Of their proceedings I and my school-fellows knew nothing. But one evening there was a large dinner-party at my tutor's house, which included the two outside professors, the Chancellor's secretary, and all the senior teachers of the school except Yakovnin. They met at a fairly late hour when I was already in bed. It was a gay and noisy party and kept me awake for a long time, as I listened to them talking loudly and exchanging congratulations: they were speaking of the new University and of the appointment of teachers in the school to be professors and assistant professors. Next morning Yevséitch told me that the party went on till three in the morning, that a great deal of wine and punch had been drunk, and that many of the guests were decidedly cheerful when they left. He added that Kartashevsky, though he had been forced to drink a great deal, showed no sign of it—' was not drunk even in one eye' was the precise expression of Yevséitch. Never had our sober mansion witnessed such a scene before; and Yevséitch and I were very much surprised. But the cause of it was now clear. Yevséitch had overheard—and indeed I could tell him as much myself—that my tutor was appointed assistant professor in the new University, together with Zapolsky, Levitsky, and Erich. From their conversation

I learnt further, that Yakovnin had been appointed to a full professorship of Russian History, and was also to act as inspector of Government students. His colleagues unanimously disapproved of this appointment : they thought Yakovnin deficient in learning, and that he had not earned such rapid promotion. They were talking about the students, when I heard my tutor say in a loud voice, ' For my Telemachus, gentlemen, I will go bail.' I guessed at once that it was intended to admit me to the University. Such a thing was quite beyond my hopes, because I had not completed the course in the Senior Class and also knew no mathematics.

My tutor was still in bed when I went to school next morning. I made haste to tell the news to my companions, but they had all heard it already from Yakovnin's son, a very stupid and terribly fat boy. He boasted that he would be admitted too, but we all laughed at the idea. The top boys in the Senior Class, who had gone through the course of study twice, naturally hoped for promotion to student rank ; but no one dreamed of me and some others being chosen. But the list of students was published that same day, and it appeared that all the boys of the Senior Class, with two or three exceptions, were to enter the University ; Yakovnin and I were both included. Strictly speaking, about a dozen of us, of whom I was certainly one, did not deserve to be admitted, partly because we were too young, and partly because we did not know enough. Nor do I refer merely to the fact that none of us knew Latin and very few German, though in the coming autumn we were bound to attend lectures delivered in both languages. For all this, we rejoiced heartily and gave loud expression to our feelings. We embraced and congratulated one another, and vowed to work untiringly at the subjects in which we were deficient, so that we should not be ashamed in the course of a few months to call ourselves qualified students of a University. A Latin class was started at once, and most of the future students began to tackle the language. From some foolish prejudice against Latin, I did not follow this praiseworthy example. To this day I do not understand why my tutor, who was a good Latin scholar himself, allowed me to shirk that subject.

I have a sense of satisfaction and of admiration when I recall the spirit which then animated the older boys, a spirit of genuine devotion to knowledge. They worked by night as well as by day till the effect was visible in their thin and altered faces. It was necessary for the authorities to take active measures, in order to discourage such excessive zeal : a master patrolled the dormitories all night to put out candles and forbid conversation ; for even in the dark the boys examined each other in the subjects they had gone through. The teachers too were spurred on by the eager zeal of their pupils, and worked with them, not in school only but in all free hours and on all holidays. My tutor gave a course of lectures on Applied Mathematics at his house for the best mathematicians ; and this example was followed by his colleagues. Even after the college was opened, this state of things continued during the first year. Those were proud and happy days, days of pure love for knowledge and praiseworthy enthusiasm ! I can speak of them impartially ; for I did not share the eager aspirations which filled most of the scholars and exhibitioners. For some reason the pensioners stood somewhat aloof from the movement; and my own education went on as usual under the direction of my tutor. I daresay he thought I had no vocation for a learned life; and I daresay he was mistaken. He was led to this conclusion by my passion for literature and the drama which had now come to the surface. But I believe that I could have conceived an equally strong passion for Natural History, and I might perhaps have done something useful in that line. My parents, however, never intended me for a scholar's life, against which they had even a prejudice; and my tutor was only carrying out their wishes in the direction he gave to my studies.

It must be admitted that the birth of our University was somewhat premature. Six weeks after the Chancellor's arrival, on the 14th of February 1805, it was formally opened. The staff comprised only six teachers, of whom two were professors, Yakovnin and Zeppelin, while the other four, Kartashevsky, Zapolsky, Levitsky, and Erich, had the rank of assistants.

In that year, 1805, the letters from Dmitri Knyazhévitch, which were always received by us and listened to with keen interest, became more interesting than ever, for political reasons. The first war with Napoleon was then going on; and news of the campaign was for some reason very scanty and very slow in reaching us; but Knyaz-hévitch sent us early and full details. Besides this, his letters were so full of patriotic ardour and devotion to the glory of the Russian arms, that they had an electrical effect on all of us. When

Alexander Knyazhévitch called out, 'A letter from my brother!'—we needed no further summons: an eager crowd gathered round him at once; leaning on each other's shoulders, in dead silence broken at times by enthusiastic shouts, we listened greedily while the letter was read aloud. Even the boys from the school joined us and listened to these letters. The famous General Bagration was our hero; and when we heard how he and his detachment, when left at the mercy of the enemy, had forced their way through the whole French army,[1] the cheers which we raised, and the passionate enthusiasm of every one of us, are beyond my powers of description. There was plenty of life in the young men of that day, and it is comforting to think of it now.

The usual summer examinations were not held either in the school or the University, and all our time was spent in preparing for the courses of lectures to be delivered after our return. My tutor for some reason unknown to me sent me off for my holidays shortly before the speech-day. I travelled with Yevséitch to Old Aksákovo in the Government of Simbirsk, where my family was then living. The reason for this migration is also unknown to me, but I did not like it at all. Old Aksákovo was ill supplied with water; there was no fishing there and very little shooting. There was indeed plenty of black game, and it was possible to pick up a woodcock; but this difficult form of sport was still beyond my powers. Being aware of this beforehand, I laid in a stock of plays, intending to read them at leisure, and even to act

[1] After the battle of Hollabrünn (Nov. 1805). Bagration fell at the battle of Borodino (1812).

them with my family for audience ; and I carried
out this intention later with great pleasure and
success. My parents, though they found it hard to
believe it, were much pleased that I was to enjoy
the dignity of a student, and expressed regret that
my tutor had not kept me till speech-day, to hear
the list of students formally read, and to receive
my sword with the others. My dear sister was
delighted to have me back at home. She listened
with pleasure, when I recited or rather acted my
plays ; tragedy, comedy, and even opera—all
came alike to me, and I played all the parts, both
male and female, changing my voice to a lisp or
a squeak, singing bass or falsetto, and sometimes
dressing up in clothes which I fished up out of
old wardrobes. I had another occupation as well.
As I knew that after the middle of August I should
attend lectures on Natural History delivered by
Professor Fuchs who had lately come to Kazan,
I determined to collect butterflies, and made
a start in that direction during the holidays.   My
sister helped me in this ; but alas ! I destroyed a
great number of these lovely creatures, because
I did not know then how to set and dry butterflies.

Twice during the holidays we travelled to Choorassovo and spent a week each time in the house of
my great-aunt, Praskóvya Ivánovna Kurolyéssova.
The distance from Old Aksákovo was not more
than forty or fifty versts.   Praskóvya Ivánovna
was much pleased to hear that I had become
a student : she announced the fact with pride
to every visitor ; she made me put on my uniform,
and was very sorry that I had not got my sword ;
and she went so far as to give me ten roubles to
buy books. Of my dramatic activity no one would

have dared to tell her directly, for it was possible that she might not approve of it ; but she happened to hear it mentioned, and made me recite, act, and sing. To my great joy, she was much pleased and laughed a great deal. She had never been in a theatre in her life, but she was quick at picking up things, and this new form of entertainment suited her gay and lively temperament. But she liked my ordinary reading better still. Sometimes when she was at a loss for occupation, especially in winter—when she was tired of playing cards and singing the songs and ballads of those days, and tired of listening to gossip and scandal—she made someone read aloud recent novels and tales ; but she never found a reader to suit her : even my mother, who was better than others, did not give entire satisfaction. But when she heard me, she said, ' Well, that is something *like* reading ! '—and from that day, though it was summer and she generally spent that season in her splendid garden, she made me read to her for at least two hours every day. *The Miller* by Ablesímoff, and *The Hawker* by Knyazhnín were sometimes chosen ; and I remember her hearty good-humoured laughter, when she saw a mere boy representing one of the two old men from whom these comedies take their titles. I gained a full measure of her good graces, and this was a great satisfaction to my family ; for thoughts of the great fortune which she had promised to leave us could not be entirely banished from the anticipations and calculations which no man can help making. When I left, I received a gracious command from Praskóvya Ivánovna to write to her twice a month; and she got those letters regularly down to the time of her death.

CHAPTER IV

LIFE AT COLLEGE

I RETURNED with no mishaps to Kazan and was much pleased to see my tutor again ; and he greeted me affectionately. My first business was to get the sword which was part of my uniform and had been kept in store for my arrival. Alexander Panáyeff and I fastened on our swords and spent the whole of that Sunday in walking about the streets of the town. As our costume was then a novelty, we had the satisfaction of attracting the attention and interest of the inhabitants, though some menservants, as they sat at the doors and made love to the maids, being more sophisticated than the rest of their class, made bad jokes at our expense. The officers of the school had much business on their hands : students and boys were both lodged in the same building, and separate dormitories had to be arranged for the students, as well as separate meals in a second and smaller dining-hall ; and a scheme of University lectures had to be organized. By the end of August all arrangements were made, and lectures began as follows : Kartashevsky lectured on advanced Pure Mathematics, Zapolsky on Applied Mathematics and Experimental Physics, Levitsky on Logic and Philosophy, Yakovnin on Russian History, Geography, and Statistics, Professor Zeppelin on General History, Professor Fuchs on Natural History, Professor Herman on Latin Literature and Antiquities, Erich on Greek and

Latin Literature, and Evest—an assistant professor from a foreign University—on Chemistry and Anatomy. There was another professor, Buhnemann, a stout man who lectured in French on ' The Law of Nature and of Nations '; I attended his lectures but I have not the faintest recollection of them. Such was the rudimentary staff with which our University opened ; nor were the faculties properly distinct. Yakovnin, being both inspector of the students and Rector of the school, enjoyed the title and authority of Vice-Chancellor ; as chairman of the school governors, who included all the professors and assistant professors, he controlled the educational department of school and University alike. The business administration was managed by the school office ; Yakovnin was head of this also, and one of the university instructors acted regularly as secretary. With the permission from the Chancellor required by the rules of subordination, Yakovnin allotted chambers to the students and made other necessary arrangements. Many students, of whom I was one, had not completed the school course and continued to attend advanced classes there as well as college lectures ; and I was very glad of this, because it would have pained me to part from Ibrahimoff. He loved me so sincerely and took such pains with me, that the time spent in his class-room remains as one of the pleasantest memories of my youth. I ought to confess, that he gave me more than my share of his attention, and that my vanity, excited and gratified by his notice of me before the whole class, played a considerable part in the matter. Thus the transition from school to college was felt by us all, and especially by those who, like myself, continued to attend some classes in the school.

After the University opened, my friendship with Alexander Panáyeff, now a student like myself, grew by leaps and bounds, and soon there was such an intimacy between us as can only exist in early manhood ; he, however, was eighteen and consequently three years older than I. My tutor approved of this friendship. Our love of literature and the stage was one of the ties between us, and we soon acquired another taste in common, for natural history and the collecting of butterflies, though it was not till the following spring that this taste was fully developed.

During that winter the theatre attracted us to the exclusion of everything else, and this was due to the unexpected appearance of a famous actor from Moscow, Plavilshchikoff. His visit had a great influence on me. My tutor had spoken to me about him before this time ; and now he gave me leave beforehand to go to the theatre every night that Plavilshchikoff was playing ; he was much pleased that I should see a real artist, and hear that correct, natural, and powerful delivery for which Plavilshchikoff was justly famous. To go often to the pit or stalls was beyond the means of the students : a seat in the pit cost a rouble, and a stall two and a half roubles ; our regular resort was the gallery, where the price of entrance was two kopecks.[1] But for us the gallery had one serious drawback : as the play began at 6.30 P.M. and our lectures ended at 6, there was only just time to run to the theatre and get a place on the back benches of the gallery, from which it was

[1] i. e. One halfpenny.

impossible to see anything, because the front rows were filled long before the performance began. But we devised measures to overcome this difficulty. Two or sometimes three students, the biggest and strongest of us, used to go to the theatre at five or earlier ; there they sat down at the ends of an empty bench and kept off all intruders. The rest of us turned up just before the curtain rose, and took the seats reserved for us. At first there were some disputes caused by this manœuvre, but the regular visitors to the gallery soon became accustomed to the arrangement, and everything went off peaceably. Our emissaries used at first to conceal their disappearance from the class-room ; but many of the professors and teachers, when they came to understand the reason, used to wink at the departure of some of their hearers. The good-natured Ibrahimoff would often say, ' Well, gentlemen, isn't it time to be off to the theatre ? '— and sometimes dismissed his class half an hour too early. To procure playbills was the duty of the pensioner students. In those days there were no printed playbills at Kazan : written bills were supplied from the box-office to a few persons of distinction, while the public was informed of the title of the play and the names of the actors by a notice secured by four tacks to a pillar or the wall of the main entrance to the theatre. I must confess that we used to steal these notices. The method was this : you went up to the theatre steps and began to read the notice ; then, as soon as the coast was clear, you tore it off, hid it in your pocket, and carried back your prize to college. When Yessipoff, the manager, discovered this trick of the students, he gave

leave for them to get a playbill regularly from the
box-office.

To me Plavilshchikoff's acting was the revelation
of a new world in dramatic art. Unable, especially
at first, to see his defects, I was equally enchanted
by him in tragedy, comedy, and melodrama. But
he stayed a long time in Kazan and produced many
new pieces, including his comedy *The Outcast*, which
was a great success, and his tragedy *Yermak*, which
had no merit and failed entirely ; and, as he
sometimes repeated the same part two or three
times, we had plenty of opportunity for judging
his acting, and came to see that he was far better
in some parts than in others. But his real triumphs
in delivery were the parts of Titus in *The Mercy of
Titus* and of the pastor in *Lovers' Vows*.[1] The
latter performance was a perfect marvel to me.
The part used to be played at Kazan by a very bad
actor, Maxim Gulyaeff, and was thought so
intolerably dull by me and all the audience, that
the long monologue addressed by the pastor to
Baron Neuhof was cut down by general desire to
a few lines. But Plavilshchikoff restored the part
to its full importance and simply killed all the other
parts. It was really a masterly performance.
Another play which he staged at Kazan was
Oedipus at Athens, and his acting as Oedipus was
rapturously applauded.

In him I saw for the first time truth, simplicity,
and nature upon the stage, and it was a revelation
to me. I felt all the faults of my own manner of
recitation, and eagerly set about reforming my

---

[1] Readers of Miss Austen will remember that *Lovers'
Vows* was the play rehearsed but never acted at Mansfield
Park.

delivery. My tutor had said something of the kind to me and had suggested improvements, but I hardly understood him. Now, however, the moment I heard Plavilshchikoff in his best parts, I understood what my tutor found amiss in my performance—which shows how much better example is than the very best precepts. Directed by my tutor, I worked hard at this difficult task for a fortnight, and then recited to my friend, Alexander Panáyeff, the long monologue from the pastor's part. He was struck dumb with astonishment: all he could say was ' You're as good as Plavilshchikoff ! you're better ! ' Getting to college before me that day, he told them all of his new discovery ; and when I came in to attend lectures, the students crowded round me and made me recite the monologue and passages which I knew by heart from other plays. If they did not call me a Plavilshchikoff, they applauded me warmly, and some of the senior students at once conceived the idea of getting up plays ourselves. The authorities would not agree to this all at once ; and therefore Panáyeff and I put together a play of a kind—it was childishly silly, of course—and acted it, with the aid of his brothers, in the rooms which they occupied ; they lived in a biggish stone house belonging to their uncle. The title and plot of this play I have forgotten, but I remember that I played two parts in it—an old hermit in the first two acts, and a robber-chief, who got killed by a pistol shot, in the third. I distinguished myself chiefly as the hermit.

Our Chancellor lived in Petersburg, and it was long before we received permission from him to make a theatre with scenery and foot-lights in one of the University halls. In the meantime, we got permission from the Vice-Chancellor to get up private theatricals in one of the dormitories, with no raised stage and no scenery. This scheme gave rise to no end of pleasant excitement and bustle. A curtain, made of sheets sewn together, divided the long dormitory in two; the place for the stage was fenced off by bedsteads and lighted by candlesticks from the class-rooms. We acted *Serve Him Right*, a comedy by Verevkin, and the parts of the old and the young Doblestin were taken by myself and Panáyeff. The dresses were ludicrous: for instance, the old Doblestin wore a tattered military tunic, borrowed from one of our porters who was an old soldier, and a tow wig whitened with chalk; the fetters on his hands were borrowed from a watch-dog, who took advantage of his free evening to bite someone very severely. A student called Perevoshchikoff, with a pale and not young face and a hoarse voice, was excellent in the old woman's part; and parts of the kind were always assigned to him afterwards. I and my dog-chain produced a powerful effect: I was hailed as a genius, and so was Peter Zykoff, who threw the whole audience into convulsions by his comic powers. But alas! my bosom friend, Panáyeff, in spite of his good looks, pleased nobody in the part of young Doblestin. He had in fact a rather plaintive and cold delivery; and he was handicapped by a defect in pronunciation which he could not overcome.[1] This was my first public success as an actor; for our acting at the Panáyeffs' house had been private, and the

---

[1] He pronounced *o* as *o*, whereas most educated Russians pronounce an unaccented *o* as *a*.

audience very small; but now all the chief officials were present, the professors and teachers and even their wives and daughters, not to mention as many students and schoolboys as could be crammed into the room.

Soon afterwards the Chancellor sent his permission: a theatre might be made for the Government students as ' a reward for their exemplary diligence'; at the same time the inspector was charged to keep an eye on the pieces chosen, and also to see that this form of amusement did not interfere with serious study. We were all delighted. A stage and background, which could be easily and quickly removed, were put up at the cost of Government; but the students diminished the expense considerably by painting the scenery themselves. It was intended at first to construct the theatre in one of the halls; but this turned out to be uncomfortably large, and the authorities objected to the expense; and finally the choice fell on one of the class-rooms, which was especially suitable because it was divided in the middle by an arch. There had been two rooms originally, but the dividing wall had been removed some years before, and an arch, resting on two pillars at the side, was left to support the ceiling. For the erection of a stage this was a great convenience. But we were too impatient to wait for the completion of our theatre, and played a comedy by Kotzebue, *Misanthropy and Remorse*,[1] in the hall which I mentioned above. I distinguished myself in the part of ' The Stranger,' and my fame was

[1] The English version of this play is known as *The Stranger*. Thackeray's opinion of its merits may be found in chap. iv of *Pendennis*.

established on a solid foundation. Next we drew up a code of regulations and confirmed it by the signatures of all who took part in the acting; and I, young as I was, was chosen as manager of the company. But alas! I did not hold this position for long: I gained some distinction in another comedy by Kotzebue, and then an unfortunate combination of circumstances banished me from the stage for a whole year. I must describe in somewhat greater detail this tragi-comic affair.

The next play we took in hand was *Meinau, or The Result of Reconciliation*, written by some German author to express his opinion that the reconciliation between Meinau and his erring wife, which ends up Kotzebue's comedy of *Misanthropy and Remorse*, cannot restore their domestic happiness. The piece has a small part of a General who had once been in love with Mme Meinau: he happens to meet Meinau and his wife, whereupon the lady faints and the husband challenges the General and kills him in a duel with pistols. Alexander Panáyeff, after his failure as Doblestin, took little part in our performances, though he was still a member of the company; but when he heard our choice of a play, he begged me to give him the General's part. He admitted that he had no gift for the stage, but he had special reasons for wishing to have this part assigned to him. These reasons I knew: he was attached to a certain young lady who always attended our performances, and he wished her to see him on the stage, wearing a general's uniform with large epaulettes, and falling at the fatal shot. Now I knew that the rest of the company would resent my decision; and I knew that another actor, Peter Balyasnikoff, whose character and ability gave him a marked ascendancy among us, wished to have this part and would play it ever so much better; but I was led astray by the claims of friendship and allotted the part to Panáyeff, which, as manager of the company, I had a perfect right to do. The others at once declared that Panáyeff would ruin the whole play; but I replied, that the part was small and unimportant, that Panáyeff had gone through it with me very well, that I would undertake to make him perfect, and that his good looks gave him a special claim to it. Out of respect for my authority as manager, they submitted, but with much reluctance. But Panáyeff was such a failure at the first rehearsal, that it was painful to me to look at him, and the company attacked me again, begging me to choose anyone but Panáyeff for the part. I refused, urging for my friend that he did not know the part, and vouching for it that with my coaching he would do very well. But I saw trouble ahead, and privately begged my friend to resign. It was in vain: he begged me with tears not to deprive him of the opportunity to make a favourable impression on the heart of his fair one; he feared a rival, and that rival was Balyasnikoff! I was so affected by this appeal that I took an oath not to give the part to anyone else; and I promised, in case of a serious revolt, to resign my own part of Meinau. At the second rehearsal, Panáyeff, though he knew his part, acted as badly as before. Taking advantage of my powers as manager, I had excluded everybody but the actors from this rehearsal; but during the scene between me and the General, the door opened and I saw Balyasnikoff come in with several others; he stopped right in front of the stage and looked very contemptuous and insolent. I had hardly killed the General, when all the company came round me and insisted that I should give the part to Balyasnikoff instead. Panáyeff turned pale. Eager in defence of my friend, and insulted in my dignity as manager, I refused positively and used a threat : ' You are interfering in what is no business of yours,' I said, ' and if you won't obey me, I resign the part of Meinau and decline to take any further share in the acting.'

I expected to cause a sensation by my closing words. My head had been turned by praise and my high opinion of myself, till I thought that I was indispensable ; but my opponents were only waiting for the opening I had given them. Balyasnikoff at once stepped forward and made a speech : he said coolly, that I was conceited and thought myself a great actor, that I misused my power as manager and was sacrificing the play and the whole company to my friendship for Panáyeff who could not act at all. ' Our praise gave you glory,' he added, ' and we shall also rob you of it, and assert everywhere that you cannot act. We deprive you of the management and expel you from the company.' The rest unanimously expressed their agreement. Though I was expecting a revolt against my authority, I had not foreseen such a blow as this. I rallied all my presence of mind, took my friend Panáyeff by the hand with the fortitude of a hero, and left the room without saying a word. I returned home stunned by my fall and also conscious of my unfair dealing ; but I tried to comfort myself with the thought that I had sacrificed my own vanity and passion

for the stage to my friend's peace of mind. I
believed that the piece could not be acted without
me, and that therefore his hated rival could not
appear in the glittering epaulettes to steal away
the heart of the fair lady. But it was a great
blow to Panáyeff and me, when we went next day
to college and heard that the company had elected
Balyasnikoff manager on the previous evening,
that my part had been given to Dmitrieff, and that
Balyasnikoff himself was to act the General.

Dmitrieff was a pensioner student of remarkable
ability; he had been my regular rival in all our
studies, though up till now I had almost always
distanced him. In Ibrahimoff's class his compositions on the subjects set to us were sometimes
as good as mine; and Ibrahimoff, in spite of some
partiality for me, on two occasions informed the
whole class that he could not determine the order
of merit between our essays. He had also a
reputation for reciting, and I had sometimes seen
him declaiming poetry to a crowd of listeners.
Speaking candidly, I must admit that Dmitrieff
had perhaps more talent for literature and the
stage than I had; but, as neither the one nor the
other inspired in him the exclusive passion that
I felt, his gifts were unimproved and undeveloped.
Also, in his appearance, which was rather rough
and uncouth, and in all his movements, there was
visible a certain heaviness and a want of ease and
grace. It never entered my head that such an
Orson would consent to appear on the stage;
but the company appealed to him and induced him
with some difficulty to take the part of Meinau.
They gave him the book and made him read the
part aloud on the spot, and were delighted one and

all by his performance. We were told that many of his audience were reduced to tears, and that a student called Chesnoff, a bosom friend of Dmitrieff's and a great laugher and good-humoured joker, had shed floods of tears. To me and my friend this was absolute death and destruction : what had become of his love affair and my vanity and passion for the stage ? If I had acted justly and assigned the General's part to someone else, Balyasnikoff would never have got the part or the chance to appear in the glittering epaulettes ! The play was at last performed, and Panáyeff and I were a little consoled, because it was not a great success. Neither of us was present, and my report of its failure depends on the general verdict of the teachers and unprejudiced spectators, though the students and especially the actors were loud in their praise of Dmitrieff. Having seen him at a rehearsal, I am myself convinced that he was very good in the striking passages of the part, if not in all.

Torn from the stage by this combination of circumstances, I next dashed off in a different direction, towards literature and natural history. On the latter subject I attended lectures given in French by Professor Fuchs ; and I became interested chiefly in collecting butterflies, which soon was an absorbing passion with me. Panáyeff was my faithful companion and collaborator in the whole business. We spent all our leisure in wandering, net in hand, through gardens and meadows and woods, and chasing all the butterflies we came across ; the moths we searched for under boughs and leaves, in hollow trees, or in the chinks of fences and stone walls.[1]

[1] A full account of this hobby follows in the Appendix.

I went to lectures in college and kept up my
attendance at two classes in the school; and my
progress was fairly satisfactory, but not more.
I began a course on anatomy with much interest,
and enjoyed the lectures, as long as the dissection
was confined to animals, living or dead; I was even
thought likely to do well in the subject. But, when
it came to the dissection of corpses, I gave up
anatomy for good. I was afraid of dead bodies;
but my companions felt quite differently: they
ransacked the town for a 'subject', and, when one
was found and brought to the anatomical school,
they hailed it with joyful triumph. For long
I was unable to look at some of *them* without
disgust.

In describing my dramatic career, I have run
on far ahead; and now I must go back and give
an account of my life with my tutor, Kartashevsky,
and of some changes that had taken place. When
we acted for the first time, by day and in the
Panáyeffs' house, my tutor knew nothing of it;
but when we determined to start a theatre in the
college and I told him of this, he raised no obstacle
to my taking part in the scheme, and even expressed approval. Later, when he saw the comedy
Serve Him Right, he was pleased with my acting
and laughed a great deal at my costume. I must
confess that the theatre monopolized my attention
far too much; but it is also true that my tutor began
to pay less attention to me. I do not know what
was the original cause of this change, and I should
be glad if I could clear it up in my own mind. It
is true that some trifling differences gave rise for
a time to a certain coldness between us; yet I do
not believe that they could have led to such serious

and unexpected consequences, but for the evil influence of some third party.

Our first difference was caused by his discovering in my possession two novels which he had prohibited—*The Boy by the Stream* by Kotzebue, and *Nature and Love* by Auguste La Fontaine. I used to read them at night or in the unused rooms, and they gave me an ecstasy of delight. It sounds absurd, but even now the words, ' Love me, Fanny; I am kind,' or ' Months, blissful months flew by over these happy mortals ' [1]—trifling and silly as the words are in themselves—make my heart beat faster, at the mere recollection of that intense delight which they gave to the boy of fifteen. The fact is, that the words do not matter : all depends upon the feeling which the reader imports into them. I was certainly to blame ; but my tutor censured my fault too severely, and if I had believed what he said, I should have been in despair. But I could not admit that I was so great a criminal ; and so it became possible and reasonable for me to accuse my tutor of injustice and want of consideration towards me. On this occasion, however, our friendly relations were restored pretty soon.

Our second difference arose as follows. On the day before Trinity Sunday, my tutor decided to take me to Zapolsky's country-house for the week-end. But this time I did not wish to leave Kazan, because Panáyeff and I had made a toy theatre, with elaborate scenery ; it had ingenious devices for changing the scenes, and one of the scenes was a storm with thunder and lightning ; Panáyeff was a great hand at all contrivances of this kind.

[1] The quotations are from *Nature and Love*.

As a performance had been fixed for the Monday, and an audience invited, it was vexing to me to be absent, but I submitted without grumbling. On the day fixed for our departure, I asked leave of my tutor to spend some hours at Panáyeff's house. He consented, but said, that if I did not return by seven o'clock, he would start alone ; I promised to return without fail. Panáyeff and I put our toy theatre through a ' dress rehearsal ' ; but some of the phenomena would not come right : the lightning missed the tree which it was bound to strike and set fire to, the moon refused to appear from behind the clouds, and the waterfall ceased at times to fall. I was so much taken up in regulating these natural phenomena, that I did not notice when my time was up. When I became aware of this, I ran all the way home ; but still I was a quarter of an hour late. My tutor had started alone exactly at seven ; he was very angry and had left no directions for me. In what followed I was really to blame : though Yevséitch proposed that we should hire horses and follow at once, I refused flatly to do so ; I said that Kartashevsky might have waited for me or left instructions for me to come on alone. I went back to the Panáyeffs' house, and spent the whole night in working at the puppet-show. Alarmed by my long absence, Yevséitch came for me himself. We showed him the theatre, and he was not a little surprised by our cleverness ; and I went home with him at sunrise. Again he urged me to join my tutor in the country, and again I flatly refused.

On Trinity Sunday Panáyeff dined at my house, and after dinner we went off to the park which was close by, and a regular resort for a great concourse

of people at Whitsuntide. Next day the performance took place at the Panáyeffs' house and was
a splendid success : the oak was shattered and
burnt by the lightning, the moon duly rose from
behind the clouds, the waterfall foamed and
splashed without stopping. The hosts and the
spectators alike were delighted ; but I felt as if
cats were scratching at my heart.

Early on Tuesday my tutor returned. While
I was still in bed, he had a stormy interview with
Yevséitch, who told him all that had happened,
not even keeping back that he had twice over
proposed to me to follow. My tutor refused to see
me, and for forty-eight hours we did not meet,
even for dinner. I was greatly distressed, but
I also felt injured : I was nearly sixteen, and I felt
that such treatment was unreasonable except in
the case of a boy. The explanation came at last.
I had prepared myself to face it firmly and coolly,
and was able at first to meet and parry all his
harsh rebukes with an appearance of calmness ;
but when he said, ' Now, what will be your
mother's feelings when I describe your conduct
and refuse to go on living with you any longer ? '—
then my firmness melted like wax, tears gushed
from my eyes, I confessed myself entirely in the
wrong and sincerely begged his forgiveness of my
fault. But now Kartashevsky made a great
mistake : instead of catching at my sincere
repentance, he met it coldly and refused to make
it up with me entirely. Perhaps he did not quite
believe me ; but it is more likely that he acted
thus from calculation : he knew that my mind was
too quick in losing the impressions which it was
too quick in receiving, and wished by a change in

his behaviour to make me feel my fault more deeply. But the result was not in the least what he expected. While changing towards me, he expected me to remain the same ; but to my nature these cold relations were intolerable, and I soon began to think myself always in the right and him in the wrong, and my attachment to him was shaken.

At last an utterly trifling incident finally changed the former relations between us. The Bursar, Markevitch, died. I have said already that he always showed kindness to me and that I was much attached to him. But I had been afraid from childhood of the sight of a dead body, and therefore, in spite of the arguments and remonstrances of my tutor, I positively refused to attend the funeral.[1] Kartashevsky came back from the sad ceremony and brought with him Chekieff, the teacher of drawing. I ought first to say that I had a strong dislike for this gentleman, who was a great fop and annoyed me by his silly jokes. It was always a surprise to me that my tutor could be on intimate terms with such a fool ; but the simple explanation is, that they had been school-fellows together at Moscow. On this day Chekieff was more troublesome than usual : Why had I not been at the funeral ? Why had I not paid the last tribute of respect to one who was so fond of me ? He declared that my conduct proved the hardness of my heart, and so on. In a word, he teased me beyond bounds ; and when he said with a sneer, ' Confess that you are really not at all afraid of dead bodies, and that this fear is merely a selfish

---

[1] At Russian funerals it is the custom to look at the dead before the coffin is closed.

pretence '—I grew very angry and answered roughly and rudely, ' You are quite right : my fear of dead bodies is a mere sham.' Now that I consider these words coolly, I do not see in them the importance which my tutor attached to them. His features changed with displeasure ; and he said in a low but significant voice : ' After the language which you have ventured to address in my presence to my friend and guest, you can judge yourself whether we are likely to be agreeable to one another. Please go to your own room.' Not feeling myself to blame, I was naturally more angry than ever, but I left the room without a word. This took place just before dinner, when the meal was already on the table. Yevséitch came after me with my knife and fork and napkin ; he explained that my tutor ordered me to dine in my room. This redoubled my fury ; and nothing but the thought of my mother kept me from going straight to my tutor and pouring out a torrent of abuse. I must do justice to Chekieff : he went on for a long time begging Kartashevsky to pardon me, but with no effect ; this I was told by Yevséitch. After dinner Chekieff came to my door, but I locked myself in and would not admit him. Next day my tutor summoned me and said coldly and firmly : ' We cannot go on living together, and I must resign my position as your tutor ; but we must both try to lighten as much as possible the blow which our separation will inflict on your mother ; and we must manage this business without insulting one another.' I answered that he had anticipated my wish, and that I had intended to make exactly the same suggestion to him. ' Then that is all right,' he said with a sneer, and nodded to me to go. I went off to my room and gave myself up in my solitude to excitement and anger. I thought myself entirely in the right and my tutor entirely in the wrong.

And here I must confess to an action which it is difficult to excuse on the ground of irritation and impulsiveness. The following day was unluckily post-day, and I wrote a long letter to my parents, in which I showed no mercy to my tutor and spoke of him in language so insulting that I blush for it now. If I had put off writing till next post, I should have thought better of it, beyond doubt; but then, and often afterwards throughout my life, I was carried away by my impetuous nature. Next day, when the letter had gone, my conscience began to reproach me, and I kept constantly thinking of my tutor's words, that we ought not to insult each other. But what were my feelings, when, after some days during which we met only at dinner and hardly spoke, my tutor summoned me and read over to me a very long letter which he had ready to send to my mother! This letter was full of good sense and affectionate feeling: he confessed himself entirely unfit to go on acting as tutor and director to a young man who could no longer be treated as a boy and needed something different; he declared that he had no idea how to tackle such a problem; he felt that he was mismanaging it and might in this way do me harm. Then he described in detail my intellect and character and my tastes, and foretold their future development; he also described my defects; but the bright side with its happy promise for the future was thrown into relief, and he spoke indulgently of my failings, and said that time and experience would root them out. He vouched for my good principles ; it would be quite safe, he said, for me to live alone or with a friend, Alexander Panáyeff for instance, or with some professor, not as a pupil but as a young friend ; it was even desirable that I should be my own master for a year or so before entering on a profession ; it would be bad for me to pass directly from the control of a strict tutor to independence and a career divided between society and professional occupations. He ended by saying that he intended soon to leave Kazan for Petersburg, in order to take steps towards getting a post in the teaching profession there or possibly in the civil service.

The effect produced on me by this letter was positively alarming to my tutor. Conscience-stricken and repentant, I was so agitated that for long I could not speak a word. Tears at last relieved the burden on my heart, and I made a clean breast of my letter home, expressed all my old feeling of attachment, and begged and prayed him with tears to forget what I had done, and not to part with me till he went to Petersburg. I promised—and I should certainly have kept the promise—that, however severely he might treat me, I should not feel it, far less resent it. The sincerity of my repentance and distress seemed to shake his determination. He looked at me long and attentively, and then began to walk about the room ; at last he said, ' This needs thinking over,' and let me go. Two days remained before the next post went. I wrote another letter to my parents, in which I confessed that I was entirely to blame and had sinned beyond forgiveness ; I praised my tutor enthusiastically, described the whole affair in detail, and ended by saying: ' However Kartashevsky treats me—whether he lets me stay or drives me from him—I shall continue to love him as a second father.' Before I sent off the letter, I took it to my tutor and asked if he wished to read it. He refused, saying that he had already sent off the letter I had heard, and that the matter was definitely settled. To me this was a blow; I cannot say that it was quite unexpected, but it was heavy all the same : I knew that no attacks would make my tutor withdraw from his position; and any withdrawal would have been useless, because his letter was already posted. There was nothing to be done, and I made haste to send off my own letter.

The picture which my lively imagination painted of my mother's despair followed me day and night till grief made me ill. Kartashevsky frowned at this : he disapproved of all my fits of excitement, and pointed out the obvious danger of uncontrolled feeling in any direction ; but at the same time he pitied me and tried to comfort me by saying, that my mother would take it much more coolly than I imagined, that our parting was inevitable in any case, and that my second letter—I had repeated its contents to him—would wipe out the painful impression left by its predecessor. I took some comfort from his words and soon got well ; and before long letters arrived from Aksákovo, which entirely confirmed my tutor's opinion. My father and mother appreciated my repentance and forgave me for the first letter, written as it was in a fit of anger. My mother put entire confidence in my tutor's report about me, and her loving heart was filled with bright and happy hopes for the future.

She believed him also when he said that private affairs made it necessary for him to leave Kazan without delay. She was convinced that he would always be a true friend of the family, and that, after ceasing to be my tutor, he would draw closer to me and like me better; and that I should take his advice with more readiness and more in earnest, when it came unaccompanied by any flavour of authority. Nor was she mistaken: the future confirmed the anticipations of her rare intelligence.

My summer holidays were now approaching. Kartashevsky intended to leave for Petersburg in another month, and my mother asked him to make arrangements for my future residence at Kazan. With his consent—I am surprised that he gave it—I arranged with Levitsky, the assistant professor of Philosophy and Logic, that I should live in his house, paying a small sum for board and lodging and also looking after his three pupils who were pensioners in the school. All three boys were as old as myself, and great scamps, though I had no idea of this at the time. I parted with Kartashevsky with much feeling and even wept; and he was much moved himself, but tried as usual to hide his feeling by jesting and even making fun of my sensibility.

In spite of the confusion and unrest which troubled my life at this time in my tutor's house, Panáyeff and I continued to interest ourselves in literature and to collect butterflies; my friend was very neat and skilful with his hands, and could set butterflies to perfection. I wrote several poems and a prose entitled *Friendship*, and showed them to my friend. He approved of them, but made some criticisms which seemed to me unfounded.

I shall insert here my first childish verses, of which, however, I have forgotten half; and thus I celebrate my jubilee after fifty years spent in spoiling paper. I should add that I had no cruel charmer; in fact I was not acquainted with any young lady.

TO A NIGHTINGALE

O friend of Spring, dearest of songsters,
Be thou alone my comfort !
Lighten the cruel pain
That devours my passionate heart.

Sing the charms of my loved one,
Sing my fiery love for her,
Recount all my sufferings,
Recount my days of mourning.

Let her hear thy voice,
Let her know who taught thee !
It may be, the hardhearted one
For pity's sake will sigh for me.

It may be, she will learn from thee
That love for man is happiness ;
It may be, she will feel at last
That life without love is misery.

(Several stanzas are wanting).

Such were the unrhymed verses with which I made my appearance on the literary stage, while I was still a boy at school in the year 1805. But I soon considered these verses ' unworthy of my pen,' and did not give them a place in our magazine of 1806. All my subsequent poems were in rhyme ; and they are all completely devoid of any merit, even if allowances be made ; they show not the smallest sign of a gift for poetry.

I spent the summer vacation of 1805 at Aksá-kovo, and somehow I remember little about it, except that I was keenly interested in shooting and butterflies ; I seldom fished, probably because the larger fish do not take freely at that season.

I found my mother in a bad state of health, and learnt that this was the only reason that prevented her from setting out for Kazan when she heard of the breach between me and Kartashevsky. I still confided everything to her without reserve ; and, when I had told her all the minutest particulars of my life and even my thoughts, she felt happy about me. In spite of my youth, she let me go back to Kazan to live with a professor of whom she knew nothing, with a full belief in the steadiness of my principles and the blamelessness of my conduct.

On returning to Kazan, I went straight to Levitsky's house. Not long before my return, Kartashevsky had left for Petersburg, and I was much surprised to hear that he had spent a whole month of the vacation in idleness at Kazan. Until a new professor was appointed, the teaching of higher mathematics was entrusted to a student, Alexander Knyazhévitch, whose remarkable powers gave promise of a distinguished career in that branch of learning.[1] It was impossible for me to stay long with Levitsky : a fatal passion for drink had completely mastered him, and at this time he shut himself up every evening to gratify it ; his pupils were absolutely free to do as they liked and learnt nothing at all. I soon grew tired of looking after these young scapegraces ; and, with my parents' consent, I parted from Levitsky at the end of two months and took lodgings in the house of a German, named Hermann, near the

[1] He became Minister of Finance in the Russian Government.

H

theatre. Here I settled down by myself and began for the first time to live alone and uncontrolled. Panáyeff and I were almost inseparable, and we took another student, D. Perevoshchikoff,[1] into our literary partnership. We translated tales by Marmontel, those which Karamzin had not translated; we wrote original poetry and prose, and each read his translations and compositions to the other two. I had planned to translate Marmontel before I left Levitsky, and I told him so one day, before dinner, of course, while he was still sober; and I clearly remember how insulted I was by his reply: ' Translate Marmontel after Karamzin ! You are a bold man; but " fools rush in where angels fear to tread ".' But these words did not stop us. At last Panáyeff and I determined to publish a magazine in manuscript in the coming year of 1806; it was to be called *A Journal of our Occupations*, and no editor's name was to appear. This was a more serious undertaking than *Shepherds of Arcadia*, and I did all I could to keep out of this magazine all mechanical imitation of Karamzin, and to discourage the predilection of my friend for pastoral writing. Against the former I was struggling at this time with all my might, and I found support in a book by Shishkoff,[2] *A Discussion of the Old and New Styles*, which carried me to the opposite extreme. I shall speak of this in more detail elsewhere. I have preserved three

---

[1] Afterwards famous as a mathematician and astronomer.

[2] Aksákoff wrote a very entertaining account of his acquaintance with Shishkoff at Petersburg in later years. Shishkoff, an admiral and high official, was also an ardent upholder of archaic style. In private life he was the most absent-minded and most disinterested of men .

numbers of our magazine; and I see that it began in April and appeared for the last time in December. These numbers do not contain a single article, original or translated, from my pen, though I remember that I wrote many; I am sorry, because it would interest me now to see how I expressed my literary creed of those days.

Meantime, at the end of 1805 and in the following January, the students twice acted plays without my taking part in them. This deprivation was a bitter pill to me: my love for acting was ungratified, and my vanity was hurt by the success of my rival, Dmitrieff; but there was nothing to be done. The actors proposed that I should rejoin the company; but I had not yet forgotten their insulting treatment of me, and my reply was: 'You don't want me, you have got Dmitrieff who plays my parts excellently.' 'Well, just as you choose! Sulk, if you like! We can get on without you,' said Balyasnikoff the manager; and there the matter ended. There was no ill-feeling, however: I attended rehearsals and gave my advice to any who asked it. The first performance was Kotzebue's comedy, *Misanthropy and Remorse*; and Dmitrieff played 'The Stranger' with great success. He had, indeed, no idea how to hold himself; his attitudes were absurd, and his gestures still more so, because he used his right hand only while his left remained as if tied behind his back; and in ordinary conversation with his servant and the old villager, his acting was positively bad. Yet in the scene with the friend to whom he tells his misfortunes, and in the reconciliation with his wife, Dmitrieff showed such power of feeling that all the spectators, myself included, were quite carried away and expressed their delight by frantic applause. At first, I felt nothing but delight, and no trace of jealousy had stolen into my heart; but afterwards I was deeply wounded by some remarks of the students, especially the actors, and then the green-eyed monster took up its abode in my breast. They said very rudely: ' You see, we got on all right without you. You could never play " The Stranger " like Dmitrieff. The people who praised *you* had never seen *him*.' It was true that his success in the part had been much more brilliant than mine; and yet I had a few partisans who maintained that my performance was better, and that Dmitrieff caricatured the part, succeeding only in a few striking passages; I, they said, was a real actor and did justice to the part from beginning to end, from the first word to the last. This was partly true; and I conceived an intense desire to study the part of " The Stranger " and then to act it in such a way as totally to eclipse my rival.

At the beginning of 1806 the students gave a second performance in which they acted another play by Kotzebue, *Poverty and Honour*; and Dmitrieff took the part of Heinrich Blum, and scored another success, though it was not so great a success as ' The Stranger '. My champions declared that I would have been beyond comparison better as Heinrich Blum. Spurred on by jealousy and vanity, I worked up both these parts with great care and then recited them, or rather acted the striking passages of both, before a large audience of students. They were not all predisposed to favour me, but they all felt the difference between me and my rival, between his powerful but uncouth expression of feeling and my more polished and natural acting. And now two parties of equal strength arose among the students, one for me and the other against; and this was my first step on the way to triumph. There were noisy disputes which led on to quarrels and all but ended in blows. This was some consolation to my vanity; and before long a sudden turn made me the spoilt child of fortune. Dmitrieff, who was now over twenty, became discontented with the instruction given by the professors, which, to tell the truth, was very unsatisfactory. There may have been other reasons as well—I do not know; anyhow, he decided to enter the Army and left the University at short notice; being a good mathematician, he chose the artillery. The bereaved company was forced to appeal to me for aid. Taking advantage of the position, I would not consent for a long time, though they offered to reappoint me as manager. At last, when I had coquetted long enough, I agreed, on two conditions: (1) the title and office of manager were to be abolished, and a committee of three to be elected to manage the company; (2) our performances were to begin with a repetition of the two plays, *Misanthropy and Remorse* and *Poverty and Honour*. As a matter of course, they all agreed to my conditions.

The former play was performed in Easter week. Gruzinoff, an actor at the Kazan theatre for whom we all had much liking and respect, came somehow to be invited to the dress rehearsal. The piece had been acted by the students twice before; we all worked hard, and I harder than any one; and the result was fairly successful. Gruzinoff was astonished : he could not believe his own eyes and ears. He praised us so highly that Yessipoff, the manager of the town theatre, bestirred himself to get Yakovnin's permission to attend the actual performance, and not only came himself but brought with him four actors, of whom Gruzinoff was one. At last I had the opportunity which I had so long desired and looked forward to. My youthful vanity was satisfied : all the students said that I had excelled myself and quite distanced Dmitrieff. What more could I wish ? Alas for the transitory nature of earthly glory ! But two or three months had passed since the triumph of Dmitrieff ; and now only one or two of his partisans were left, who said in whispers, that Dmitrieff acted the part not worse than Aksákoff, and some passages better ; and this was perfectly true. A good many strangers saw the play, and they praised me to the skies ; but my glory derived its chief brilliance and permanence from the praise of Yessipoff and his actors, whose verdict was with justice considered to carry weight. In the other play, *Poverty and Honour*, which had been acted already early in the year, I hoped to win a still greater triumph ; and the reader will see presently that I was not disappointed.

I must now go back in my narrative. Kartashevsky, owing to his long delay in Kazan, outstayed his leave of absence and was more than a month late in returning. He did not present any medical certificate or state any urgent reasons which might have justified or at least excused his absence. The University authorities were displeased at his conduct and passed a vote of censure at their council : they fined him and entered on his certificate the fact of his absence without leave. He was offended and asked leave to resign his post. After some delay, he was allowed to resign ; but it was resolved to enter his offence and punishment on his leaving certificate. He refused to accept such a certificate, left the place, and entered the public service at Petersburg without any certificate ; the department he joined was the Legislative Commission. After a long time and much trouble, he procured an order from the Minister of Education, that the University should issue a certificate without the objectionable particulars. I often saw my former tutor before he left Kazan, and I felt at parting that he was a kind friend older than myself, whom I had to thank for the purity of my ideals and convictions. What my mother had foretold was beginning to come true.

In the year 1806 another event took place, the importance of which was long unrealized by me, though its consequences entirely changed the position of my family. Praskóvya Ivánovna Kurolyéssova died, after suffering for nearly a year from dropsy. During all this time my parents lived at Old Aksákovo with their other children ; I mean, that the children lived at Aksákovo, while my father and mother never left the sufferer who was at Choorassovo ; but when she was removed to Simbirsk, our whole family went there too. Praskóvya Ivánovna was a remarkable woman : she bore her grievous illness with astonishing patience, calmness, and even cheerfulness, and she faced death with a degree of fortitude of which few are capable. She had twice been tapped for dropsy; when the operation had been performed a third time, her doctor, a Jew, looked at the wounds, and expressed much satisfaction with the result. 'None of your lies, Jew!' said the patient; 'I can see that the end is coming. There is a great change in me, and that is erysipelas on my skin. I do not fear death; I got ready for it long ago. But tell me, thou seed of Jacob, how long I have to live.' The doctor, though he was accustomed to be addressed in this fashion, never failed to resent it; he answered in relentless tones, 'You will live four days more.' 'Thank you for telling the truth,' answered the patient, and this time she spoke quite politely; 'now goodbye! I thank you for your trouble and beg you not to come again. I shall order your fees to be paid at once.' Then she assembled all the household, and announced that she was dying; she refused any further treatment and asked to be left in peace; no one was to stay in the room, except one person to read the Gospel aloud. She turned to my father and asked, 'Have I done all that ought to be done? is nothing more needed?' 'Nothing, aunt,' he replied; 'you settled everything long ago.' 'Well, that is all right,' said the patient; 'I wish no one to be distressed about me. Now, please leave the room.'

Praskóvya Ivánovna lived on for five days. She spent the whole of that time in repeating prayers, or singing part of the Church service, or listening while the Gospel was read. About worldly affairs she did not speak a single word to anyone. By her desire, all took farewell of her in silence, and she spoke just four parting words to each member of the household, even to her hall-porter—

' Forgive me, a sinner ! ' I heard of all this by letters from my family ; but they told me nothing more. Before long, I heard that I had a third sister, and that, though my mother had been desperately ill, all was now going on well. I was alarmed at first, but then took courage ; and further letters set my mind completely at rest on the score of my mother's health.

Panáyeff and I went on zealously with the old occupations—working at literature, visiting the theatre, and collecting butterflies when the spring came on. I must confess with shame that, apart from these hobbies, I was idle enough, and that my distractions from study were frequent and absorbing.

Among these distractions I may reckon the formation of a small Literary Club, with Ibrahimoff as president. The founders and original members were Ibrahimoff, Bogdanoff, a teacher in the school, and six students, including Panáyeff and myself. We met every Saturday to read our compositions and translations in verse and prose. Every member had the right of criticism, and the articles were sometimes corrected on the spot, if the author admitted the justice of the improvements suggested ; there was never any quarrelling. If any piece was accepted, it was copied out in a book which we started for the purpose. After I left Kazan, the membership was increased and byelaws drawn up ; and finally ' The Society of Lovers of Russian Literature at Kazan University ' was formally opened by permission of the Imperial Government. It still exists, but, like all our Literary Societies, in a state of suspended animation. I have still the distinction of ranking as an honorary member.

There happened about this time at Kazan a remarkable incident in which I was directly concerned. A private school for boys and girls was kept in the town by a German couple, of the name of Wilfing. Having no children of their own, they had adopted a destitute orphan, Marya Kermik, who was now grown up and very pretty. Kartashevsky sometimes called on the Wilfings and took me there twice; but, at the time I am speaking of, I had not been there for more than six months. A chance meeting in the course of a jaunt out of the town renewed the acquaintance; and the girl's beauty soon asserted its influence over me. I naturally revealed my secret to my bosom friend, Panáyeff; he was delighted, embraced me warmly, and congratulated me on ' beginning to live '. He used every effort to fan the spark which had dropped upon my youthful heart. As Marya was a very quiet modest girl, all her many admirers sighed for her at a respectful distance; and of my feelings she had of course no idea. Visionary hopes and visionary disappointments, which I expressed in wretched boyish verses, were still going on when suddenly a mysterious traveller, a Swedish Count, turned up at Kazan for a short stay. He made the acquaintance of the Wilfings and charmed them all; he went there daily and spent the whole day at their house. He was a handsome man of about thirty-five, clever, pleasant, and lively, a skilful artist and a master of many languages, and an author as well both in verse and prose. In three days, the Wilfings were raving about him; in a week, Marya had fallen in love with him; and, at the end of another fortnight, he married her and carried her off with him to Siberia, where he had been sent by Government to conduct some scientific investigation, with an official to act as interpreter, because the Count himself did not understand a word of Russian. The Wilfings found it hard to part with their adopted daughter, whom they loved as if she had been their own; but they did not venture to complain of a match which seemed so enviable, so astonishing, and so dazzling. She was a baker's daughter, and she had married a Count, who adored his wife and was richly endowed with every gift of nature and education. People less simple than the Wilfings might easily have been seduced by an event so wonderful.

But alas! the riddle was soon explained. The Count had conferred this title on himself; he was a notorious swindler and adventurer, well known for his exploits in Germany under the name of Aschenbrenner. From Germany he had fled to Russia for fear of the police; he became a Russian subject and spent several years in the western provinces, where he was implicated in many frauds and finally banished to Siberia. The official who accompanied him was a police officer with a German name, whose business it was to convey his charge incognito to Irkutsk, and hand him over personally to the governor there for rigorous supervision. But all these facts were somehow kept from the public and from the Wilfings. The traveller had no need of an interpreter; for it was afterwards discovered that he spoke Russian very well. In the course of his journey he himself wrote to the Wilfings and informed them of the imposture; he said he had been driven to it by the irresistible power of love; of course he called himself the victim of calumny, and hoped to be cleared and compensated for his undeserved sufferings. His wife wrote too: she said that, though she knew all, she still thanked God for her happiness. Later, some one sent to the Wilfings a German work in two volumes, which contained a narrative of the sham Count's adventures written by himself. The man was the Vidocq [1] of his time. The old Wilfings were inconsolable. I never could find out what was Marya's ultimate fate. Such was the sorrowful ending of my first love-story.

For the summer vacation I went again to Old Aksákovo, where my family then was. I arrived late in the evening, when every one was in bed; but my mother expected me on that day, and when she heard the sound of my arrival, came out to meet me on the steps and took me straight to her bedroom, where I embraced both my parents and found much to tell and many questions to ask. Then I went to sleep on the sofa in their room. When I awoke rather late, I overheard my parents talking in subdued voices of some business which was a mystery to me. Then my mother noticed that I was not asleep, and said in a low voice to my father, 'We must tell Seryózha the whole story; of course he is still quite in the dark.' 'Do, my dear,' said my father. 'Are you awake, Seryózha?' 'Yes, mother,' I answered. 'Then come here beside us. We must tell you of something that has happened to us. We have become rich.' I got off the sofa and sat down on their bed; and they told me fully and in minute detail what I shall try to convey in a few words.

[1] François Vidocq (1775–1857), first thief and then thief-taker, published his own *Memoirs* in 1828.

When Praskóvya Ivánovna suddenly became seriously ill of dropsy, she lost no time in making my father the legal heir to all her property, real and personal. The whole affair was settled in the course of a few days; all the district judges travelled to Choorassovo for the purpose, and some persons of credit in the town came as witnesses. In the presence of them all Praskóvya Ivánovna signed the necessary documents, and confirmed them by a verbal declaration. When all was done, she ordered champagne to be served, took a glass herself, and proposed the health of her heir in cheerful terms. I ought to say that she was dangerously ill at the time, and that the doctor who had been summoned at once from Simbirsk, the best doctor at that time and a Jew, had no hope of her recovery. He determined to relieve her by tapping, though he would not for a moment guarantee the result of the operation; but she retained so much natural force that she soon conquered the disease and was perfectly well in a very short time. Unfortunately Praskóvya Ivánovna did not believe in the danger of chills and regarded diet as a mere whimsy of doctors. Therefore, she resumed her former life and caught a chill, which was followed by indigestion and a return of dropsy. A second operation was less successful and only postponed the fatal event. The patient was taken to Simbirsk, where after a third operation she died; but of this I have spoken already.

Our accession to wealth had surprising results: it was sand in the eyes to people in general, and it raised a ferment of envy in the breasts of near friends and even of relations.

Praskóvya Ivánovna had sundry poor debtors. When she was reminded of this on her death-bed, she said that her money was not stolen or ill-gotten, and she did not intend to give it away. My parents, however, forgave debts of this kind to the amount of 20,000 roubles, and gave the debtors to understand that Praskóvya Ivánovna had changed her mind and wished them not to be worried for payment. But this generosity disarmed no enemy and earned no gratitude for people who had inherited wealth ; and my parents, much mortified, went off after a few months to Aksákovo, intending to live there.

I can honestly say that change of fortune produced no impression at all upon me. I spent the whole vacation partly in shooting, partly in studying plays. When I went back to Kazan, I was just the same thoughtless and far from wealthy student that I was before ; and for a long time I forgot even to tell my bosom friend, Panáyeff, of the fortunate change in our circumstances. But in my family I noticed a change. There was some talk of going to Kazan for the winter ; a letter was sent to Moscow, asking an old friend there to discover and engage a French-woman as governess to my sisters ; and there was even a plan of going ourselves to Moscow for the following winter, and to Petersburg in the summer, that I might enter some department of the civil service. In order to carry out this last plan, it was settled that I should leave college in the following year, i. e. 1807. To all this I listened with tolerable indifference : I felt no vocation at all for the civil service and no desire to go to Petersburg ; I even thought it was all mere talk and speculation, but I was mistaken. A month after I returned to Kazan, I got a letter from my father, telling me to make inquiries and take a large house, with comfortable accommodation for all our family, and separate rooms as well for two half-sisters of my mother's, who had lived till then at Kazan with other relations. My mother added that, as she intended to go into society on their account, she must make acquaintance with the best people in the town. I was very glad, both on my own account and for my aunts, whom I met fairly often and was really fond of. Without delay I took a large stone house, belonging to a merchant named Komaroff, and moved into it myself; I occupied one snug room on the first floor, and waited for the family to arrive.

In the University life went on as before. There were four new professors, two of them Germans. The Russians were Kamensky, an assistant professor in the department of medicine, a man of remarkable eloquence, and Gorodchaninoff, a teacher of small capacity and old-fashioned ideas, who lectured on Russian Literature. (I forgot to say that his predecessor, poor Levitsky, died of dropsy due to his excesses and was sincerely regretted by us all.) At his opening lecture Gorodchaninoff began with a silly pompous greeting to his audience, and then, in order to improve his acquaintance with us, proposed that each of us should name the Russian author he liked best and also his favourite passage in that author. As such a question is difficult to answer on the spur of the moment, each of us gave whatever answer came into his head. Many named Karamzin, but the professor frowned and expressed his regret at

finding the atmosphere of a University infected
by so dangerous a writer. My neighbour then
whispered to me, ' Watch me, Aksákoff, playing
up to the old gentleman ! '—and when his turn
came, he actually got up and said in a loud voice,
' Of all writers I prefer Sumarókoff, and I rank
highest of all his poetry the dying words of Dmitri
the Usurper in the famous tragedy of that name :

" Go down to Hell, my soul, to lie in chains for aye ! " '

Then he pretended to stab himself with a roll of
paper, and added the following line :

' I would that all mankind might share my fate this day ! '

The students could hardly help laughing ; but the
professor was so delighted that he jumped down
from his raised platform, called my friend up,
shook hands with him, and expressed a desire for
their better acquaintance. Thereupon he observed
that no literature in the world could show a more
powerful verse than the second of these. My turn
came next. I said that Lomonossoff was my
favourite author, and that among all his writings
I preferred the Ode from *Job*. The professor's face
shone with satisfaction. ' May I trouble you to
repeat something from that noble poem ? '—he
said. This was exactly what I wanted, for I hoped
to petrify the professor by my reciting. But fate
punished me cruelly for my vanity and my love
of bygone writers. I meant to begin with two
famous lines by Lomonossoff—

> ' O man, who vainly in thy sorrow
> Dost murmur at the will of God '—

but with incredible carelessness I came out with
a familiar parody of the verses instead. ' My dear
sir ! ' cried out the professor ; ' that is a shocking

travesty of the noble poem!' I blushed with confusion, tried again at once, and repeated my mistake! The whole room burst into a roar of laughter; I could not understand how I had done such a thing; I was burning with shame and stupefied with annoyance and confusion. The professor contemptuously told me to sit down and went on questioning the other students. The lecture lasted two hours, and I seemed to sit on hot coals all the time. At the end I had an interview with the professor and tried to convince him that my unlucky mistake was an accident and a surprise to myself; I had heard the accursed parody twice and had repeated it once myself just before his lecture; and this was the result. I proved to him that I really knew Lomonossoff by heart and had named him as my favourite from personal conviction. When he learnt further that I was an admirer of Shishkoff, he soon made friends with me, being himself a passionate 'Shishkoffite'. Thus I had put myself right in the eyes of the professor, but I could not escape from the banter of my companions, which went on till they were tired of it. They laughed less at my mistake than at the similarity of taste between me and the professor. For several days running, a number of them greeted me with low bows and congratulated me on having found a kindred spirit, by which they meant a worshipper of Shishkoff and an opponent of Karamzin's innovations; each asked me, ' How is your friend and patron, Gorodchaninoff? when did you last see him? when will you see him again?'—and so on. Their mockery annoyed me, but quarrelling did no good and patience was the only remedy.

Meantime the play, which I had settled on long before, and in which I hoped to score a final triumph over my rival Dmitrieff, was getting into shape; it was Kotzebue's *Poverty and Honour*. We invited the actor, Gruzinoff, to two rehearsals; and though he now and then stopped the others and suggested improvements, he passed no criticisms on my acting, only saying from time to time, 'Very good! Excellent!' At last the play was acted, and brilliant success crowned my hopes: there was not one admirer of Dmitrieff's who was not obliged to admit that I had played the part of Heinrich Blum infinitely better. The manager of the Kazan theatre gave me a free ticket of admission for every performance. This was the last piece in which I acted at college, my last stage triumph at Kazan. I am not ashamed to say that the recollection of it still awakens pleasant echoes in my breast. There is a fascination which is difficult to explain, in arousing the enthusiasm of an audience. To move a crowd of spectators, to dominate their minds, to compel them to share the feelings which you are expressing and to live your life for the moment—this is a pleasure which fills the actor's heart for long and can never be forgotten.

There was another play, *The Robbers* by Schiller, which we had long intended to act; and all the company and the other students were ardently desirous to have it performed, but the thing dragged on, because the enterprise was difficult and beyond our powers. I was not very eager about it myself; for I attached much importance to the general effect of each performance, and we had no good actors to take the principal parts, those of Karl and Franz Moor. At last a Karl was

found in a young man who had never appeared on
a stage before ; his name was Vassilieff, and he
was then a teacher in the school. His reading of
the part delighted everyone except me. The
students were very fond of him, as he had been
a popular boy at school ; and they were attracted
by his appearance, especially his expressive face,
flashing black eyes, and fine voice. But I thought
him deficient in art, and also that he did not
possess that fire which nothing can take the
place of—that visionary reckless passion which
alone can give meaning and character to the part
of Karl Moor. Our Franz Moor was positively
bad. I took the part of the old Count, their father.
We rehearsed the play to the best of our ability
and intended to perform it in Christmas week.
My family had now been for some time at Kazan,
and I was pleased to think that they would see me
act, and particularly anxious to be seen by that
dear friend, my pretty young sister ; but just a week
before the date of the peformance, an order was
received from a very high quarter, forbidding us to
act *The Robbers*.

My family had come to Kazan in the middle of
November, as soon as the snow made travelling
possible. My mother settled down in the town,
installed her sisters in our house, and made
acquaintance with the best society of the place ;
then she paid visits and received them, took her
sisters out to balls and parties, and gave small
parties and dinners at home. I pass rapidly over
this, and indeed I paid little attention to it all ;
but I remember how one of these dinners was
interrupted by the arrival from Moscow of our
first governess, an elderly French lady, called Mme

Foissier : she flew straight into the dining-room and began to complain of the cabman, and we were all taken aback, because none of us could speak French and she knew no Russian.

The year 1807 began. Russia was now definitely at war with Napoleon. A militia was enrolled for the first time in our history ; young men crowded into the army, and some of the students, especially the pensioners, asked permission of Government to leave the University for active service against the enemy ; among these were my friend, Panáyeff, and his elder brother, Ivan, our lyric poet. I blush to confess that I never thought at that time of ' rushing, sword in hand, to join the fray ' ; but the senior Government scholars, who were all destined to enter the teaching profession a year later, were burning to join the ranks of our armies ; and the career of learned activity, to which they had voluntarily devoted their lives, suddenly became distasteful to them. They were required to serve six years in that profession, and now the obligation seemed an intolerable burden. Contrary to all expectation, their eager desire was very soon granted, and scholars were permitted to enter the army. This happened after I had left college. Science lost in this way many remarkable men, and only a few remained faithful to their former calling. Many received commissions in the artillery, and almost all of these met with an early death.

In January 1807 I sent in a petition for leave to retire from the University and enter the civil service. I ceased to attend lectures after this, but I went to college daily and spent all the time of recreation in eager and animated conversation with my companions. Sometimes we played scenes from Schiller's *Robbers* : ' Karl Moor ' tied himself to a pillar, to serve for a tree, and declaimed the fiery rhetoric of Schiller's young days ; then he was released from his tree by ' Schweitzer ', and all the band of robbers loudly swore to die with their chief.

In March I received my leaving certificate, which, to tell the truth, I did not deserve. Of scientific knowledge I carried away little from the University, not because it was new and small and insufficiently organized, but because I was too young and childish and was drawn aside by my impetuous nature into one hobby after another. Throughout my life I have suffered from a lack of scientific information and solid learning, and this deficiency has been a great hindrance to me both in my profession and in my pursuit of literature.

The day for my departure was fixed ; and on the previous day I went to say a last farewell to the University and my companions. Walking in a long chain, arm in arm, we visited all the dormitories, lecture-halls, and public rooms. Then followed a long and close embrace with each. To take a final farewell, a crowd of students and even of schoolboys poured forth and escorted me to the outside staircase ; I went slowly down the steps with a heavy heart ; I turned round for one more glimpse of my friends and of the building, and then I made off almost at a run, while the sound of familiar voices rose behind me—' Goodbye, Aksákoff, goodbye ! '

And I too say goodbye to that season of youthful noise and youthful study, to those early irrevocable years when the blood may be hot and the judgement unripe, but men can hear the voice of honour and follow unselfish aims. That brightness has not yet been clouded over by the claims of society or the petty cares of domestic life. The walls of the school and University and my companions—these made up a whole world to me. There, the problems that puzzle young minds were solved; there, ideals were realized and emotions satisfied. Judgement was passed there, and condemnation or triumphant acquittal pronounced. The rule of the place was complete contempt for all baseness and meanness, for all worldly wisdom and selfish aims, and hearty respect for every high and honourable ideal, however visionary. The memory of years so spent accompanies a man through life; unfelt by him, it lights and directs his path to the very end; and even if circumstances drag him into slippery paths and miry ways, that memory restores him to the high road of truth and honour. I at least, for all of good that survives within me, count myself indebted to the public education of my school and University, and to the stimulus which I carried away with me when I left them. I am convinced that a man who was never at a public school or University is a defective man, that his life is incomplete, and that he lacks a kind of experience which must be felt in youth or never.

Just before the snow melted in spring, we travelled to Aksákovo; and there I found spring and outdoor sports. Nature was awaking from her winter sleep, and the migratory birds were returning. It was the first time I had really seen and really felt that season; and the effect was to banish from my head for a time all thoughts either of the war with Napoleon or of the University and the companions I had left there.

APPENDIX

BUTTERFLY-COLLECTING
AN EPISODE OF COLLEGE LIFE

BUTTERFLY-COLLECTING

To collect butterflies was one of the hobbies of my youth. It did not last long, but for a time I had a perfect passion for it, and it has left on my memory a deep impression which remains fresh to this day.

From childhood I was fond of Natural History. A little book in Russian—I forget the title—with poor illustrations of beasts, birds, and fishes, fell in my way while I was still a schoolboy; and I worshipped it and learnt it by heart from beginning to end. Then, because I realized that the book did not contain just what my own peering childish eyes had noted, I tried myself to write descriptions of the wild creatures with which I was most familiar. These were the first feeble attempts of a child, who thinks that every fact which he has found out for himself is a complete novelty, a precious and important discovery which must be written down and communicated to others. I cannot now look unmoved at these two note-books, each containing four pages of thick blue paper such as you could not get nowadays. They contain descriptions, written in a hand as childish as the style, of the following creatures: the hare, the squirrel, the snipe (three kinds being distinguished), the roach, the minnow, the gudgeon—these were clearly the earliest acquaintances of the young observer. But my attention was soon called off by a host of those new interests and exciting objects in which youth is so rich; and I gave up describing my beasts and birds. Yet I still retained my strong love of Nature and of living creatures, and, fifty years later, rich in the experience which I had gained in my enthusiastic pursuit of shooting and fishing, I looked back with interest to my childish days, and supplemented the attempts of my boyhood by books written when I was sixty years old—'Notes on Fishing,' and 'Notes of a Sportsman with the Gun in the Government of Orenburg.'[1]

While still a child I learnt from *Reading for Children* about caterpillars and their changes into chrysalises or cocoons and finally into butterflies. This certainly made butterflies more interesting to me, but I loved them even before. And indeed, of all the insects that inhabit God's earth, of all the little creatures that creep or hop or fly, the butterfly is the most beautiful and the most charming. It is, in real truth, 'a flying flower,' either painted with the brightest hues and glittering with gold or silver or mother-of-pearl, or speckled with elusive colours and patterns which are just as lovely and attractive. And they are as harmless as they are beautiful, feeding on the honey of flowers, which they suck with a tongue, either short and thick, or long and slender like a hair and coiled up when not in use. How delightful is the first appearance of the butterflies in spring, first the white and then the yellow! What life they lend to the landscape on its first awaking after the long cruel winter! There is hardly a green blade or leaf then to be seen; the sight of the bare trees and withered autumn vegetation would be

---

[1] Published in 1847 and 1855: a long and interesting review of the later book will be found in Turgénev, vol. x, pp. 401–16 (ed. of 1897).

depressing, but for the pleasant warmth and the
thought that all the earth will soon break into leaf
and flower, that the living sap is already rising
from the roots through the trunks and branches
of the trees, and that the young shoots of grass
and plants are spearing up out of the moist warm
soil ; and these thoughts bring peace and happiness to man's heart.

The charter of the University of Kazan was
confirmed in the year 1805 ; and a few months
later, in the beginning of 1806, the college was
opened with a small staff of professors. One of
these was Karl Fyodorovitch Fuchs, professor of
Natural History, who delivered his lectures in
French. By that time I could read French easily
and understood French books even on abstract
subjects ; but the conversational language and
the oral discourse of the professor puzzled me
a good deal at first. Before long, however, I got
accustomed to it, and listened with eager attention
to the lectures. They were the easier to follow,
because Fuchs used Blumenbach's text-book, of
which we possessed printed copies in a Russian
translation. This book, in three parts, bears the
following title : ' Introduction to Natural History,
by Dr. Joh. Friedr. Blumenbach, Professor in the
University of Göttingen and Privy Councillor of
Great Britain. Translated from the German into
Russian by Peter Naumoff and Andrew Teryayeff,
teachers of Natural and Civil History and Geography ; printed by Vilkovsky at the Government
Press, St. Petersburg, 1797.'

One of those who attended Fuchs's lectures was
Vassili Timyansky. During his school-time he had
worked harder than any of us at languages, Latin

as well as French and German, and was therefore
a great favourite with Erich, who had taught us
these languages in the upper forms of the school.
Erich had now been made assistant-professor in
the University and lectured on Latin and Greek
literature. We all believed him to have a profound
knowledge of ancient and modern tongues ; but
his appearance and manners were extremely odd
and comical, and he spoke Russian in such a way
that it was impossible to hear him without laughing. He tried it, however, only in despair, and
after recourse to every other language he knew,
in the endeavour to explain his meaning to some
pupil who could not understand him. He named
us all after a fashion of his own. Thus he addressed
Bezobrázoff, one of the students, as ' Herr Abra-
zantsoff,' and me as ' Herr Achakoff ' or ' Aksayeff,'
and never by my real name, though he knew me
very well and often paid visits to Kartashevsky in
whose house I lived. Timyansky could mimic
Erich to perfection. I too could represent my
tutor with some skill, and the pair of us sometimes
entertained the other students by acting a meeting
of our teachers in the street and their greetings to
one another.

But I must apologize to the reader : recollections
of youth have led me astray from my subject, to
which I shall now return. Timyansky, though he
probably did not know much Latin then, was
considered our best Latinist and soon attracted
the attention of Fuchs, who was pleased with him
for his knowledge of the language,[1] and invited
him to his house, a fine house which the professor

---

[1] Fuchs was evidently a German, who understood Latin
and French better than Russian.

rented in the outskirts of Kazan. I was present
one day when Timyansky mentioned that he had
seen a large collection of insects, including butterflies, in the professor's house, and that the professor
had promised to teach him how to catch butterflies, set them, and preserve them. This was in
January or February of 1806. But I had just seen,
for the first time in my life, men fighting with
their fists, and came back eager to describe to my
companions what I had been seeing, and in my
excitement I paid no attention to what Timyansky
had said.

In those days in winter at Kazan, the ice
on the great lake Kaban was the scene of famous
encounters with fists between Tartars and Russians.
They lived on opposite sides of the lake, and the
Russians were weavers and serfs of a landowner
named Osokin.[1] These contests were sometimes
waged with ferocity, and the feeling of nationality
certainly contributed something to the zeal of the
combatants. But the fight I saw was conducted
within proper limits and according to certain rules
which were always kept unless when the Tartars
happened to get the upper hand. The combatants
were drawn up in two long lines with a respectful
distance between them, and remained there for
a long time inactive, while the small boys on both
sides ran out into the middle space and fought,
amid the jeers or applause of their elders. At last
a famous Tartar champion called Abdulka strode
out in front, and was immediately faced by
Nikita, a doughty Russian boxer; the Tartar

---

[1] The Tartar quarter and the weavers' quarter still
exist at Kazan; but the serfs are of course free labourers.
(*Author's Note.*)

went flying to the ground, and his place was taken by another. Meantime other single combats took place at different points along the line, and neither side could claim the advantage. Both Tartars and Russians measured their length on the ice, and got up again, with hands pressed to their sides or faces; and some had to be carried off. But suddenly with a wild yell, the whole Tartar line advanced and closed with the enemy, and a tremendous hand-to-hand encounter took place. The Tartars did not hold out long: they were forced back and fled to the banks of the lake, pursued by the Russians. The conquerors then came back in triumph. I was told that, when the Tartars prevailed, they pursued the Russians into their very houses, and that the contest was renewed there with fresh fury, the old men and women and children joining in with any weapon they could lay hands on; and these engagements always ended in the rout of the Tartars.

In the spring of 1806, when I learnt that Timyansky and another student called Kaisaroff were beginning to collect insects, and that they secretly possessed implements for catching butter-flies and boards for setting them, I remembered for the first time what I had heard before on the subject, and conceived a sudden and strong desire to collect butterflies myself. I told my bosom friend, Alexander Panáyeff, also a student, and aroused a similar desire in him. Then I turned first to Timyansky and asked him to instruct me how to proceed, but he refused and said he would not reveal the secret till he had made a considerable collection; he only showed me a few specimens of butterflies and other insects preserved. This added fuel to my fire, and I decided to call at once on Professor Fuchs, who was also a doctor of medicine and starting a practice in the town.

I explained my visit by the pretext of some imaginary symptoms. On the walls of his study there were boxes with glass lids, and inside I could see, stuck on pins and in splendid condition, the loveliest butterflies I had ever beheld. I was perfectly enraptured, and made haste to explain to the professor as best I could my passion for Natural History and my eager desire to collect butterflies; and I begged him at the same time to teach me how to set about it. The professor was much pleased and willingly described all the details of the art, which, though not difficult to master, needs care and patience and neat-handedness. He showed me there and then all the requisite implements both for catching and setting the insects. I knew that Panáyeff would do all this much more skilfully than I could; for he was a capital hand at all mechanical work with his fingers. I therefore asked leave of the professor to bring Panáyeff with me next day; and he promised that, if we brought some live butterflies with us, he would set them at once in our presence. And further, as I wished not only to catch butterflies but to rear them from the caterpillar stage, he gave me hints on the way of distinguishing them from the grubs of other insects; he told me how to keep them and feed them and in general how to manage them. Panáyeff and I, in our turn, resolved to keep our undertaking a secret, not only from Timyansky but from all the students.

Next day we caught a few miscellaneous butterflies in the garden and then went off to Fuchs's house. He began by setting two of them while we looked on and then gave the third to Panáyeff to set, thinking it best to watch the first experiment himself. The operation was performed as follows. The professor took the butterfly cautiously by the under side between his thumb and forefinger, and squeezed it rather hard; this was necessary to make the insect unconscious; otherwise it might flutter and rub the painted dust off its wings. A special steel forceps was often used for this purpose; but the professor said and proved to us that we could get on very well without it. Next he took a pin corresponding in size to the size of the butterfly and ran it through the insect's back from above, letting the point project sufficiently for sticking it into a wooden frame. He passed the point of the pin through a card and heated it for a moment over a candle—a necessary precaution, in order to dry the insect's body and prevent it from turning on the pin. Then he took a smooth board of lime-wood—this is the softest kind of wood—with holes cut all along it, larger and smaller to suit the different size of the butterflies' bodies.[1] The professor inserted the body of this butterfly in one of these holes, and drove in the pin to such a distance that the wings rested exactly on the surface of the board. Finally he took narrow strips of writing-paper shaped for the purpose, placed one of them over the upper and under wings, and secured the strip with a pin; and then with a special implement like a bodkin or an awl—a large long pin can always be used as a substitute—he straightened each wing separately,

---

[1] Nowadays the setting-board has a continuous groove with a cork bottom. (*Author's Note.*)

so that they lay flat and even, and the upper wing touched the under without hiding it. He ended the operation by pushing a pin into the lower end of the paper and into the wood, to keep all fast. The only part of the business which required practice and dexterity was the arrangement of the wings : it was essential not to tear or crumple them or rub the dust off them. In a few days the butterfly would be dry ; and then the strips of paper would be carefully removed, and the insect transferred to the box or cabinet where it was to remain. Panáyeff set the third butterfly ; and though he was a beginner, he did it so well that the professor, after repeating many times ' Bien, très bien, parfaitement bien ! '—at last solemnly pronounced the word ' Optime ! '

And now Panáyeff and I went to work with the eager enthusiasm of youth. Seasoned boards of different sizes, made of lime-wood, were planed smooth under his personal inspection, and he carved the holes very neatly and cleverly himself. We procured stout pins for setting the butterflies and securing their wings, and tough writing-paper which did not tear as the professor's had done. We made nets of two kinds, some with long bags of gauze or muslin, and others flat like the battledores used with shuttlecocks. With the first kind it was necessary to strike the butterfly in the air and entangle it in the pouch, with the second to strike it to the ground or cover it as it perched on some plant or flower. The first method is clearly the best, because the dust on the wings is less likely to be rubbed off ; but it required more activity and skill to work with the bag-net. Thanks to my eager and unremitting exertions,

I

and also to the efforts and intelligence of my partner, everything was ready in two days; and the contrivances which we planned and executed were much superior to what we had seen at the professor's house.

The setting of the butterflies was undertaken exclusively by Panáyeff; when he had set a few more specimens, he was quite perfect in the art. We determined to hunt together, as a rule, for butterflies outside the town; and I undertook as my special charge to rear caterpillars till they chrysalized, to collect chrysalises already formed, and to mind them all till they hatched into the perfect insects. I had a peculiar pleasure in observing the habits of living creatures in general, and also I was encouraged by Professor Fuchs, who said that artificially reared butterflies would afford the best specimens, because they keep the original freshness and brightness of their colours in perfection. He said that when the insects begin to fly about the fields, exposed to the wind and rain, they soon deteriorate by rubbing or shaking off the coloured dust which covers their wings in the shape of minute scales, as soon as they creep out of the envelope of the chrysalis or cocoon and expand their compressed limbs and crumpled wings.

As I have told in more detail in another place, after spending two months in the house of Professor Levitsky, I found it impossible to stay there any longer, and was now living, for the first time in my life, all by myself in my own lodgings. I rented rooms from a Russianized German named Hermann, whose son Alexander had been at school with me and was now employed in the post-office at Kazan; he shared my rooms and was often my companion and sometimes my guide, when we went to places of public resort and entertainment, for which he had a great liking. At the time I am speaking of it was spring, and an annual fair of a peculiar kind was going on at Kazan. As soon as the Volga rises above its banks and inundates its flat side—its waters sometimes spread more than ten versts in that direction—it unites with Lake Kaban which is about three versts from the channel, swells its stagnant waters and drives them into a canal called the Bulak, which runs through all the lower part of Kazan and joins the river Kazanka. In summer the Bulak is shallow, muddy, and ill-smelling; but in spring swarms of large boats, laden with small wares of different kinds, take advantage of the flood to leave the Volga and cross Lake Kaban; they gather in the canal and literally cover it. This is the only fair held at Kazan, and the inhabitants look forward to it with impatience: the news that ' the boats have come ', throws all the town into excitement at once. The fun of the fair is at its height along the canal; its muddy dirty banks are thronged by the people and curious sight-seers, just as a part of Moscow is in Easter Week. Oranges and lemons and many other things are offered for sale, and especially vast quantities of glass and earthenware, and what is called ' grass-ware ', which is covered over inside and out, or inside only, with green enamel. A great number of children's toys made of glass or clay, such as ducks and geese, whistles and squirts, are sold at the fair; and crowds of boys and girls may then be seen in all the streets and especially round the canal, all provided with new toys bought on the boats. With joy on their faces and wild with excitement, they rush up and down, blowing their whistles with all their might and discharging the contents of their squirts at each other or the passers-by; and this goes on for nearly a month. It is a purely popular festival which the aristocracy of Kazan visit from curiosity; and the variety of costumes worn by Russians and Tartars, townspeople and countrymen, makes it very picturesque.

Hermann and I often went to the canal; and he was much vexed when I explained one day that I did not intend to waste any more time there. My mind was full of something else, I said: all my free time was to be devoted to collecting butterflies, rearing caterpillars, and hunting for chrysalises; and I should be very glad if he would help me. He disapproved of my intention, and would much have preferred to accompany me to the fair. But I was stubborn, and he was obliged, with his will or against his will, to assist me in my new occupations. I had a good many rooms at my disposal, and one of them, which was quite apart from the rest, I gave up exclusively to caterpillars. There were several tables in the room, covered with glass boxes with cardboard lids, cardboard boxes, and large glass jars; and in these the caterpillars were to live, sufficiently provided with their proper food-plants. The lids of all these receptacles were perforated with a large pin, for ventilation. In all these tiresome and minute preparations Hermann gave me his assistance. Later, when my collection of caterpillars became rather large, the smell in this room became so strong, that it was impossible to stay there long without an open window. I liked to spend much of my time in watching my nurse-lings; but Hermann ceased to go there at all and even declared that the whole house reeked of my caterpillars; but that was a calumny. I had also boxes for chrysalises, keeping butterflies and moths apart.

My lodgings had this further advantage, that the house stood apart and between two grassy valleys which went down to the river Kazanka. I examined them at once with great care, and was pleased to find various butterflies flitting about. Panáyeff lived with his four brothers in a house of their own by the Black Lake, with easy access to a rather large garden which had been partly con-verted into a market-garden; it was in a state of utter neglect, but that did not prevent butterflies from visiting it. Thanks to these advantages and opportunities, Panáyeff and I, during the first two days and without leaving the town, were successful in catching about a dozen butterflies, which, though they were common enough, were worthy to take a place in our collection.

I said that we intended to keep our occupation a secret from all our companions. But alas! few secrets are strictly kept, and the other students knew of our enterprise the very next day. I suspect that Panáyeff's younger brothers, Vladímir and Peter, who were then pensioners at the school, let the cat out of the bag. We decided to drop concealment, and our example was followed by Timyansky and Kaisaroff; but open rivalry went on just the same. Timyansky's collection had this advantage, that it got the start of ours and contained thirty specimens before we had a single one; but we had more leisure and more money and soon caught up our rivals. The students were soon divided into two camps—one backing the collection of the pensioners [1] (Panáyeff and myself), and the other the collection of the scholars.

As if to spite us, we were prevented for several days from going out of town into the woods and gardens beyond the Arsky Park. My impatience increased every hour. Though I had never yet properly experienced the satisfaction of catching butterflies, especially rare or remarkable specimens, my whole soul was given up to this new excitement; and I thought of nothing else at this time but hunting for caterpillars and chrysalises and catching butterflies. Panáyeff shared the new pleasure with me, but always kept within the limits prescribed by good sense and moderation. At last the day came. Panáyeff had spent the night with me, because I lived much nearer the Arsky Park, and at dawn we sallied forth. Each of us held one net firmly mounted on a wooden stick, and carried another in reserve, strapped over our shoulders; and each had a cardboard box, in which to deposit the captured butterflies. I doubt if I ever felt such intense excitement in later years, when I had become a passionate lover of the gun, not even when bad weather had kept me indoors for several days and I took the field at last with my gun and dog, to shoot over a bog abounding with snipe! It was a lovely bright spring day, and the sun rose to greet us from behind a wood and soon filled all the landscape with floods of burning light. We ran over the Arsky Park as quickly as if the ground scorched our feet, and soon the Bolkhovsky

---

[1] Pensioners: i. e. students paying their own expenses; scholars were maintained by the Government.

garden lay before us—an old neglected place with
dark avenues of ancient trees, rickety fences,
and fields full of flowers. The chorus of birds'
voices, drowned by the song of the nightingales,
was the first thing that struck me, but I soon forgot
it. We stopped to draw breath and to settle our
plan of attack.

A wide grassy opening lay before us, and we
decided to walk along it, keeping about a hundred
yards apart. I started, and my feet were soaked
by the heavy dew in one moment. When I had
gone a few yards, I saw Panáyeff running and
brandishing his net. I forgot the arrangement that
we were not to keep together or pursue the same
prey: I rushed towards my companion and saw
that he was in the act of catching a splendid
butterfly which was new to me. He cried out to
me to keep off and not hinder him; but I flew to
his assistance. His warning came too late. The
butterfly, alarmed by our pursuit and especially
by my rapid approach, rose straight up, fluttered
over a line of trees, and disappeared. Panáyeff
was very angry; he scolded me severely and said
positively that if I did it again he would never go
out with me in future. He declared that the butterfly was an unusually fine one, possibly a *Purple
Emperor* or a *Peacock*.[1] Feeling very penitent and
self-reproachful, I promised and even took an oath
that it should never happen again. I kept this
promise scrupulously. We parted, each to follow
his own line at the appointed distance; and
soon I saw my companion running again. He

---

[1] Here and elsewhere the English names have been
substituted for the Latin or Russian names given by
Aksákoff.

caught something, stopped, and began to take it
out of the net; it cost me a great effort to stand
still, because I was panting to know what he had
caught and to see it for myself. But suddenly there
flashed before my eyes a large butterfly, throwing
its dancing shadow over the grass and flowers;
it was dark in colour, but its burnished wings
flashed in the sunlight. I flew in pursuit and very
quickly succeeded in catching it; my hands shook
so in my excitement that for some time I could
not squeeze my captive's thorax, so as to paralyse
it; this regrettable precaution was necessary, to
prevent it from fluttering in the box and spoiling
its velvet wings. I recognized this butterfly at
once: Timyansky had it already in his collection,
it had been identified from Blumenbach's book,
and the professor had confirmed Blumenbach. It
was a *Camberwell Beauty*. But what a wretched
description Blumenbach gives—' a striped butterfly, whose wings are pointed and black with a
whitish edging '—and that is all. Such a description conveys no idea of the insect; and, besides, it
is not striped at all. The *Camberwell Beauty*, in
spite of its sober colouring, ranks for size alone
among the finest European butterflies. Its
burnished wings, of a dark coffee-colour, look like
velvet owing to their thick covering of painted
dust, and are covered near the body with a
rust-coloured down of very fine hairlets; all four
wings are bordered with a whitish-yellow straw-
coloured edging, rather broad and curving in
festoons; there are two small spots of the same
colour near the upper edge of each fore-wing;
and on both wings there is a row of bright blue
spots inside the straw-coloured border; the eyes

and club-shaped antennae are large, compared with those of other butterflies; the whole body is covered with dark-coloured down; the underside of the wings is inconspicuous—the background is dark and chequered with fine white veins.[1]

I was delighted that we had got such a prize. I caught a few more butterflies, whose names I did not know and which I had never seen close, and then I joined Panáyeff. He also had caught a *Camberwell Beauty* and some of the small butterflies, bright blue and copper-red, which I had in my box. I had also found several caterpillars, one of which, a very hairy creature, commonly known as a ' Priest's Dog,' [2] promised to develop into a beautiful moth; I recognized it by the token that these caterpillars have generally eight pairs of legs. Much pleased by our successful beginning, we sat down to rest in the impenetrable shade of some old lime-trees, and even made a meal on some bread and cheese which we had been prudent enough to bring with us. After our lunch we fixed a rendezvous, and started off in different directions. We knew this garden well:

[1] All my descriptions are taken either from the originals or from drawings or from Blumenbach corrected and supplemented by us at the time. They may contain some discrepancies from those given in the text-books. This is due to a fact which we did not know then—that there are two flights of many butterflies, in spring and in autumn; and the colours of the spring butterflies, which have hibernated, are much less brilliant. In general, I do not correct the mistakes which we made; the science of entomology has made great strides in fifty years. (*Author's Note.*)

[2] What we call a ' Woolly Bear ', the larva of the Tiger Moth.

the students used often to amuse themselves there and also in the Neyólovsky garden which lay close beside it.

It is fifty-two years since I last saw these gardens. I picture them now as vast and mysterious enclosures and some parts of them as an impenetrable jungle. But it is very possible that I am quite wrong, and that they are not even large. More than once I have seen, after a long interval and when I was grown up, a place where I often ran about in childhood or a house in which I lived for long ; and I have always been surprised to find them so much smaller than their images which lived in my memory. I fear the same might happen with these gardens ; and therefore I warn my readers that I describe all objects as they appeared to me fifty years since.

First I wandered for a good while about the clearings and grassy spaces, and caught a number of butterflies, including several quite unknown to me ; some of them I imagined must be valuable from the peculiarity of their shapes and colours. Then I began to search for caterpillars, chrysalises, and moths ; these last attracted me even more strongly than butterflies. When I found a caterpillar, I always broke off the plant or twig on which I found it, that I might know how to feed it. I might have collected a number of grubs ; but my box was full enough already and I had nowhere to put them. I turned my attention therefore to chrysalises and moths : I examined the underside of the leaves of all tall broad-leaved plants, the hollows in old trees and all the crevices and depressions in the bark, and, finally, the cracks in the tumbledown fences. I succeeded beyond my expectation, and was forced to stop my search, for want of room to stow away any more. I hastened back to our rendezvous, and found that Panáyeff had been waiting there for me a long time.

I guessed at once from his face that he had been successful. But he would neither tell me anything nor listen to my report: he only said: ' If we delay any longer, those butterflies which have had their thorax squeezed too hard, will shrivel up, and it will be impossible to set them.' Though I wanted very much to rest, the reason he gave was so weighty and convincing that I agreed to make an immediate start for home. We made straight for Panáyeff's house on the Black Lake, intending to deal at once with the fruits of our activity, and hoping that we might possibly eclipse our rivals at the first go-off. The thought lent us strength, and we walked manfully along, telling of our achievements and failures, and discussing at the same time the remains of our bread. How happy we were on our way to the house! Panáyeff had four brothers—two older and two younger than himself. They all took a lively interest in the collection and were awaiting us with impatience. As we were dying of thirst, they first gave us some *kvass* [1] to drink and then made us sit down to our task. Panáyeff had to set the best butterflies and all that we had not got already; the duplicates were left to me, and the common sorts, and also those which we called 'reversible', i. e. those which were set upside down so as to show the under side of the wings. The professor told us that in museums a specimen of every butterfly is set in this manner; but we only

[1] A popular Russian drink, made of malt and rye.

did it when the under side was rather conspicuous ; in some butterflies the under surface is even more beautiful than the upper.

On reviewing our bag it appeared that both of us, and I especially in my haste and excitement, had sometimes squeezed the thorax of the insects too much or too little. Some were quite dead ; others had fluttered in their confinement and rubbed the colour off their wings ; but we were glad to find that our best butterflies were well preserved. Twelve new specimens were added to our collection, and half of them we were able to identify on the spot from Blumenbach, which we knew almost by heart ; but the rest puzzled us, because Blumenbach is very brief and inaccurate in his descriptions and leaves out many butterflies altogether. For instance, there is not a word about the small blues or orange-golds which glitter like burnished silver and gold, yet they occur at times in large numbers. I once saw a large blue butterfly of this kind ; but I regret to say that I failed to capture it.

I will enumerate the butterflies which we were able to identify with certainty. (1) *The Large Cabbage White*, with black wing-tips and two small black patches ; this must not be confused with the common Cabbage, of which there are several sorts. (2) *The Peacock*, rather large, very beautiful, and rare ; the indented wings are of a dark cherry-colour, with a large bluish-purple eye on each and five small white spots along the margin ; the eyes on the fore-wings have an incomplete yellow ring ; on the hind-wings the ring is buff, and so is the under-surface of the wings ; the edging of the wings is black. On the fore-wings there is a dark interval and then a yellow spot between the eye and the body. (3) *The Marble White*, with indented wings speckled with black on a pale straw-coloured ground; on the under surface of the wings there are colourless eyes, one on the upper wing and five or more on the hind-wing. This butterfly does not occur now at Kazan. (4) *The Comma*. We were much pleased with this butterfly which Panáyeff caught. We had read the description with surprise and some incredulity: was it possible that a butterfly should have on its wings a white letter C, and a comma after the letter? It is of moderate size; the much indented wings are reddish-yellow, chequered and spotted with black; and the white C, followed by a white comma, is very clearly marked on the upper surface of the hind-wings. (5) *The Dark Green Fritillary*. The wings are roundish and yellow-brown, with black spots regularly arranged like columns of figures; the under surface, according to Blumenbach, has twenty-one silver spots; but they can hardly be called spots, and the real colour is mother-of-pearl, divided by dark streaks into dice of different sizes and shapes, some of them being roundish. (6) *The Grizzled Skipper*, also called the *Mallow Butterfly*, because it breeds on that plant; the wings are dark with white spots and indented along the margin. (7) *The Oleander Hawk-moth*. Though Blumenbach says that this insect breeds on the oleander, and it ought not therefore to exist in Russia, yet the green pointed wings with pale or dark or yellow stripes and spots, faithfully described by Blumenbach, leave no doubt of its identity and its existence in the Government of Kazan. (8) *The Spurge*

Hawk-moth. This beautiful creature has rather
large brown wings, with a pale pink stripe across
the fore-wings and a red stripe across the hind-
wings. (9) *The Six-spot Burnet Moth,* of two kinds.
I caught the first ; and I mistook it for an emerald
green beetle as it flew past ; but when it settled
on the grass, I had a good view of it and was
enraptured by its beauty. Its upper wings are
just like green velvet, shot with blue, and there are
six crimson spots on each ; the under wings are
much smaller and crimson with a narrow black
edging ; the whole body is greenish-blue and
iridescent. The other kind of *Burnet* (10) was
caught by Panáyeff. It is rather smaller ; the
fore-wings are greenish-brown with the same
beautiful spots ; the hind-wings are pale pink or
yellowish-pink. These moths were long our pride
and glory, because our rivals sought for them in
vain. But my chief delight was in a *Ghost Moth*
(11) which I found in the hollow of an old lime-tree.
The head is shaped exactly like an owl's, the body is
reddish-yellow, and the wings white as snow above
and dark brown beneath ; to crown all, it was as
fresh as if it had just been hatched. According to
Blumenbach, it was a male ; for the female has
reddish-yellow wings.

We set our butterflies and admired them to our
hearts' content. Then, after a hasty meal with my
partner—his brothers, knowing that we should be
late, had dined much earlier—I hurried home.
I had about thirty caterpillars and as many
chrysalises to stow away. The butterfly chrysalises
I tried to attach to the sides or lid of my boxes,
which opened at the side for this purpose. But it
was a difficult operation, because the sticky stuff,

like raw silk, by which the caterpillars fasten their tails to the under side of leaves or the bark of trees, had dried up by this time; and, though I removed the chrysalises very carefully with a penknife, the gum had got wetted and refused to stick on the lid or even the sides of the box. Panáyeff later devised a plan of sticking them on with cherry-tree gum, which proved very successful. The cocoons of moths, which were wrapped up in a sort of nest of fluff, I put in a box by themselves, and covered them over with tufts of cotton wool, to protect them from the light, because I knew that they were always found in thick shade.

Next morning my partner and I went down to college half an hour before lectures began, wishing to report our own acquisitions and to discover how our rivals had got on; for we knew that they also had planned an expedition to the country. I admit that we were in a sanguine state of mind and anticipated that the advantage would be on our side. But as soon as we entered the dormitories, several students who took a special interest in the venture of Timyansky and Kaisaroff hailed us loudly as follows: ' It's simply marvellous, the butterflies that Timyansky and Kaisaroff have caught! You fellows have no chance beside them! And what a host of rare insects of all kinds they've got! They're busy with them now upstairs in Fuchs's lecture-room. They've actually got a *Swallow-tail*!' We were sadly discomfited and taken aback by this news; the mention of the *Swallow-tail* in particular was a crushing blow. Our friends were quite ready to talk, and we now heard that our rivals, with three other students, had spent the whole of the previous day in the country, near the Zilanty Monastery, about four *versts* from Kazan; they had taken with them a large box on purpose to hold setting-boards for the butterflies and drying-boards for other insects; and they had collected specimens of seventy different kinds! We went upstairs and were soon convinced by the evidence of our own eyes that our rivals had triumphed. Of all the butterflies which we two had caught, except the *Burnets* and the *Ghost Moth*, they had got several specimens; and they had also caught a dozen species unknown to us, including two *Orange Tips*, which are found near Kazan but not every year; and, above all, they had captured a *Swallow-tail*. When I looked at it, spread out on the setting-board in all its size and beauty, my heart beat fast with admiration and envy! The great butterfly kingdom contains, according to Blumenbach, only four kinds of *Swallow-tail*.[1] The first of these, *Priam*, he describes as follows: ' the wings are indented and green above with black patches; the hind-wings have six black spots. It breeds in the Molucca Islands. This and the following species are the finest and largest of all butterflies.' Of the second, *Ulysses*, he says: ' the wings are brown with tails or spurs; but the upper margin is bright blue and indented; each hind-wing has seven eyes. This also breeds in the Moluccas.' Even from this short and meagre description, one can imagine the glorious beauty of these two insects. Fuchs, who had

[1] Ten species are now known to breed in Europe; but the Chinese *Swallow-tails* are four times as large as the European insect. (*Author's Note.*)

seen them, said that they were the size of a bat
and beautiful beyond description. ' The other
two species breed in Europe,' continues Blumenbach ; and a specimen of one of these two our
rivals had been lucky enough to find ! We could
not but envy Timyansky his good fortune ; for we
did not know then that these two species breed
in all parts of Russia and are not very rare.

Timyansky noted our confusion and said with
a smile of triumph : ' Well, now that I have
shown all our butterflies, you might as well show
yours.' My partner answered that we had few
specimens and nothing particular to show ; ' But
if you like,' he said, ' we will bring what we have,
to-morrow or next day ; the insects will not be
dry till then, especially a very fat *Ghost Moth*.'
' A *Ghost Moth* ! ' said Timyansky surprised :
' have you got that ? Why, it 's a rarity.' I said
that I had found it in a hollow tree, and that it
was a perfect specimen. It was obvious that it
was now his turn to be jealous of our *Ghost Moth*,
and this cheered us up a good deal. When we
left the room, Panáyeff said to me in quite good
spirits : ' I say, did you notice how badly all their
butterflies were set ? Why, they're not fit to
black the boots of ours ! ' I had not taken any
special notice of this defect ; but when thus
reminded, I was convinced that Panáyeff was
perfectly right ; and we both marched off to
attend our lectures very much easier in our minds.

The very next day we succeeded in increasing
our collection by the addition of three very
beautiful moths, so tiny that we had to stick them
on lace-pins of the smallest size ; it needed all
Panáyeff's skill and neatness to set them. I caught

them in the grassy valleys near my lodgings, where
I had chanced to give a look round. Though the
sun was high, there was shade there already and
the moths were abroad.

Two days later we took our cabinet, now
containing thirty-five specimens, to college for
our companions to see. A crowd collected in
a moment, and the superiority of our collection,
in respect to the perfect condition and neat setting
of the butterflies, was admitted by every one. In
particular, it was impossible not to admire the
charming little new moths : they seemed actually
alive ; for the tiny pins on which they were stuck
escaped the eye altogether. It must be added that
everything about our cabinet—the lining, the
glass lid, the lock and handles—was very trim and
neat, thanks to my partner's supervision. All the
spectators were naturally impressed by these
external advantages ; but Timyansky was quite
able to perceive and appraise what I may call the
intrinsic value of our collection. With some
vexation and, perhaps, envy he gave faint praise
to our specimens, especially the *Ghost Moth* and
the *Six-spot Burnets* ; but he made this criticism—
that the insects were set too stiffly, on purpose
to be shown off, as it were, and that the position
given to them was not natural. If there was a grain
of truth in the last objection, we were not to
blame : we had only followed the universal method
of naturalists. I said this at once in our defence ;
and I added, in defence of naturalists in general,
that living butterflies often adopt the exact position
in which they are set ; moths, it was true, did not
expand their wings on perching but held them
erect like a fan, so as to conceal the hind-wings ;

but they would lose half their attraction if set in that position, because the under-wings are often their chief beauty; and the upright position conveyed no true notion of the insect. Then Panáyeff struck in: ' Your own way of setting is just as unnatural. Did you ever see a butterfly with the fore-wings erect and the hind-wings hanging down ? ' But Timyansky would not give way. He tried to prove that his method was less artificial than ours; there arose a dispute between the supporters of the rival theories; and even if we did not quarrel openly, we did not part as friends. They soon gave us the nickname of ' the wealthy amateurs ', and called us by it even to our faces. I confess I resented this, chiefly because it was entirely undeserved. Our cabinet might perhaps be called smart, but it was not in the least sumptuous: its chief merit was its perfectly clean and neat condition—a point on which Panáyeff laid great stress, and to which he attended carefully. Then one of our opponents called our collection ' the aristocrats' collection ', and this nickname too became fashionable, because it so happened that all the opposite party belonged to the common people, whereas Panáyeff and I wore, while we were schoolboys, red collars on our jackets as a sign of noble birth. This was very distressing; because none of us had ever before said a single word about differences in social position, or even alluded to the subject. But I am thankful to say that all this disagreeable friction passed off in course of time, and the competition was carried on in a friendly spirit and without mutual jealousy. Timyansky had got already, not only upwards of fifty butterflies and moths,

but specimens of nearly a hundred other insects;
some of these had brilliant iridescent colouring,
chiefly beetles and dragonflies, ladybirds and
Spanish flies; and others were remarkable for the
peculiarity of their appearance. But I liked none
of them, and even felt a disgust for them. Butterflies, and nothing but butterflies, were the object
of a passion which grew stronger with me every
day.

At the first opportunity, my partner and I sallied
forth again and visited various parks and gardens
on the outskirts of the town. In one of these we
found few butterflies but spent a long time in
watching the rabbits. There were hundreds of
them, and a highish mound—whether natural or
artificial, I do not know—was given up to them
entirely and enclosed by a strong fence. They
bred there in immense numbers; the whole
mound was riddled with their burrows; swarms
of them ran to and fro, and it was pretty to watch
them at play; but whenever we made a noise or
called out, as we did on purpose from time to
time, the timid little creatures took fright and
vanished into their holes.

Another of our resorts was the clearing made in
the woods for beehives, and the hilly ground on
both sides of it. There are deep dells there,
covered in those days with young trees; we
students used to call the place 'Switzerland', and
the name has stuck to it. I have even been told
that half of it is now called 'German Switzerland',
and the other half, nearer the town, 'Russian
Switzerland'. Our researches were more or less
successful, and by degrees we added to our
collection all the specimens possessed by Timyan-

sky, with one exception—the *Swallow-tail*. We
even despaired of ever getting it, because it was
then believed to be of rare occurrence in the
neighbourhood of Kazan. That *Swallow-tail* was
a thorn in our flesh! It was some time before we
got the *Orange Tip*, which is a very charming
creature, though its colouring is not specially
bright or varied. Its wings are rounded and
milk-white, and covered with a peculiar soft down;
each fore-wing has a single spot of bright orange
on the top corner; the reverse of the hind-wings
is mottled green. Among our most beautiful
butterflies I may mention first the *Purple Emperor*.
Its wings are somewhat indented, of a shining
dark-brown which changes with the light to
a brilliant purple; a white band runs half across
the fore-wings, and each hind-wing has a white
eye at the upper edge; it has this peculiarity, that
the under surface of the wings is an exact repetition, in paler colours, of the upper surface. Still
more beautiful is the *Red Admiral*. It also has
indented wings of a lustrous black variegated with
white spots; a bright scarlet band runs all across
the fore-wings, and a similar band, with small
black spots, edges the curve of each hind-wing.
It must be confessed that both collections contained a number of anonymous specimens, which
we could not identify out of Blumenbach, and to
which Professor Fuchs could give no Russian
names.

My breeding-cages had long been filled to over-
flowing with caterpillars. Many turned into
chrysalises, and many died, probably for want of
fresh air or proper food. It was difficult to
provide the exact plant which they preferred,

because we seldom knew the name either of the caterpillar or its food-plant. As a rule I picked plants of all kinds and tried to change them as often as possible. I found great enjoyment in watching my charges several times a day. Those which were near their change when I caught them hardly ever died on my hands. The butterfly grubs, which were all smooth-skinned, fastened their tails, by means of some sticky stuff discharged from their mouths, to the sides or lid of their box. At first I thought they were dead and was much distressed. But as a rule the dry and shrivelled caterpillar-skin fell off in twenty-four hours, and the chrysalis was left there hanging. Imagine my joy, when, instead of a wretched and apparently dead caterpillar, I suddenly found a pretty chrysalis ! Many of them were golden in colour ; they had little horns and visible outlines of the wings, and all the lower part of the body was thorn-shaped. The caterpillars of twilight moths were all more or less hairy ; they set to work at the top corner of their box or under a leaf of their food-plant, and wound round their bodies fine threads of the same sticky stuff, with some of their own hairs in it. These threads were sometimes downy like cotton wool, and sometimes covered with a white shiny glaze which made them look like a fine transparent wrapping. The grubs of the true moths, which, with few exceptions, were very hairy, made themselves shell-shaped cocoons, where they lay down, sealed themselves up, and turned into chrysalises. With each of the last two kinds, the dry cast skin of the caterpillar always lay beside the chrysalis in the nest. The chrysalis was oval and smooth, with no points or projections ; but here too it was possible to see the outlines of the head, wings, antennae, legs, and segments of the body. They are always dark in colour and, in the case of some true moths, quite black.

Before the time of their transformation, which differed greatly with different kinds, my caterpillars, if they did not die of starvation or want of fresh air, changed their skins two or three times; before this change they always fell into a kind of sleep or swoon, and did not fasten themselves on to anything. I believe I threw some away at first, thinking that they were dead. The rejuvenated caterpillar seemed weak or ill at first, but he had more hair and much brighter colour, and soon attacked his food with intense voracity, and recovered his health very quickly. Some of the chrysalises which I had collected hatched out into creatures like winged black-beetles, of most repulsive appearance. They must have been very like butterfly chrysalises, as I could see no difference. Some of the butterflies came out deformed— with a dwarfed wing, or only one wing, or a wing which remained furled and would not expand. The professor could not give me a satisfactory explanation of these phenomena. But I suppose that the chrysalises had been somehow crushed or bruised, so that the wing on the injured side could not develop normally. It very often happened that a butterfly, when nearly dead and while being set, laid a quantity of eggs, which developed in due time into tiny grubs. Nor is this surprising, as the female may have been fertilized before she was caught; but it is surely remarkable that a moth, which I bred myself and set a few hours later, laid eggs on the setting-board, and the eggs proved fertile. A surprising discovery of the same kind was made not long ago with regard to bees, not only the queens but the workers also,[1] and afforded a remarkable proof of Nature's care to provide for the multiplication of her creatures.

As soon as our collection was inferior in no respect (except, alas! for the *Swallow-tail*) to that of our rivals, and far superior in the condition and arrangement of the specimens, we took our cabinets—we had two by this time—to the professor for exhibition. He was profuse in praise of our skill, and especially admired the small moths which were just as well set as the large ones. He expressed much regret that we did not intend to collect other insects.

Meantime spring came to an end, and summer began to reign instead. The nightingale sang his last strains, and almost all the other song-birds became silent; only the mocking-bird continued to mimic and mix up the notes of other songsters, and even he soon had to stop. The larks alone were left: hanging at an invisible height in the sky, they poured down their music from above and gave life to the sleepy stillness of sultry summer. Spring with the sound of all its voices was over—spring, the season of careless merriment and song and love. The summer solstice passed by, the 12th of June, when, according to the Russian saying, the sun takes the turn to winter and the summer to heat. Their busy season had begun for the birds—the season of constant cares

---

[1] *Three Discoveries in the Natural History of the Bee*, by K F. Roulier, Professor in Moscow University; printed at Moscow 1857. (*Author's Note*.)

and perpetual alarms, of instinctive self-sacrifice and parental love. By this time the young of the song-birds were hatched; they had to be fed, and then taught to fly, and defended at every moment from dangerous foes, from birds and beasts of prey. The parent birds sing no longer; they talk instead. They never stop calling to summon their stupid little young ones, who can only gape with their hungry bills and answer with a plaintive monotonous cheeping. The change took place in little more than a fortnight, during which time I was kept in town. I was struck and even saddened by it when I went out early one morning in the second half of June and walked with my inseparable companion to the shady Neyolovsky Park. I had never in previous years noticed such a complete change in the life of the birds.

Our captures on this occasion were insignificant; indeed failure and disappointment made this expedition live long in our memories. Panáyeff saw a *Swallow-tail* but failed to catch it; and I utterly destroyed a splendid red moth, whose name I don't know, but I remember its appearance perfectly well, chiefly because my memory was refreshed by a later incident. It was very large, thrice the size of the common red moths which often singe their wings at a lighted candle. The insect I spoilt was a rare one: all its wings, head, and body were covered with velvety dust of a bright red colour, but its brilliance was dimmed by thin yellow streaks which covered it all over. I took it up carefully, squeezed its thorax, and somehow dropped it in the grass. While searching for it, I trod on it and destroyed the lovely creature. It makes me smile, when I recall how intensely grieved I was by this loss, and how long I took to get over it. In the year 1810, when I was walking in the Summer Park in Petersburg, I saw an exactly similar moth perched under a broad leaf of an ancient maple. The old passion revived in me : I caught and set it and made a present of it to a naturalist.

Time heals all wounds, and Panáyeff and I became reconciled to the thought that we did not possess, and perhaps should never possess, a *Swallow-tail*. Timyansky also ceased to resent the general opinion that our butterflies were better than his, and consoled himself with the thought that he collected all insects and was superior in this way to us who confined our attentions to one kind.

The examinations which now came on were not, and could not be, conducted under the conditions usual in other Universities. They were of the nature of domestic and friendly tests, or I might call them a review of all that the professors had found time to impart and the students to acquire. There were no separate faculties, and consequently no prescribed courses of study and no transferences from one to another. Ours was a very young and rudimentary institution : but nevertheless, there was a genuine desire for knowledge among us, and much solid laying of foundations for further acquisitions. If the amount of scientific information absorbed was small, yet it became a part of the learners, was fully appropriated by them, and contributed to the independent development of youthful intellects. The subjects of instruction were so much mixed up, and the council of examiners were so tolerant of

the confusion, that Zapolsky, for example, the
professor of Applied Physics, made us read aloud
before the examiners our essays on philosophical
or even purely literary subjects; and no one
thought this strange. Zapolsky himself set up for
a philosopher: he was a disciple and admirer of
Kant, and never delivered a lecture on Physics
without bringing in the *Kritik der reinen Vernunft*.
One day he launched out into ' efficient causes '
and ' final causes', and then proposed that all who
understood him and took an interest in the subject
should write something on it and show it up to
him. Ten students, of whom I was one, wrote
essays; and what was my astonishment, when
the compositions read aloud at the examination
included my three pages on efficient and final
causes! They showed, I have no doubt, a most
childish and superficial comprehension of the
subject. Levitsky, assistant-professor of Russian
Rhetoric, was down on the lecture-list for a course
on Philosophy and Logic; but he had long ceased
to give lectures and hardly ever came to college.
Yet he managed to drag himself down for the
examination, and looked so ill that he alarmed us
all. He examined us, not in his own subject of
Russian Literature but on Logic, which he used
to teach us formerly from a manuscript text-book
in a very compressed form; he warned us beforehand to prepare for an examination in Logic.
It was a great day for the professor of Natural
History: our butterflies and caterpillars and the
other insects were all triumphantly displayed.
Timyansky gained much credit by his wide knowledge and the good Latin he spoke; and I too
had to set forth my observations on the rearing

of caterpillars and their transformations. And I got much applause, even from those professors who knew no Russian and therefore could not understand a word I said. The mathematical examination, conducted by Kartashevsky, was undoubtedly the most successful; but I had no share in that glory and did not even sit for the examination. Among all our subjects mathematics was taught with special brilliance and success.

The examinations diverted our thoughts for a time from butterflies; and another circumstance contributed to the same result. I had a violent quarrel with Panáyeff's elder brothers, though we had always hitherto been on very good terms. One of them, the eldest, applied to me a term so rude and insulting, that in my anger I solemnly vowed never to enter their house again until the offender apologized. He never thought of apologizing, and I stayed away for a whole week. My chosen friend, Alexander Panáyeff, came to see me nearly every day, but what he told me of his elder brothers only increased my resentment. I was specially vexed with Ivan Panáyeff, the chief poet among us; he was an excellent comrade, kind and just; in his family he was considered the flower of the flock, and he was fond of me. And yet he did not take up the cudgels in my defence, but actually justified his brother instead of forcing him to apologize! But great events happen just when they are least expected, and unravel in a moment the tightest knots, which might otherwise take a long time to undo or never come undone at all.

On one of the last days of June, when our examinations were drawing to a close, I went back from college to my lodgings. I should have dined at once, but some mysterious motive made me take my butterfly-net and walk out, in spite of the burning heat, into the grassy valleys which stretched near the house. I felt a desire to make a round there before dinner; but why I felt this, I cannot tell to this day. The valley to the left of the house was nearest, and I had got about halfway down it, nearly suffocated by the heat of this hollow where no breeze could penetrate, when I saw within two yards of me, fluttering from flower to flower, a splendid *Swallow-tail*! At first I was so surprised that I could not believe my eyes; then I recovered and brushed the butterfly with a hasty swoop of my net off the top of a thistle still in flower. It disappeared; I examined the crumpled folds of the net, but there was nothing there! It flashed into my mind that I was dreaming, when suddenly, at the very bottom of the gauze, I saw my inestimable prize, the *Swallow-tail* which I had longed and prayed for; he was lying with folded wings, in a position which made it easy for me to seize him and squeeze his thorax. I did so at once, and then, without taking him out of the net, ran home half-crazy with excitement.

My servant Yevséitch was waiting for me by the steps, and I began yelling to him from some distance off—'Fetch a cab! fetch a cab!' Alarmed by my tones and unusual appearance, my kind Yevséitch ran to meet me. I made haste to explain what I was about, and implored him to order a cab at once. His alarm gave place to surprise: he shook his head and smiled, but went off to do what I told him. I went into the house, laid my net on a table, and fixed my gaze upon my prize; and now for the first time I was convinced that there was no dream or vision about it—I had actually caught a *Swallow-tail*, and there it lay before me! To make assurance doubly sure, I squeezed its thorax a second time; then I lowered it gingerly into a pill-box, covering it with paper and filling the box up with cotton-wool, that no jolting might shift its position. Yevséitch came back and said the cab would be ready at once; he was still smiling. I had time now to embrace my kind Yevséitch and impart to him all my happiness. Though his knowledge of my character might be called extensive and peculiar, he was taken aback by my wild enthusiasm. In vain I assured him of the importance of securing a *Swallow-tail*; in vain I pointed out how extraordinary it was that the insect should find its way into the centre of a large town and that I should take that hot walk in the valley for no reason—my attendant heard me to the end with complete indifference. He had ceased to smile but went on shaking his head. At last he said: ' No, no, my little falcon! You are terribly young and green still, and need a lot of schooling yet, before you are fit for a man's work.' His lecture was cut short by the sound of wheels, and a moment later I was galloping along the road straight for Panáyeff's house. I thought of his surprise and delight, which would be all the greater, because it was barely half an hour since we had parted.

The twenty minutes during which that drive lasted seemed to me like a whole long day. But there it was at last—the familiar house with its weather-stained white walls. I ran up the steps and upstairs to the parlour. Just as I opened the door, my friend rushed out of the drawing-room, with blood on his face, and pressing a hand to his eye. ' What is the matter ? ' I cried out. ' I'm done for ! ' he answered in a voice of despair ; ' it was an accident ; Peter has just hit me right in the pupil of my eye with a splinter of glass. If I lose an eye I shall blow out my brains. I am off to the well, to bathe it with cold water.' I ran beside him. He was so afraid of finding that his eye was injured and his good looks gone—he was really very handsome—that he could not make up his mind at first to remove his hand and bathe the wounded eye. When I induced him to do so, I was much relieved, but less than he was, when I saw that only the lower lid had been cut and the white of the eye slightly scratched. Just as I was embracing my friend and congratulating him on his fortunate escape from such an alarming accident, his brothers came running to the spot. I was able to reassure them, and they soon convinced themselves that there was nothing serious the matter. In our joy we all embraced one another. All the brothers were present except Peter who had done the mischief : in his grief and fear he had crept away to an attic, but he was now sent for to join our party.

Suddenly my friend asked me : ' How did it happen, my dear fellow, that you arrived in the very nick of time, just when this horrible thing was so near happening to me ? I suppose some instinct told you of my despair and made you forget all and rush to help me.' And now I remembered for the first time, that I was not on speaking terms with his brothers and had ceased to visit their house, and also that I had caught

a *Swallow-tail*. ' You are wrong,' I said; ' it
was not a case of instinct this time. Something
else has happened to banish all feelings of un-
pleasantness from my mind. Half an hour ago,
in the valley near my lodgings, I caught a most
splendid *Swallow-tail*. I will show it you '—and
off I ran to the drawing-room where I had left the
pill-box lying on the table. They all followed me
with shouts of joy; and when I opened the box
and displayed, lying just as I had placed him,
a really exceptionally large and splendid *Swallow-
tail*, their shouts pealed out again. I need hardly
say that I told over and over again the history of
this happy event. When my friend had bathed
his eye with rose-water and bandaged it with
a very smart cambric handkerchief, he sat down
at once to set the butterfly, which turned out to
be quite perfect and not rubbed anywhere. ' Well,
there is no doubt now of the superiority of our
collection over Timyansky's,' he said with a smile
of triumph. He set to work with care and pains,
while we five stood round and followed every
movement of his skilful fingers, never taking our
eyes off him and hardly daring to breathe freely.
He called out that we were hindering him, that he
had no room to move and was being stifled, but
none of us stirred and his protests were vain. At
last the setting was successfully accomplished,
and then I remembered that I had had no dinner.
The brothers had dined already. Every trace
of unfriendliness had disappeared : they begged
me to stay and offered me what remained of their
dinner. But I could not accept their invita-
tion, because I had not seen my caterpillars and
chrysalises that day, and some change might

have taken place or some butterfly hatched out !
I remembered also that I had to read through
a note-book, with a view to an examination the
next day. But I felt unwilling to part so soon
from my friends and—I must admit—from my
Swallow-tail, the captive of my bow and spear.
I thought of a plan to meet all the difficulties :
I said I would examine my breeding-cages, eat
my dinner, and pick up my notebook, all in half
an hour, and then come back. My friends were
most cordial and made me repeat more than once
my promise to return within the hour. How
happy I was, as I got into the cab and drove off to
my solitary lodgings !

The proverb which says that misfortunes never
come singly is true enough alas ! at times. But
the reverse also is fairly common, and one piece
of good fortune is often followed immediately by
another. When I got home, as soon as I opened
the box containing my chrysalises, I saw before
me a very large and beautiful moth, which must
have hatched out in the night, as its wings were
fully expanded. To judge by Blumenbach, it was
the *Privet Hawk-moth*, which he named thus from
the plant it breeds on ; but I do not assert this
positively ; Blumenbach gives no description at
all of the fore-wings ! I discovered later that the
very pretty caterpillar of this fine moth feeds
chiefly on gooseberry or barberry leaves. The
fore-wings are dark grey with white spots or dull
white with dark spots ; I give the alternatives,
because both colours are present in an equal degree
and it is hard to determine the prevailing tint.
The hind-wings are blood-red with three black
bands ; the body also is red with black rings

covering the whole abdomen—these parts are fairly well described in Blumenbach. We always afterwards called this very fine insect the *Barberry Moth*. It is common enough, but I had never seen it before, and to me it seemed a marvel of beauty. And besides, it was the very first moth I had bred myself from a chrysalis which I had collected. The large size and dark colour of the chrysalis had made me suppose it to be a moth of some kind. I sat down to a late but happy dinner. Yevséitch waited on me, as usual; and I noticed that the rather peculiar smile which his face had worn earlier was still playing about his mouth. From time to time he made some disparaging allusion to my passion for catching butterflies and taking trouble over ' those stinking caterpillars '; and I was heartily amused by these sarcastic comments. When I had dined, I went back to my friend's house and carried my new-born beauty with me, taking every precaution that the virgin gloss of its lovely hues might not be dimmed. Panáyeff's delight over the moth was almost as keen as over the great *Swallow-tail*; and he lost no time in setting it. It was destined to add fresh lustre to our collection.

Next morning all the University heard of our new and splendid acquisitions; and though all the students were more or less preoccupied by the examinations, yet they took a keen interest in the new butterflies. But Timyansky, especially when he saw them, was a good deal put out. ' Well, you *are* lucky people ! ' he said; ' just to please you, a *Swallow-tail* flew into the town. And we used to laugh at you, Aksákoff, for messing about with those silly caterpillars; but a man might go far enough and never catch such a perfect specimen of the *Privet Hawk-moth* in all his life.'

When examinations were at an end for the students, they were still going on for the school-boys. Seven students, of whom I was one, still went to the school to learn Russian Literature from Ibrahimoff, and had therefore to present themselves for the school examination in that subject; and this was to be the last of all the examinations. My companions resented this necessity, but I looked forward to it with pleasure. In general, the school examinations were more thorough, more orderly, and kept more closely to the programme. The examination in Russian conducted by Ibrahimoff was a brilliant success. We read our compositions aloud, discussed ancient and modern literature, and reviewed the works of our best authors. My talent for declamation was also called into play. Ibrahimoff was hurt at not having been promoted to a professor's chair, and therefore we all with one accord heaped praises upon him and congratulated him on the success of his pupils. Never shall I forget the pleasure that shone in his small Tartar eyes, or the smile that split his large Tartar mouth from ear to ear. The thought of this excellent teacher is always connected in my memory with my happiest recollections of youth and youthful study. ' Thank you, Aksákoff,' he said ; ' I have always found it a pleasure to teach you. You have shown your gratitude to me in the best way.' I embraced him, and assured him that I was deeply conscious of my debt to him and would never forget it.

The last examination was over. I was to spend the summer vacation at Old Aksákovo in the Government of Simbirsk, while the Panáyeffs

were to join their mother and sisters at their place
in the Government of Kazan. It happened to me
for the first time that the joy of going home for the
holidays was disturbed by a special anxiety that
filled my mind. Our butterflies Fuchs had advised
us to deposit in the school library, to be looked after
by the attendant; but what was to be done with
my caterpillars and chrysalises? It was impossible
to take seven boxes and three glass jars with me
in the travelling carriage: twenty-four hours
would be enough to shake up all the caterpillars
and detach the chrysalises and make general
havoc; and besides there was simply no room
to stow away such bulky packages. But then it
was equally impossible to leave my foundlings with
no one to attend to them. Who was there on whom
I could rely? I was leaving no servants at Kazan
except a coachman in charge of a horse. Who could
take my place? I confess too that I was loath to
tear myself away from the constant observation
and anxious attention which I was accustomed
to bestow upon my nurselings; and it made me
sad to think that the final transformation into
some splendid butterfly new to me might take
place without me to see it. But this was inevitable,
and I had already become resigned to the thought.
It only remained to settle who was to have the
charge of them. I was inclined to give them over
to Alexander Hermann: he was to stay behind
and occupy my rooms; I had pressed him into
my service in this way already; and he was not
likely to refuse. But he was exceedingly careless,
and I was afraid to trust him.

Suddenly I thought of Timyansky. He had no
relations or home to go to, and was to spend the

vacation at college, as many other students did. Why not ask him? According to my view, our rivalry need not prevent him from minding my caterpillars and chrysalises, in which he as a naturalist could not fail to take some interest.

I was not mistaken. The moment I spoke to him of my difficulty, Timyansky frankly and goodnaturedly volunteered to look after my charges. I told him that I had intended to ask this favour of him, feeling sure that he would not refuse to oblige a fellow-student and relieve his anxiety; and I thanked him heartily. I felt as if a mountain had rolled off my shoulders! I knew that a whole room near the physical laboratory was at his disposal for drying his butterflies and insects, as well as Fuchs's lecture-room, of which he had a key. Thus he had abundance of room. Then the house next to the college, which had been bought for University purposes, possessed a garden where he could gather a daily supply of fresh leaves and plants for the caterpillars. So I thanked him once again for his friendliness and willingness to take my troubles and anxieties upon his shoulders, and then set off to tell Panáyeff this good news. But my friend did not take it quite as I expected. He was rather distrustful and even suspicious; and though he did not attribute any evil design to Timyansky, he hardly expected him to put his heart into the task of increasing and adorning our collection. He agreed, however, that the plan was the best we could hope for in our present situation. That same day we carefully conveyed the butterflies to the library and my chrysalises and caterpillars to the room near the physical laboratory, where we personally delivered the latter to the rival collectors. When I begged Kaisaroff also to keep an eye on my breeding-cages, he promised to do so; but, true to his custom and his temper, he gave the promise very stiffly; I felt no confidence in him, but there, to my great satisfaction, I was entirely mistaken. Kaisaroff was always dry and unsociable; I doubt if he had an intimate acquaintance, let alone a friend, among the students; there was no real intimacy between him and Timyanksy, and it was a surprise to me when they became partners in collecting insects. Timyansky said at parting: 'Now, look here. I will look after your things carefully, but of course I don't guarantee success. It is quite possible that the grubs and chrysalises will die before their change; in that case, don't blame me. Any butterflies that hatch out I shall set as well as I can and preserve. And, by the way, butterflies in cases are often injured by moth—Fuchs told me this and advised to drop a little spirit of camphor on the abdomen with a camel-hair pencil. You might as well do this at once to the butterflies you are leaving in the library. I have the materials here at your service.' The suggestion of this precaution convinced even my partner that Timyansky was to be trusted. We availed ourselves of his offer with gratitude and went at once to the library, where we took a last look at our splendid butterflies, applied the camphor, locked the cabinets, and gave the keys, in case of emergency, to Timyansky. We said a cordial goodbye to him, assuring him that we relied upon him entirely, and should be grateful to him, whatever happened. We also said goodbye to the other students who were not leaving the college, and set off accompanied by their good wishes.

We went first to the Panáyeffs' house, where I said goodbye to my friend and his four brothers. Their horses had long been put in, and they were only waiting for their brother to return ; indeed they scolded us, and me especially for my fussing over grubs and chrysalises, in their impatience to start for home and the country. And it was natural that they were panting to be off, when, after ten months of study and discipline, they were exchanging the dust and summer heat and perpetual smells of a town for clean fragrant fields and cool shady woods, for family life and the place where they were born, or, at least, had spent the unforgettable years of childhood. I watched them start. All the five of them took their seats on an old *lineika* [1] drawn by horses sent from home. My friend held a fair-sized box on his knees, containing a score of butterflies which he had chosen out of our duplicates as a present for his sisters. The two youngest brothers, who sat on each side of him, complained loudly that they would be squashed by the box ; but their youthful voices were drowned by the loud rattling made by the old *lineika* as it started. They intended to camp out that night, and had fishing-rods and even guns with them. I felt sad and envious. I had been told to travel home this time on a courier's cart with hired horses ; and, worst of all, my destination was not my dearly loved New Aksákovo, with its waters and meadows, marshes and coppices : the family was at Old Aksákovo in Simbirsk, a tiresome place,

[1] A long four-wheeled cart with a single seat running lengthwise.

without water and surrounded by forest, where we had not even a decent house to live in.

I went back to my lodgings and found all preparations made for departure. The hired horses were harnessed already; the bells, loosely tied to the wheeler's yoke, jingled at his least movement; the servants, dressed for the journey and holding their caps in their hands, were waiting for me by the steps. While I was changing into light clothes for travelling, the thought that I should soon see my family and especially the darling sister who was looking forward with intense eagerness to my arrival, flashed through my mind and filled me with pleasant excitement. Then the smell of tar and matting, which came from the cart, transported me in one moment to the country, and my heart grew light and happy. Yevséitch took his seat beside me in the cart, Little Ivan jumped up on the box, the driver shook his reins and whistled, and off flew the horses.

When we had climbed up the long suburb that leads out of Kazan, the heat of the day was over, and a splendid summer evening breathed coolness over the parched earth. There had been no rain for a long time, and everything was very dry. I had never before properly experienced the pleasure of fast driving; and when the coachman, wishing to please the young gentleman and earn his tip, urged his three horses to their utmost speed, I felt for the first time an inexpressible delight and a kind of nervous excitement. Yevséitch was much pleased too: ' Well, this really is something like ! '—he said with a smile ; ' and yet the horses are nothing to look at. But you're not afraid, are you ? ' he went on, when I said

nothing and he saw that I was breathing hard.
I was horribly vexed, but I controlled myself and
tried to assure him that, on the contrary, I was in
excellent spirits—my heart was beating hard for
joy, and I found my breath come short. This
was the exact truth; the voice with which I spoke
was trembling with excitement. I should have
liked to fly like a bird—I felt such an eager desire
to move forward, such a delightful but indescrib-
able nervous tension. Meantime evening came
down over us. Longer and longer grew the shadows
of the flying carriage and horses, of the coachman
and Ivan who had by this time struck up a song.
The shadows grew fainter by degrees and were
lost at last in the darkness of the ground. All the
surroundings combined to affect me strongly, and
I felt a kind of agitation which I could not explain
to myself.

At the post-house I refused to drink tea,
although Yevséitch quickly opened the canteen
and Ivan placed our travelling *samovar* on the
table. My refusal caused great uneasiness to my
kind attendant. He had never known me refuse tea
before; and here there was a special inducement;
for I was very fond of cream, and a pot of cream,
thick and wrinkled and cold, stood on the table
before me. Thinking I was unwell, he began to
worry me with questions, till I contented him by
eating a whole plateful of cream with Kazan
biscuits. The fresh horses were soon ready, and
we started again. Yevséitch was haunted by the
idea, so mortifying to me, that I was frightened
by the pace, He told the driver to go slow,
that we might not upset in the dark, and bored
me exceedingly by his tiresome questions and

comments. I shut my eyes—a rather unnecessary precaution in the dark—and pretended to be asleep; I even snored, until my anxious guardian fell asleep himself in the process of observing me. I remained awake till long after sunrise, and this sleepless night, with the glow of evening followed by the glow of dawn, brought me many new and delightful feelings. Sleep at last mastered me, slowly and imperceptibly; but I slept so soundly that I was unconscious of our changing horses and was only roused at nine in the morning by a peal of thunder.

When I became conscious, I saw a large thunder-cloud drifting rapidly overhead towards a bank of cloud, dark-blue and black, which had covered half the sky already and was growing larger every moment. One edge of the large cloud was whitish, and there the rain was already falling in torrents; a dull menacing sound and a feeling of fresh moisture came from that quarter. 'Can that be hail?' cried Yevséitch; 'the Lord have mercy upon us! The people will lose their last grain of corn!' The large cloud, which appeared to be moving sideways, now suddenly wheeled straight towards us, and big drops began to patter on the dusty road and the dusty matting of the carriage. The servants made haste to protect me and themselves too. Yevséitch told the driver to go at a foot-pace; he said it was dangerous to drive fast in a thunderstorm. The cloud soon came over us. Blinding flashes of lightning played like serpents over the sky, followed immediately by deafening peals of thunder. Each crash sounded close to the carriage. At first the three men bared their heads and crossed themselves at each flash;

but when the lightning became almost continuous, they gave it up. Suddenly a storm of thick large hailstones and heavy rain came up, and all the atmosphere was turned into a white watery powder. I could not look without fear on this majestic but terrible sight. There is something awful in the rage of the elements. At that moment they displayed all their mighty power of destruction, and the feebleness and defencelessness of man was so clearly revealed and forced upon me, that I could not keep my composure. In my childhood I had once been frightened by thunder, and the terrible impression of that time had not yet disappeared. A feeling of inexpressible relief and joy went through me, when the thunder began to come at longer intervals and farther away. The black cloud shifted from south to west, and one side of the sky became blue and bright. Yevséitch and I were all right, but the other two men were soaked to the bones. The clouds cleared away and the hot summer sun soon began to dry their wet clothes, while each laughed at the other's plight. To us it seemed that the very centre of the storm had passed over our heads ; but as we trotted on ahead, we saw that the rain and hail had been much heavier here than with us : there were pools on the road, and the mown hay-fields were flooded ; the big hailstones had not melted yet and were lying in many places, especially in hollows, like white patches. We drove past crops which were all, more or less, ruined by the hail ; and some fields were as much beaten down as if a flock of sheep had grazed there for weeks—not only the ears but the straw also appeared to be trodden into the mire. Nor was this all. Two columns of smoke were rising from a village near the road—a certain sign that houses had been struck by lightning—and some stricken trees were smoking in a wood hard by. These awful traces of the storm's swift passage were peculiarly impressive, now that the air was still and fresh and the sun shone bright in a clear sky. ' This is where the real storm was,' said Yevséitch; ' it only grazed us with the tip of its wing.' My companions were distressed chiefly by the injured crops; the driver belonged to the village ahead of us, and even knew who were the owners of the fields; as fortune would have it, they were very poor, and to them this loss meant utter ruin. The three men discussed the disaster for some time, and Yevséitch's words showed the unfeigned kindness of his heart. ' Dear, dear ! ' he said, ' if I were rich, I would help them. But the loss there runs to hundreds and thousands of roubles,[1] and what will kopecks do in such a case?' We soon reached the post-house and brought the bad news with us. No hail at all had fallen in the village, though they had heard the noise; and their terrible calamity was a complete surprise. The women began at once to weep and wail, and some of them set off immediately for the fields to see their misfortune themselves before they would believe it. Yevséitch admitted to me afterwards that he had given his kopecks to one of the most destitute families.

Our next change of horses was at a settlement whose inhabitants made a strong impression on my mind. They were Tartars, who had been converted to Christianity, as far back, I was told,

[1] A rouble was worth two shillings : 100 kopecks = 1 rouble.

as the reign of Ivan Vassilyevitch.[1] Both sexes
wore Russian dress and spoke Russian; but their
whole appearance had something forbidding and
depressing about it, as if they were lost creatures,
a sort of homeless and helpless air. Even their
clothes seemed not to fit them, and a sort of
timidity was visible in all their movements. They
were very poor, though the surrounding villages—
Russian and Tartar, Mordvinian and Choovash—
were prosperous enough. Yevséitch had been in
this village before, and had come across similar
converts in other places. ' They're all alike,' he
said, ' and all poor; they've given up their own
ways and not caught on to ours; like Cain, they
are fugitives and wanderers in the earth.' His
words gave me much food for thought, and I
lingered on after the horses were ready, trying to
study the people of the house and enter into
conversation with them. I talked also to their
neighbours—the old people and even the children.
These last were livelier and more cheerful: the
sadness and moroseness which marked all the
grown-up people was less noticeable in them. The
Tartar type of face, though still traceable, had
become less pronounced; there were no shaved
heads among them, but also no long hair; they
all looked like peasants whose hair has just been
cut before they enlist in the army or enter on the
personal service of their masters. They understood their own condition to some extent but
considered their case hopeless. There was a
tradition among them, that their ancestors, when
sentenced for some crime to flogging and penal
servitude in Siberia, obtained pardon by changing

[1] i. e. Ivan the Terrible, who reigned 1533-84.

their religion, and were then transferred to a new
settlement ; but they could never prosper, because
the curse of Mahomet clung to them. These people
and their story made a strong impression upon me
at the time ; but as I never again happened to
visit a settlement of converts, by degrees these
sufferers vanished entirely from my mind. But it
would be interesting to know, whether later
generations still suffer this terrible punishment for
the sin of their ancestors, who changed their faith
without conviction and merely to save their skins ;
or whether these innocent victims have at last
become assimilated to the Russian settlers with
whom they live, and have appeased by their
patient endurance the stern sentence of moral
justice.

Of rain or hail there was not a trace on the
rest of our journey. We travelled very fast, and
when night came on, we were within thirty-five
versts of home. I went sound asleep and slept on
through our arrival, and might have slept much
longer, if I had not been awakened by the kisses
and caresses of my sister. Waking at six o'clock
and hearing that I had arrived at dawn and was
asleep in the carriage, she ran down and waked
me. Most of the household were still in bed.
I went to her room ; and she told me at once that
she had caught and collected a number of butterflies and caterpillars for me. She knew by my
letters all the details of my new hobby. She kept
the caterpillars—but many of them were grubs
of other insects—in her own room, in little boxes
and glass jars and tumblers turned upside down.
The butterflies inhabited a window which was kept
shut and fenced on the inside by a muslin curtain.

This was not a bad idea, but it had one disadvantage, that the butterflies beat against the panes and spoilt their wings. Another idea of my sister's was less successful. She raised the lid of the piano and showed me a number of butterflies which she had placed there : most of them had died for want of air. Piles of fresh leaves and plants were a proof of the care with which my kind sister attended to the caterpillars, though she disliked them herself and would never touch them. I examined carefully these unexpected acquisitions, and found several species unknown to me ; many were dead and even dried up, and many were spoiled ; but there were a fair number which I began at once to set, having brought setting-boards, pins, and paper with me. Though I advised my sister not to watch, and told her she would not like it, she was unwilling to leave me and curious to see how it was done ; but when I held the insects over the candle, she fled and for long after was unwilling to look at butterflies even in cabinets.

By this time all the household was awake. I shall not speak of the general rejoicing or the especial joy of my mother, when she saw me for the first time as a University student, no longer a boy but a young man leading an independent life of his own. She saw too that I was perfectly frank with her and quite unspoiled. My kind father too was rejoiced to see me again, and I noticed, though he said nothing about it, the satisfaction with which his eyes rested on me while I eagerly described my life at college. The first days were given up to conversation, and we told each other all our news. I heard much that was new and, from the worldly point of view, very important and agreeable. When it came to my turn, I told of the new and old professors, the new subjects of study, our theatrical and literary occupations and plans for the future, and finally I spoke of my passion for collecting butterflies and of the advantage that might accrue to science by means of such collections. Later we paid visits to some friends and neighbours, including the Minitskys and my cousin Alexandra Kovrigin, who had been brought up by my great-aunt Praskóvya Ivánovna, and now had a house and a small estate of her own.

When these visits were over, country life went on in its usual course, with such amusements as the district offered. But it could not be denied that there was no comparison between Old and New Aksákovo. At the latter there were bathing and fishing in the river and large pond, and very varied shooting. But here there was hardly any water— even the drinking-water had to be fetched from springs two versts away—and though the shooting was very good, it was all in woods, and I was too young for that, and besides I had no dog. My father took me out once or twice in pursuit of capercailzies; one of the peasants, Yegor Filatoff, knew how to find their coveys and flush them without a dog. But we were among trees all the time, and before I could raise my gun to the shoulder, the young birds had scattered in every direction, though Yegor and my father always contrived to knock over some of them. I only once succeeded in shooting a young capercailzie which was stupid enough to perch on a tree within range. There were a great number of woodcock also, but the season for them had not yet come.

Still, Yegor used sometimes to bring in both old and young woodcocks : the young ones he caught in his hands, aided by a dog which he owned ; but how he managed to slay the old birds, I don't know to this day ; for he could not shoot flying. Snipe also bred in numbers round the Mossy Lakes in the woods ; but I was absolutely unable to hit them, and also the soil round these lakes was treacherous and sank so much when trodden on, that I was afraid to go there. We sometimes drove in a body to the woods, to pick berries or mushrooms or nuts ; but such expeditions had little attraction for me. Thus I was forced back upon a single occupation—collecting butterflies ; and to this I directed all my attention and activity.

It turned out, to my joy, that the district contained a great abundance and variety of butterflies, and, still more, of moths. Caterpillars were becoming rare, and I did not trouble about them, because it was now too late in the season for them to hatch out, August having begun. I began by searching in the old orchard, along the shrunken stream of the Maina, in the clearings of the forest, and round the little springs which bubbled up here and there in the old channel of the river ; and I found not only the butterflies which bred near Kazan but many others which were quite new to me. I lay in wait for the twilight moths at dusk ; and even by day I pursued them in the darkness of the forest, where they fluttered from tree to tree, unconscious of the bright sunlight outside. The true moths I used to search for by day in hollows of trees or crevices in fences and buildings ; and I used to decoy them after dark by means of a light. I made a small lantern and tied it to the

top of a barberry or gooseberry bush or lilac or
low apple-tree. Then I stood still with my net
ready and swept it over the moths when they came
flying to the light and circled round the lantern.
Before long, I had caught about twenty new
species; but, in spite of all our trouble, my sister
and I found it difficult to identify them out of
Blumenbach. I do not vouch for the accuracy of
the names which I adopted from certain indications
and a general resemblance to the descriptions;
I took them from our German authority, and they
seemed to me at the time to be right. I shall name
some of my most important captures in the order
in which I got them.

My first, which is not described in Blumenbach,
was, as I now believe, a *White Satin Moth*. It was
small, without being one of the smallest; its
wings were round and white as snow, and covered
with a thick down, which is still thicker on the
head, back, and abdomen; this white down shows
off the jet-black eyes and long hairy proboscis, the
thick antennae and the legs. When I first saw it
slowly rising and falling near a tree in the forest,
I took it for a particle of down floating about in the
close windless air; but when I saw it the second
time sticking to a leaf, I went closer and, to my
great joy, discovered that it was a moth. It cost
me a world of pains. It needed much dexterity to
catch and set it, without crushing it or rubbing the
down off the wings. My next prize was a butterfly,
according to Blumenbach, a *Ringlet*. It was of
moderate size; its purplish wings were angular
and much indented, and each of the four had white
spots; on the reverse of each hind-wing were three
bright circles or eyes. It was rather pretty or,

perhaps I should say, uncommon. Then I caught a *Death's Head Hawk-moth*. About this there was no possibility of mistake: its characteristic mark is so peculiar : on the back, close to the head, there is something resembling a human skull and cross-bones. The fore-wings are bright brown, the hind-wings yellow with two black bands running along them. These were by no means all my novelties ; but my most precious acquisitions, which each in turn drove me wild with delight, were two—the *Scarce Swallow-tail* and the *Great Peacock Moth*. I must describe how I obtained these two treasures.

I was walking one day along the dried-up channel of the Maina, when I saw in a little hollow, where a spring had been parched up by the heat and the bottom was still wettish, a whole heap of common cabbage-butterflies. Many were already dead or dying ; others were sitting on the heap, able to creep but not to fly ; and the rest were fluttering above them. It was not the first time I had seen a sight of this kind. I had noticed that certain kinds of butterflies—the Small Whites and Blues, for instance—collect in heaps in order to die together. Yet I went close to them from curiosity ; facts like that which one cannot explain are always interesting. Suddenly I saw a large yellow butterfly resting on the ground, in the middle of the others which were perched or crawl-ing about. I leaned over to examine it—and it would be difficult to convey to my readers the excitement and joy I then felt. It was a *Swallow-tail*, and not the common *Swallow-tail*, because the black transverse bands, broad above and narrow below, were clearly shown on the under surface of its fore-wings, which is not the case with the common *Swallow-tail*; and also the ends of the spurs were quite different. It must therefore be the *Scarce Swallow-tail*! Such an extraordinary piece of good fortune made me dizzy. Then, as if to remove my last doubt, the butterfly opened its wings, crawled forward a few inches, and then closed them tightly. From drawings and from the single specimen which Fuchs possessed, I was well acquainted with the distinctive peculiarities of this butterfly, and felt quite convinced that I saw it before me. I lost no time in throwing my net over it; then I could breathe more freely and find some relief from my agitation. I began to consider how I could get hold of my precious prize without damaging it. First I tried to frighten it, intending to catch it in the pouch of the net when it rose; but it never stirred. Then I understood that it was in the same condition as the white butterflies—in the sort of faintness or sleep that precedes death; and I pushed my right hand under the net, very deliberately caught the *Swallow-tail* by the thorax with my finger and thumb, and squeezed it; and off I ran home, keeping it in my hand all the way. While setting it, I was vexed to find that the upper side of the left hind-wing was rubbed; and, in general, close examination showed that the butterfly was old and rather faded, with much of the brightness and freshness of its colour gone. But, for all these defects, the *Scarce Swallow-tail* might be called a valuable prize.

I think it relevant to clear up at this point a mistake into which we fell in those days, with regard to the two Swallow-tails, the Common and the Scarce, also called *Podalirius* and *Machaon*.

Having at hand Blumenbach, Ozeretskovsky, and Raff (all these books were known to me in early days and to other students who had a turn for Natural History), and having before me at this moment preserved specimens and drawings of the *Swallow-tails*, I perceive on a careful review of all the evidence that we called the two species by the wrong names. At first sight there is, certainly, some resemblance ; but it was not this resemblance that misled us ; it was Professor Fuchs. He gave to *Machaon* the name *Podalirius*, and we, relying on his opinion, read the descriptions in our authorities with insufficient attention. Accordingly, the first *Swallow-tails* caught by Timyansky and myself were *Machaons*. Here is a description from nature, as detailed and exact as I can make it.

Machaon is one of our largest butterflies. Its wings are not round ; they are rather long and pointed, with a yellow ground variegated with black spots, streaks, and squares. The fore-wings are marked with three short black bands along the upper edge ; and on the side edge, over a broad black border, there are eight small yellow semicircles in a row ; next to the body and the roots of the wings there are black triangles, about half a finger in width ; the yellow ground is seamed all over with black veins, and all the black parts seem to be lightly dusted with yellow. The hind-wings are between oval and round ; the rims are festoonshaped with a black border, and have six yellow semi-circles larger than those on the fore-wings ; immediately above them are broad black curved patches, with six dark-blue rings which run into one another ; a seventh ring, the nearest to the inner edge, is of a red-brown colour with a tinge of white at the top; from the second yellow semicircle proceed the long black appendages called spurs, and very like spurs. *Podalirius* is also yellow but much paler, variegated with black; the upper wings have black bands from top to bottom, broad at the top and tapering to a thread below. The hind-wings have small red circles with a dark-blue centre, and a pattern of blue semicircles on the outer edge. It also has long black spurs with yellow tips. *Podalirius* is generally smaller than *Machaon*, but, in my opinion, even more beautiful.

The *Peacock Moth*, an insect of rare size and beauty, came to me unsought. A fortnight before I left home, we had visitors staying with us. At nine in the evening we were all sitting round the *samovar* in the drawing-room, drinking tea; my mother was pouring it out herself. Though the evenings were getting cool, the windows were open, and four candles were burning in the room. I happened to look up and saw on the ceiling the dancing shadow of something flying about. I thought at first it was a bat: they bred there in quantities and often flew at the windows in the evening, attracted by the light. My mother had an unconquerable aversion to bats, and I was on the point of advising her to leave the room until we turned out this uninvited guest. But when I looked again and more attentively, I saw it was no bat but a very large moth. With a wild cry, I rushed instantly to shut the windows and doors. My mother was vexed and began to scold me for the start I had given to the party; but when I began, choking with excitement and pointing to the ceiling, to call out in an agonized voice—

' A moth! an enormous magnificent moth! Do allow me to catch it!'—every one else laughed, and my mother, who knew my frantic excitement over my hobby, could not help smiling. She gave me leave to catch our visitor, my 'enormous magnificent moth'. But it did not prove quite so easy to do this. The moth was flying just under the ceiling, perching from time to time on a curtain to rest. I ran for my longest net, placed a chair on the table, and clambered up on it. In order to leave room for my operations, my mother took our visitors to the parlour, while my father and sister stayed behind to help me. He held the chair on which I was standing, and she climbed on to the table and held a lighted candle in each hand—the other two we had blown out; with her arms raised above her head and standing on tiptoe, she gave me light and at the same time tried to attract the moth. My arrangements were crowned with success: the moth began to circle round me, and I soon caught it. It was a *Large Peacock Moth*, almost the size of a bat.

I shall not attempt to describe the joy and happiness I felt over my prize. I had often heard Fuchs speak of the *Large Peacock* as a great rarity; and this was the insect, beyond all doubt. The description in Blumenbach is very defective, and, with regard to the shape of the wings, quite wrong. This is what he says—' The *Peacock Moth* has comb-like antennae and no tongue; the wings are rounded and dark-grey in colour, with some (?) stripes and several transparent eyes or rings.' But my moth, which was afterwards identified by Professor Fuchs as well, was not like that. Its wings were long rather than round, with small, hardly perceptible indentations along the edges ; they might perhaps be called dark-grey, but that gives no true idea of the colour ; they were very beautiful, with darkish and whitish fringes along the edge, and shades of such a lovely pattern that one could feast one's eyes upon it. The hind-wings, of a cloudy ash-colour, were no less beautiful. On each of the four wings was one brilliant eye, like the eyes on the long tail-feathers of the peacock ; and hence the moth has got its name. The under side of the wings was plain grey, with white streaks ; and the eyes, though not so brilliant, were visible there too, with a tinge of pale crimson which was entirely absent from the upper side. Though it would have been more desirable to set the moth by daylight, I was afraid to postpone this operation for two reasons : if the insect died from compression of the thorax, it might shrivel before morning ; and if it revived, it would struggle and might rub the painted dust off its wings. So I determined to set it on the spot. I lit several candles and set my noble *Peacock Moth* satisfactorily, while my father and all our visitors watched my proceedings with interest.

As a matter of course, I had already made a fine cabinet with a glass lid, lined with white paper, and with a bottom of soft lime-wood, for convenience in sticking in the pins that held the butterflies. By degrees this cabinet became filled with really beautiful and even rare specimens. But now I was faced by a difficulty : how was it possible to convey the cabinet safely to Kazan ? The jolting of the carriage might loosen the pins, and then the vagaries of a single specimen would spoil a number of others. There was only one resource—

to hold the cabinet myself throughout the journey : it would be over in twenty-four hours, and I could keep awake all night !

On the morning of August 13th I was already speeding along the road to Kazan, duly holding my cabinet. At each post-house I looked to see whether the pins were firm. I stuck to my resolve and remained awake all night, though in the morning I yielded to the entreaties of Yevséitch when he offered to hold the butterflies himself and urged me ' to take forty winks '. By dinner-time I reached my lodgings at Kazan without mishaps. The Panáyeffs had not yet arrived. I set off at once for college and of course took my butterflies with me.

I found Timyansky recovering from an illness : he had been suffering, poor fellow, almost all the summer from fever. Our butterflies in the library, and also the chrysalises and caterpillars, were in perfect order. Kaisaroff had looked after them all the time, and I did not know how to thank him sufficiently for his pains. Except a few that had died, the caterpillars had turned into chrysalises, and many of the chrysalises had hatched out ; of the butterflies none was remarkable, but they had all been set. The collection I had brought from home astonished and delighted Timyansky and Kaisaroff, as well as the other students who were interested, more or less, in our pursuit. As lectures began on the 16th of August, nearly all the students who had spent the vacation elsewhere, returned to Kazan by the 15th. During my absence, not much had been added to Timyansky's entomological collection, partly owing to his illness, and partly because the immediate neighbourhood of Kazan did not offer any special advantages for the acquisition of new and rare species. As far as butterflies were concerned, it was now beyond dispute that Panáyeff and I, leaving out of account what my partner might bring with him, had far outstripped our rivals.

I was exceedingly impatient for the return of my friend, Alexander Panáyeff, wondering what captures he had made, and what he would say when he saw my butterflies. I sent again and again to inquire if the brothers had arrived, and went myself several times for information on this point. At last a message came from their house late on the 15th of August, that ' the young gentlemen had arrived'; and I reached the Black Lake a few minutes later. Of course I took my cabinet with me, but I covered it with a handkerchief, intending to display it suddenly with better effect, at a moment when the undivided attention of the whole party was fixed on my precious acquisitions. When the first embraces and greetings were over, my friend and I burst out simultaneously with the same question—' Well, what have you got ? ' I answered in a voice full of meaning : ' I have got something that you will like very much '; and he answered much in the same fashion with a complacent smile. But his brothers could not control their eagerness : all four of them began at once to boast of their butterflies and said they were sure I had nothing as good to show. ' Very well, let me see,' said I. ' No ! you must show yours first,' said my friend, and we disputed in this fashion for some minutes. At last I gave way and opened my cabinet. The boasters were crushed and confounded ; and Alexander, in his joy, rushed into my arms. The *Swallow-tail* and the *Peacock Moth* were a complete surprise to them all. ' Well,' said Panáyeff, after a more careful examination of my butterflies, ' it's hardly worth while showing you ours after this. And how well you set them too, as well as I do!' But this was undeserved praise : though I had certainly learnt to do it better, I was still far less skilful than my friend. He afterwards noticed, and indeed I pointed out to him myself, many mistakes due to impatience and awkward handling. At last he showed me his cabinet, and the perfect condition of the specimens was really astonishing as well as the excellence of the setting, but there were no butterflies as rare as my two. There were about a score of new species and several perfect duplicates of what we had already. I shall name some of the best he had got.

The first we identified out of Blumenbach as the *Large Tortoiseshell*. It was a large butterfly, with pointed wings of a red-yellow colour with black patches, and four large black spots on the forewings between the tip of the wings and the body. A second butterfly we identified, also out of Blumenbach, rather doubtfully as a *Silver-washed Fritillary*. It was a fairly large insect, with indented orange-yellow wings marked with brilliant dark-blue patches. This was a very beautiful butterfly ; but it had none of the ' silvery streaks across the under surface of the hind-wings' described by Blumenbach, though this might be due to mere accident. Two of the moths also might be called remarkable. First, there was a *Vapourer Moth*, rather large, with very flat wings of a fine dark-red colour, and a white crescent or spot in the hind corner of each fore-wing. The other new moth was at once recognized as a *Geometer Moth*; it had whitish wings varie-gated with circular black patches, and a yellow pattern with black specks on the hind-wings. Panáyeff's moths of middling size were especially good. The first we identified out of Blumenbach as a *Vine Hawk-moth*. Its fore-wings were grey and smoke-coloured, with a long line or rather two lines joined together, one white and the other black; the hind-wings were red close to the body, with six spots on each. Blumenbach says the caterpillar breeds on the vine; but where the vine does not grow, it probably breeds on other plants. Another insect we could identify as a *Humming-bird Hawk-moth*, from the tufts of hair on the abdomen and the reddish-yellow colour of the hind-wings. The fore-wings do not bear out Blumenbach's description: they are not white and black, as he asserts, but of a plain grey—the usual colour of the common moths that fly to a candle at night. There were other moths, very beautiful and not common, which Panáyeff had caught; but we were unable to identify and name them.

When we had combined the contents of our four cabinets, and put them in proper order, by arranging the insects according to species, number-ing them, and making out a list of names and descriptions, then our collection might really be called in many respects excellent, though not, of course, complete. All the students were at last unanimous, and there was no kind of dispute as to superiority between the two collections: Panáyeff and I had triumphed over Timyansky and his ally.

Meantime lectures began; and I, feeling that I had got rather behindhand owing to the excessive attention I had given to butterflies since the spring, set myself eagerly to the task of overhauling my companions; and Panáyeff did the same. Our passion, however, had not yet cooled and old habit was strong: a week later we settled to take a trip into the country, hoping that we might fall in with some prizes and specimens to us hitherto unknown. But we got nothing new, and even the familiar butterflies were hard to find, because August was drawing to a close and the weather had grown much colder. That day saw the last of our campaign against the butterflies, and we never began another. Surly autumn soon came, and we devoted all our leisure to literature, producing with much enthusiasm a manuscript magazine which we called 'A Journal of our Occupations'. I became deeply interested in acting also. We got up plays among ourselves in college, and my reputation as an actor became established. Butterflies began to take a second place; yet Panáyeff and I still looked at them and admired them daily, and recalled with pleasure the capture of our chief prizes and the joy we had felt at the time. But these recollections became daily rarer and fainter. By degrees butterflies were forgotten, and the passion for catching and collecting them began to seem to us too childish for our years. And I felt this more than Panáyeff, though I had been infinitely more excited and enthusiastic over the pastime than he had ever been.

Before long my destiny was settled by my parents: at the beginning of 1807, a few months later, I was to leave college and enter on the civil service at Petersburg.

In those days the University of Kazan was filled with a warlike spirit. A majority of the Government scholars were eager to join the army, in order to take a personal and active share in the war against Napoleon; but they despaired of getting permission. My chosen friend and his brother Ivan Panáyeff, our college poet, were equally ardent in their martial zeal: they determined to leave the University at once and seek commissions in the cavalry. They only waited for their mother's consent. Apart from patriotic ardour and devotion to the glory of the nation, there was a special reason for the state of feeling among us. Peter Balyasnikoff, one of the Government scholars, was a remarkable personality—an excellent mathematician, with a fiery, undaunted, and enterprising temperament and a will of iron. His premature death cut short a glorious career: when Napoleon crossed the Berezina, Balyasnikoff had risen to be a colonel and commanded a battery of horse-artillery; he caught a chill there and died of fever. At all times he had a strong influence over the rest of us, and now he breathed martial ardour into all his companions, even into those whose weak health and mild temperament made it seem unlikely, or even out of the question, that they should serve their country in arms. Mihail Fomin was exceptionally intelligent and industrious, devoting himself chiefly to literature; and Peter Zykoff was much valued by me for his remarkable gifts as a comic actor. No one supposed that two men of such poor bodily development and unwarlike tastes would enter the army; but they did. Timyansky and Kaisaroff, however, remained faithful to their intended career and continued their studies.

Before entering on my profession at Petersburg, I had one more opportunity of greeting the advance of spring at my dear Aksákovo. The mere recollection of the spring I had spent there as a boy of eight years old always filled me with excitement when I thought of the return of the birds of passage; and now, when I carried a gun, my longing for this season was so intense that I prayed for patience to live till it came, and for strength to live through it. There was no longer room for butterflies among the dreams and desires that then filled my head and heart. At first, I gave my share in the collection to Panáyeff, and he gave me beautiful drawings of the best specimens, which he had made from the originals with great skill and accuracy. Then, when he fixed his thoughts on the army, we made over our butterflies to Timyansky, to have and to hold in his own possession. I do not know whether he kept them himself or presented them to the museum of Kazan University.

My passion—there is no other name for it—for collecting butterflies was violent while it lasted, though it did not last long. My excessive enthusiasm went so far as to be ridiculous ; I believe that for several months it prevented me from attending to my lectures. But I cannot say that I regret it.

Every unselfish ideal or exertion of a man's powers is morally good for him. The recollection of that time, of those many happy blissful hours, is a treasure that has lasted all my life. My pursuit was carried on under the open sky and amid natural scenes that were varied and beautiful and wonderful. The hills and woods and fields where

I wandered with my net, the evenings when I lay in wait for moths, and the nights when I lured them to the light of my lantern—these passed unnoticed at the time ; but the eternal beauty of Nature was mirrored in my heart without my knowing it ; and such impressions, when they rise later to the surface in brightness and harmony, are full of blessing, and the recollection of them calls forth a consolatory feeling from the depth of a man's heart.

Moscow, *July* 21*st*, 1858.